T0036787

# THE HIDDEN HINDENBURG

*The Untold Story of the Tragedy, the Nazi Secrets,
and the Quest to Rule the Skies*

## MICHAEL McCARTHY

LYONS
PRESS

Essex, Connecticut

An imprint of Globe Pequot, the trade division of
The Rowman & Littlefield Publishing Group, Inc.
4501 Forbes Blvd., Ste. 200
Lanham, MD 20706
www.rowman.com

Distributed by NATIONAL BOOK NETWORK

Copyright © 2020 by Michael McCarthy
First Lyons Press paperback edition published 2022

*All rights reserved.* No part of this book may be reproduced in any form or by any electronic or mechanical means, including information storage and retrieval systems, without written permission from the publisher, except by a reviewer who may quote passages in a review.

British Library Cataloguing in Publication Information available

**Library of Congress Cataloging-in-Publication Data**

Names: McCarthy, Michael, 1962- author.
Title: The hidden Hindenburg : the untold story of the tragedy, the Nazi secrets, and the quest to rule the skies / Michael McCarthy.
Description: Guilford, Connecticut : Lyons Press, [2020] | Includes bibliographical references and index. | Summary: "The story of a German conman who misled the world about the Hindenburg to bury his own Nazi connections"— Provided by publisher.
Identifiers: LCCN 2019059472 (print) | LCCN 2019059473 (ebook) | ISBN 9781493053704 (cloth : alk. paper) | ISBN 9781493066681 (paper : alk. paper) | ISBN 9781493053711 (electronic)
Subjects: LCSH: Eckener, Hugo, 1868-1954. | Aeronautical engineers—Germany—Biography. | World War, 1939-1945—Collaborationists—Germany—Biography. | Hindenburg (Airship) | Aeronautics—History—Germany—20th century. | Germany—Politics and government—1933-1945. | Aircraft accidents—New Jersey—History—20th century.
Classification: LCC TL540.E35 M36 2020 (print) | LCC TL540.E35 (ebook) | DDC 363.12/465—dc23
LC record available at https://lccn.loc.gov/2019059472
LC ebook record available at https://lccn.loc.gov/2019059473

∞™ The paper used in this publication meets the minimum requirements of American National Standard for Information Sciences—Permanence of Paper for Printed Library Materials, ANSI/NISO Z39.48-1992.

*Glory to the Father, and to the Son, and to the Holy Spirit*

*Hunting truth is no easy task; we must look everywhere for its tracks.*

—St. Basil the Great

# CONTENTS

# Author's Note

THE IRON AGONY IN THAT VOICE.

This book began a decade ago, when I taught journalism history at a college in Chicago. I told all my students that they simply had to hear the stunning and dramatic radio report of the *Hindenburg* disaster. We're back in May of 1937, I told them. A muddy landing field in New Jersey. A rain-soaked young announcer with slicked-back hair begins narrating. Herb Morrison is describing the giant Zeppelin's uneventful arrival. Suddenly, the heat and the glow of the *Hindenburg* afire erupts over him. Overcome, he begins hyperventilating into his microphone. *It's burst into flames . . . It's a terrific crash, ladies and gentlemen . . . The smoke and the flames now . . . Oh, the humanity!*

Semester after semester, I played the staticky recording in class. We all listened together. It was a remarkable record, I told them: one of the most vivid, raw, human reactions ever to seeing a tragedy unfold before one's eyes. One witness simply saw, spoke. His delivery was impulsive, true, a child's.

Back then, I took a cursory look into the *Hindenburg* tragedy to try to explain to students what happened. To my surprise, the official federal government investigation never came up with a conclusion. It ruled that an atmospheric electrical charge ignited highly flammable hydrogen gas that was leaking from the famed ship—somehow. Why there was a leak was anyone's guess.

Then, a few years ago, I began wondering about the *Hindenburg* again. I think listening repeatedly to Morrison's newscast over the years haunted me. Somehow hearing the recording over and over made me wonder if there were something more to the story. That voice seemed to travel through the decades, to me, and ask the question: *What happened?*

I dove into that old, cold case. Two years of research followed. And then, when I arrived in Germany to wrap up the work in 2017, the entire story exploded. I discovered that previous books about the infamous *Hindenburg* were riddled with myth, with facts and episodes purposely twisted by a German legend, a world-renowned aviation pioneer desperate to conceal his war secrets. It all boils down to a fabulously successful lie.

Hugo Eckener, a goateed aviator and father of the *Hindenburg*, was as famous in his day as the world-renowned American pilot Charles Lindbergh. In the Roaring Twenties, the German impresario with pouchy eyes flew one of his cigar-shaped Zeppelins around the globe, met with U.S. presidents Coolidge and Hoover, and landed on the cover of *Time* magazine. Americans recognized his gravelly voice on the radio. In the early 1930s, in Germany, he was expected to run for president, a rival candidate to Hitler.

But the memoirs the early patriarch of aviation wrote after World War II, which would become the backbone of every subsequent Zeppelin account, are replete with undetected falsehoods that rewrote history and, along the way, hid the true cause of the *Hindenburg* disaster. No one caught on.

With never-before-published records from the National Archives, aviation libraries, and archival sources in Germany, I found evidence that the 800-foot-long *Hindenburg* was on a path to self-destruction back to its blueprints. Today, it's hard to imagine just how large the *Hindenburg* actually was. Eight Goodyear blimps could have easily fit inside of it. Driven to beat the Americans to the largest, most luxurious aircraft ever—with staterooms, a promenade deck, and a tinkling piano on board—the German Zeppelin men had inadvertently created something that proved, over time, too big to fly.

In the winter of 1936, they belatedly discovered that their trusty techniques had somehow failed, leaving the massive *Hindenburg*, nearly three football fields long, dangerously vibrating. Under pressure to start the 1937 flight season, they tried hasty repairs. The Zeppelin men were flying a highly visible ornament of Nazi pride and propaganda, and suddenly in a dire race to keep it from rattling apart in the skies.

From start to finish, the *Hindenburg* was so intricately tied up with the Nazis, Eckener would need a contorted account to unravel it all. His revisionist memoir worked. Eckener portrayed himself as Day, when in fact he was Night.

Minor discrepancies in Eckener's accounts put me on the long trail of his deception. The more stones I turned, the more muck I found. It all added up to something remarkable: Hugo Eckener, a global celebrity in between the world wars, had led a double life. His fanatical desire to build the largest aircraft ever, the *Hindenburg*, first connected him with chilling figures including Joseph Goebbels and Hermann Göring. Then, step by step, behind the scenes, Eckener skulked along a crooked road to spy flights, to rocket bombs, to slave labor from the notorious Dachau concentration camp.

Unlike Nazi allies who slipped into Argentina or elsewhere after the war, Hugo Eckener hid in plain sight. He used his prewar fame to hoodwink the public, brazenly taking the spotlight to declare himself a hero, who, given his self-proclaimed vocal opposition to the Hitler regime, supposedly came within a hair of losing his life in Nazi Germany.

The Eckener pretense began to crack in German scholarship on World War II arms production and slave labor after the mid-1980s, with the opening of archives on judicial procedures aimed at identifying and purging Nazis from public life. Eckener's name surfaced. I paired that research with other, primary sources: corporate memos and reports in Germany, the *Hindenburg* investigative files at the National Archives in Washington, personal letters, and declassified U.S. Army documents.

I discovered that the *Hindenburg* itself was the reason Eckener emerged as an early and vocal Hitler supporter, and his allegiance only darkened through the war. When Germany lost, he shifted to denial. To escape any wartime suspicions, he would slickly alter *Hindenburg* history to fabricate an anti-Nazi record. In the end, he used the *Hindenburg* as his getaway vehicle.

There is imposing evidence on the *Hindenburg*'s demise. A month after the disaster, a whistleblower's revelatory letter to investigators, alone, could have blown the case wide open way back in 1937. Instead, a U.S. Navy officer nicknamed "Rosie" stepped in to cover it up. With that and other crucial evidence buried for decades, sensational sabotage theories bubbled up. But the only thing actually sabotaged was the truth.

I have been a professional writer for more than three decades, twenty-two years as a reporter and editor at the *Wall Street Journal*. I have never encountered a single story with such scheming, duplicity, and lies. We'll be talking about more than just an old flying machine. We'll be talking about facts and lies, about truth and fiction, and the cost of failing to distinguish between them.

So much has been wrong for so long, the facts so twisted beyond recognition, that we simply have to go back and start over. This isn't merely a revision. This, finally, is what really happened, the story of the hidden *Hindenburg*.

—MM

# AIR

*For our struggle is not with the flesh and blood but with the princi-palities, with the powers, with the world rulers of this present dark-ness, with the evil spirits in the heavens.*

—EPHESIANS 6:12

# 1

# Dealing with Demons

THE SILVERY ZEPPELIN GLIDED OVER THE LONG COAST OF BRAZIL. As palm trees swayed below, the cigar-shaped balloon nosed along the Atlantic Ocean. Saturday evening, the last day of June 1934.

The easy tropical winds delighted the captain, a stooped man with a goatee in the middle of life. Hugo Eckener loved flying the South American route. It offered a respite from the hardship of the Fatherland, the bone cold. He was in his fifth year skippering the *Graf Zeppelin*, a marvel more than two football fields long that weighed seventy-five tons but could float across the sky like a feather.

The *Graf Zeppelin* was his magic carpet. He had ridden it around the entire globe, shadowing whole city blocks, crowds cheering in exotic tongues, spirits lifting from the Great Depression. The famed Zeppelin, a high-wire act with flammable hydrogen, landed the daring aviator on front pages across the globe.

He wanted more. Back in Germany, he had begun meeting with Joseph Goebbels, a man of ambition in the new government with a lush bank account. Eckener wanted to own the skies, with a ship of dreams. He wanted a new aircraft bigger than the *Graf Zeppelin*, one that could ferry a hundred people, with a dining room and white-gloved waiters, with beds and staterooms, the largest flying object the world had ever seen. It didn't even have a name yet, but *Hindenburg* had a nice ring to it.

Eckener looked down from the bridge, his blue eyes twinkling, his face nicely tanned. Gulls wheeled far below. He watched the sandy shore whiten with waves at the port city of Santos, Brazil. He was riding high. All was calm.

Suddenly, the Zeppelin's radio operator appeared on the bridge, a window-enclosed room brightly lit with electric bulbs. He was anxious. He whispered to Eckener, "Everything in Germany has turned upside down."

From his headphones in the radio room, the young man had just picked up bulletins from British radio. The news came in bursts. Ernst Röhm, a celebrated Nazi official, had been arrested. Kurt von Schleicher, the former chancellor, had been shot. Many more, slain.

Berlin awaited the return of Hugo Eckener.

Hours earlier, a black Mercedes made its way through southern Germany. The new chancellor was riding in silence, his hour come round at last, riding into the day he became Hitler.

Headlights broke the cold morning dark as his car pulled up to the Hotel Hanselbauer. It was in the lakeside town of Bad Wiesse, about thirty miles from Munich. Hitler marched up to the second floor, a revolver in his long leather coat. He hammered his fist on the door.

His longtime friend and ally, a cofounder of the Nazi Party, was inside. Roused from his bed, Ernst Röhm, a tubby man wearing only pajama bottoms, opened up. Hitler rushed in with several black-uniformed officers and looked Röhm in the eyes.

Tired, dazed, Röhm stood bewildered, an old scar running from his nose to his chin. Hitler then startled the half-awake leader of the SA, a national guard of sorts in Germany that had arisen since the last war. The SA was composed of storm troopers known as the notorious Brownshirts. Hitler spat a barrage of insults, accused Röhm of treason, and shouted that he was under arrest.

Throughout the hotel, filled with vacationing Brownshirts, Hitler's SS police struck open doors, rousing the troopers from their sleep and herding them into the hallways. The SS men commandeered all the Brownshirts into military trucks. It was just before sunup. Sitting shoulder to shoulder, the captives spoke anxiously among themselves, no idea they had been double-crossed.

Hitler motioned to his chauffer, and they were off to a second stop, the storm troopers' Brown House. The Nazi Party had bought the old mansion and converted it into the headquarters for the SA. The street in front had just been cleared by the police.

Several dozen SA troopers were sleeping on benches. Some had kicked off their boots, unbuckled their cross-belts. Some snoozed in their unbuttoned brown shirts. They had been out drinking, singing and carousing in the beer gardens into the night. Some were still awake, hung over and murmuring in the halls, when they noticed extra guards quietly stationed at the doors. There was no whiff, yet, of danger.

The SA had, up to this point, been a tremendous ally of Adolf Hitler. The paramilitary group, street thugs really, helped bring him to power. Hitler was the brains of Nazi policy; the Brownshirts were the brawn to back it up. But the Brownshirts had grown to be an enormous alliance, three million strong, a formidable army in its own right that could unseat Hitler at any given moment. Hitler decided to short-circuit this threat, using his elite paramilitary group, the SS, known for their black uniforms. In effect, he chose the goons in black shirts to snuff out those in brown.

The puny man with a smudge of a mustache had used his hypnotic voice to ride his Nazi Party's popularity into Germany's parliamentary government. By the summer of 1934, the nationalist party with the crooked-cross flag had achieved remarkable power. It was even, at that moment, somewhat reputable.

Germany's beloved president, an old field marshal and hero of the great war, Paul von Hindenburg, had to admit it: The Nazi Party had made vanquished Germany, in very short order, feel great again. Hindenburg had personally chosen Hitler to be his chancellor only eighteen months earlier. Adoring the spotlight, Hitler met with foreign dignitaries, delivered radio speeches, and posed for photographs with chubby babies and boys in lederhosen.

On that dewy morning in Munich, there were new orders at the Brown House: Any SA storm trooper who wanted to come in could enter at any time all throughout the night, but no one was allowed to leave after 5:30 a.m. Some asked why, but were given only a one-word reply: Orders.

At the top of the three-story Brown House was an enormous swastika in a circular sign. The stony building was stately, resembling a courthouse, with wrought-iron balconies on the second floor. Perched on the window ledges that Saturday morning, weary SA officers looked through the misty light of a tall streetlamp out front. Truckloads of police and black-uniformed militia had begun to surround the building. No one could leave.

By ten in the morning, Hitler showed up. He knew the Brown House well. For many years, he kept an office at the party headquarters there. Munich, in fact, was the first soil for Nazism. Hitler's limping lieutenant, Goebbels, who had been riding with his boss all morning a witness to the fledgling purge, spoke excitedly about the cover story he would provide the press. Anxious and sleepless, Hitler stared ahead blankly.

When they stepped through the tall front door, with a stone triangle above it, Hitler was finally ready to speak. He motioned to Goebbels, his slight, skeletal Minister of Propaganda. Goebbels was to call the other conspirator in this murderous scheme, Prime Minister Hermann Göring. Goebbels had a code word for the operation to proceed. He asked the operator to put him through to Berlin, and breathed three syllables into the receiver: *Kolibri*, the German word for hummingbird.

Flabby in his military uniform, Göring had been waiting for the call. With Hitler and Goebbels rounding up top SA leaders in Munich, Göring began unleashing strike forces in northern Germany. In Berlin, in Munich, in Silesia, all over Germany, SS assassins began breaking the eagle and swastika seals on their envelopes and reading their orders, the names of the people they were to execute. The blacks would begin taking out the browns, all German brothers.

From his office in Berlin, Göring, with a few sparing words from his moon face, impulsively condemned anyone who had ever crossed him or Hitler. To one triggerman, he simply said, "Find Klausener and kill him." The SS assassin clicked his heels, knowing who that was, and was gone.

At the Brown House, which would become Hitler's headquarters for the looming massacre, Hitler looked over a list of SA leaders. Most SA members had full-time jobs as plumbers or factory workers, but they moonlighted as mercenary soldiers. The Brownshirts had become so large that the actual German army, limited to only 100,000 soldiers by wartime treaty, felt threatened as well.

Hitler decided to side with the army. Having the German army as his ally would help him succeed the aging, frail Hindenburg. He needed to purge the SA leadership, so he concocted alarmist stories that Röhm and his SA were planning a revolt, which had to be put down before it started.

Sitting at a desk, Hitler looked at the SA list. Angrily, he marked an X in front of one name. Then quickly another, then another. At times, he paused at a name, thought about it, then drew a crisscross. The silence was broken only by the pen scratches. One of those checked off was Karl Ernst, the SA leader in Berlin. He would be some trouble to find, as he was on his honeymoon. Hitler then handed the list to a lieutenant and said, "Take six men and an SS officer with you, and have the SA leaders executed for high treason."

The dragnet was now in full swing. Hitler would employ the Gestapo, his secret police, and the SS, his elite military guard. Working in teams of two and three, coordinating by telephone and teleprinter, Gestapo and SS operatives fanned out through Berlin, Dresden, Munich, and elsewhere.

Late in the morning, two cars pulled up to the Munich villa of Gustav Ritter von Kahr. He had crossed Hitler over a decade ago, and hadn't been in politics since. As von Kahr opened the door, three men seized him and shoved him into a car. Afraid, the man of seventy-three with a handlebar mustache said nothing. They were headed seventeen miles north, to a new prison, at Dachau.

Wilhelm Eduard Schmid pulled the bow across his cello as his wife interrupted to announce four men wanted to see him. They nabbed him from his Munich home in front of his anguished wife and three children. Schmid, peering through his round glasses, assured her it would all be straightened out. They drove off, with the music man's protests falling on deaf ears. In the morning's mayhem, the SS men were supposed to arrest a different man, named Schmitt.

Around 11:30 a.m., Kurt von Schleicher was in his study outside Berlin. He heard his doorbell ring, then footsteps. The housekeeper had let several men in. The former chancellor, a dapper dresser who preceded Hitler in the high public office, was speaking on the phone. His cane was in the corner. On the other end of the line, his friend heard von Schleicher say to someone: "Yes, I am General von Schleicher." Then, a burst of firearms. One of the intruders hung up the phone. Von Schleicher hit the carpet, blood spreading. Hearing the shots, his wife, Elisabeth, dropped her knitting and ran to the study. They had been married only eighteen months. Seeing her husband sprawled on the floor, she cupped her face in her hands and screamed. Startled, the men in black shot her. She hit the carpet.

Erich Klausener, the man Göring condemned with the sparse phrase, "Find Klausener and kill him," was in his office at the Ministry of Transport. He was a prominent Catholic in Berlin who once helped write a speech critical of the Nazis. Two SS men stepped in and told him he was under arrest. He barely stepped from his desk when one of the men shot him, and then, under orders, placed the pistol in his hand to stage his death as a suicide.

At the Brown House, Hitler manned the phone, and, as the names of those executed came in, he crossed them off his list. Further north, in Berlin, Göring began having lunch in his office, with beer and sandwiches. Between beer bottles, Gestapo agents occasionally dropped little white strips of paper with the names of those arrested. Delighted as the slips came in, Göring shouted, "Shoot them! Shoot them!"

The daylight executions continued. Bernhardt Stempfle, a Catholic priest believed to have known about some of Hitler's sexual indecencies, was dropped in a forest outside Munich, shot three times through the heart. His neck was also broken. Von Kahr perished nearby. He met his end mutilated, hacked to death. Röhm was shot in a prison cell. At Dachau, the coffin of Schmid, the music critic taken by mistake and tortured to death, was nailed shut for return to his wife.

That afternoon, SS men caught up with Karl Ernst, the chief of the Berlin Brownshirts. He was on the west coast of Germany and headed on his honeymoon to the resort island of Madeira. Ernst, bug-eyed like the screen star Peter Lorre, could not believe he was under arrest. Hitler himself had stood as a witness at his wedding. Orders, he was told. The SS flew him to Berlin, where he was driven twenty miles southeast and held for hours in a dank cellar at the Lichterfelde Barracks, an old Prussian cadet training building that the Nazis had taken over. There were one hundred other SA officers packed in the cellar with him, sweaty, anxious, cursing or praying, as the blood drained from their faces.

Evening turned ghastly. Ernst and the names of three other men were called out, and the four were led from the cellar to a large courtyard. They were marched to a red brick wall. Eight sharpshooters stood at the ready. Backs to the wall, they faced the firing squad. Other groups of four had been called previously, and the men in the cellar heard the shots. But now, as his group appeared, Ernst's bulging eyes saw blood covering the wall. Still taking that in, their shirts were torn open. The only words spoken: "By order of the Führer. Aim. Fire." Stiff-jawed or cowering, the men added their spattered blood and hunks of flesh to the wall, which the SS men did not clean between executions.

The scene became so gory that the teams of eight SS riflemen, sickened, had to be replaced repeatedly. Later the SS men loaded the piles of bodies onto a horse-drawn meat carriage and drove them off to be burned.

It would be a week before the *Graf Zeppelin* would return, on July 6, 1934, to a very different Germany. During the eighty-one hour and twelve minute crossing, the Zeppelin's radio man reported regularly to Captain Eckener on the latest with the countrywide executions.

Word of the bloody treachery, which transpired the previous weekend, spread throughout Germany, between neighbors, in offices, at outdoor markets. Reporters, however, were silent. In the year since he was installed as Hitler's Minister of Propaganda, Goebbels had established complete control over newspapers and radio. Crossing him could mean being locked up at Dachau. But he could not control the foreign reporters. The world had come to know Hitler and his Nazi Party in the past eighteen months for arrogant bullying, for menacing the Jewish population. The latest dispatches from Germany horrified the world.

Details were sparse. That a hundred or more were killed wouldn't come out for years. But the callousness of the few known executions, men dragged off into the night without judges or courts, seemed more like the crimes of medieval marauders than the actions of a legitimate government in a great modern nation.

From the interior of the American continent, a newspaper in the Mississippi River town of St. Louis sounded off: "Hitler . . . has begun to kill. He has sent his bullets against men who, former friends or not, arouse his fanatic moral conscience. Nazis now have begun to kill each other. . . . And today Germany asks: where, when and with whom will the killing stop?"

The truth is Hitler had made a deal with the army to annihilate the leadership of the rival paramilitary group, the SA. And Goebbels and Hitler had fabricated a story that Röhm and some of his SA leaders were on the verge of a military coup, tossing in charges of homosexual "debauchery" in an attempt to repulse the nation and justify their being stamped out. Göring ordered all records of the operation destroyed.

After two weeks, Hitler himself finally had to make a public address. President Hindenburg, who was ill with cancer, was consigned to his estate in Neudeck, Germany. And more and more, Hitler was becoming the face of official Germany.

Clutching the lectern at the Kroll Opera House in Berlin, Hitler unleashed his bombast, spit flying in his rapid-fire delivery: "Mutinies are judged by their own laws. If someone asked me why we did not use the regular courts I would reply: At that moment, I was responsible for the German nation; consequently, it was I alone who, during those 24 hours, was the Supreme Court of Justice of the German people." Hitler spoke before members of the parliament called the Reichstag, who were nervously applauding, seated under sparkling chandeliers, with black-uniformed SS men stationed all around.

Hitler then sought to strengthen his connection to the nation's beloved Paul Ludwig Hans Anton von Beneckendorff und von Hindenburg, who, at six-foot-five, had been a mythic figure in Germany since the Great War. Hindenburg so soundly defeated the larger Russian army at the Battle of Tannenberg on the Eastern Front in 1914 that the Russian commander committed suicide on the spot. Into his eighties, Hindenburg, a man of Victorian times with a deep voice and a handlebar mustache, still wore a chest full of medals and an anachronistic pointed helmet with gold tip.

From the podium, Hitler reminded them that the great Hindenburg himself had chosen him. "Since the Marshall's confidence has placed me where I am, I am aware only of a great concern for the present life of our people and its future."

Within two weeks, Hindenburg, elected twice by the German people as their president, died at age eighty-six. Hitler moved swiftly to vacate the president's office, saying no one could fill boots as grand as Hindenburg's, and he consolidated the power of both men into himself, into a dictator, a position he called the Führer.

Neighboring countries grew nervous. Border patrols were stepped up, and diplomats gathered to plot responses. Editorialists throughout Europe sounded alarms. The *Times of London* warned of the new regime's "savagery . . . disregard for all the forms of law . . . political methods of the Middle Ages."

In short, Goebbels had a public-relations disaster on his hands. Though his savagery would worsen, Hitler would always desperately crave respect, legitimacy. So, Goebbels decided to mastermind a campaign to show the world that all of Germany was behind Hitler: this man of high morals who stamped out debauchery, saving the German people from chaos and scandal, this misunderstood leader. German citizens would be asked to approve the fusing of Hindenburg's power into the person of Hitler, into the Führer. A referendum was scheduled for late August.

The world press that summer couldn't shake what history would come to call the Night of the Long Knives. Thomas Mann, a German novelist and Nobel Laureate who left Germany the previous February, looked back on his homeland with shame. He called Hitler a "dirty swindler and murderous charlatan . . . a gangster of the lowest sort."

Goebbels needed to deflect the criticism. "Everywhere we're falling into discredit," he lamented in his diary. Hitler was slumping. The vote legitimizing the Führer needed to be strong. Goebbels needed to whip up zealous support. He needed to have other prominent Germans, luminaries whom the public respected, endorse Hitler. Goebbels immediately thought of Dr. Hugo Eckener.

The two had met briefly after Goebbels accompanied Hitler to power. Just the summer before, Eckener was in his Propaganda Ministry office in Berlin. Goebbels didn't care much for him, but the famous Zeppelin commander could be an important cheerleader for the Nazi cause. Goebbels himself had ridden on the world-renowned *Graf Zeppelin* a year earlier in grand style to Rome, to introduce himself and the new ruling party to the fascists in Italy.

As the summer of 1934 deepened, Goebbels knew that Dr. Eckener's voice was as well known throughout Germany as Hitler's. After building the *Graf Zeppelin*, the largest flying machine in its day, Eckener piloted it around the world in 1929, making headlines from Europe and the United States to Asia and Russia. Airplanes, still in their infancy as flimsy stick-and-cloth contraptions, couldn't touch the voyage. Eckener was as world-famous then as Charles Lindbergh, who crossed the Atlantic alone in his *Spirit of St. Louis* plane in 1927.

The sheer audacity of Eckener's globe-trotting flight startled the world, and stoked embers of respect for Germany. New York City had celebrated Eckener with two ticker-tape parades. *Time* magazine put pouchy-eyed Eckener on its cover, and the National Geographic Society awarded him a special gold medal.

Even U.S. presidents were star-struck by the commander of the renowned *Graf Zeppelin*. Invited to the White House, Eckener had met with Calvin Coolidge and, later, Herbert Hoover. And everywhere Eckener landed, flashbulbs popped and a flock of reporters circled. His broken English made him sound exotic to radio listeners in the United States. His celebrity was nearly unparalleled around the world.

Yes, this was the man Goebbels needed. When the two met at the Propaganda Ministry the year before, 1933, Eckener was in financial trouble. Construction was being delayed on his new ship, designed to be one-third larger than the *Graf Zeppelin*, one so big it would challenge the old laws of physics and the newer theories of aeronautics.

Eckener's Zeppelin factory was running low on money. Meeting with Goebbels, Hitler's trusted lieutenant, Eckener explained that he needed two million Reichsmarks to continue building his dream ship. Goebbels thought something could be worked out. Eckener would need to consider himself indebted to Hitler, to the new regime. The grand new Zeppelin could be dispatched for party propaganda, for flyovers of parades, marches, and rallies.

With the fat check from the Nazi government, construction was stepped up at the famed factory in Friedrichshafen, a little shoreline town on Lake Constance, or the *Bodensee* in German, far south in Germany. It was called the *Luftschiffbau Zeppelin*, or the Zeppelin airship maker. The plant, which had constructed more than one hundred crayon-shaped Zeppelins over thirty years, had hired hundreds of new workers. Giant, round girders were in place, and tons of a special light type of aluminum were on order. The big, new ship was finally going to happen.

With Hitler in trouble by the summer of 1934, Goebbels wanted to collect on the donation the Nazis made to the Zeppelin company. Eckener needed to deliver a three-minute speech that would be broadcast across Germany, in his familiar voice, oddly high-pitched for a man with a thick torso. He needed to endorse Hitler in the upcoming nationwide vote. To complete his futuristic *Hindenburg*, Eckener would have to deal with demons.

This was surely a predicament. With all his celebrity, Eckener himself had briefly considered running for president of Germany, against Hitler, in 1932. Newspaper articles wondered if Eckener would step in as a candidate. Friends had suggested he do so, but he really wasn't political. He mostly enjoyed the cheering crowds, the adoring politicians and reporters, the cameras, the microphones. Worse, Hitler was frightening. How could Eckener commend him, after all the murders, to his fellow countrymen? How could he portray a butcher as a statesman? Would the world ever forgive him if he helped bring a madman to power, and the tide of blood rose?

# 2

# "The Pope"

IT WAS ALL BUT IMPOSSIBLE THAT THE *HINDENBURG* EVER CAME TO BE built. Zeppelins began as a scandalous instrument of war. The slender, dark balloons had dropped bombs on London, Paris, Brussels, and Antwerp among other places during the first world war. It was the dawn of aerial warfare, hatred falling from clouds. Zeppelins brought war to civilians in a way never before seen, terrorizing innocents on the ground. With lights flicked off to hide from the new flying machines, townspeople huddled at night, cursing what they called "Baby Killers."

After Germany fell in defeat in World War I, the Allies wanted to wipe out any hope that it could rearm itself. By treaty, German weapons production was severely limited, as was its army. Zeppelin production was effectively banned. It was only by luck, poor memory, and shrewd deception that Hugo Eckener managed to keep the famed Zeppelin factory alive and running.

From the top-down mentality in Germany, where authority came from on high, the Zeppelin melded mind and machine perfectly. The first Zeppelin was developed by an old cavalry officer, a nobleman named Ferdinand Adolph Heinrich August Graf von Zeppelin. *Graf* is the German word for the rank of Count. And Count Zeppelin, with a shiny bald head and a white walrus mustache, had one particular passion: war. Along with much of Germany before the Great War, he was petrified of France someday marching across the border, and he hated England and all its global power, the empire on which the sun never set.

Interested in learning the latest in military tactics, Count Zeppelin headed to the United States in the spring of 1863, with special permission from the Union army to observe the Civil War being waged in Virginia. His visit was a gesture of military goodwill between America and Germany. Zeppelin later set off for St. Paul, Minnesota, and in August of 1863 he had an opportunity to ride in a large balloon inflated with coal gas. It rose to a height of 600 feet or so, offering stunning panoramic views.

The Union balloon corps had the inflatable contraptions for reconnaissance, an eye in the sky on Confederate troop and weapons movements. There on the American frontier, Zeppelin feared that he had glimpsed the future of warfare. Germany would have to have dominion of the air, or be dominated from it.

With no schooling in science, Count Zeppelin had to hire engineers to help him realize his vague ideas. As the 1800s came to a close, the self-styled aviator was nearing sixty and the designs were shaping up. On the calm currents of the Bodensee, he had workmen construct a large rectangular floating shed. Inside, he began building balloons that were elongated, with large inflatable sacks called gas cells. His first model, the LZ 1, differed from previous balloon-craft in that it was not a single gas-bag, but had multiple gas cells lined up and held together with a series of light-metal ribs. The whole shebang was enclosed within a fabric envelope. Filled with hydrogen, the balloons were sturdy and slim like link sausages, and they were powered with propellers affixed to the sides.

The French had similarly been developing so-called dirigibles, or steerable balloons, elevating the Count's anxiety. The Count's aircraft, with all its components, was so different a balloon design, there was no name for it. It wasn't a blimp, which is a bouncier, nonrigid balloon. He decided to give it his own surname, Zeppelin.

The Count believed his Zeppelin could serve as a weapon of terror for the German military to dominate other countries. In a memo to the German emperor in 1887, Zeppelin first detailed his three-part formula for the perfect war balloon. It needed to be able to fly against headwinds, remain airborne for at least twenty-four hours to handle broad reconnaissance flights, and provide enough lift to carry soldiers, supplies, and explosive projectiles. Those three imperatives, he wrote, will require larger gas containers of some kind, and therefore large airships. "Were it possible to solve these problems, then airships will become enormously useful in the conduct of war," he promised Wilhelm I, the German emperor.

Zeppelin's first few models barely got off the ground, though, and he quickly became a laughingstock: the crazy Count with his wobbly sausages. His first airship, the LZ 1, rose above the Bodensee in July 1900 and flew seventeen minutes before being forced to land. It was grounded and dismantled the following year, after three flights totaling two hours and one minute. The LZ 2 wrecked on landing in 1906.

With trial and error, along with heavy new funding from patriotic-minded industrialists who shared his vision of superior weaponry, the Count found his way, advancing the Zeppelin to the point it could fly hours and hours without refueling, reliably covering distances of hundreds of miles. Enemy territory was then within reach.

The Zeppelin probably wouldn't have gotten much further but for the energy and determination of Hugo Eckener, thirty years younger than Count Zeppelin. Eckener was born in a speck of a Baltic seaport town, Flensburg, in 1868. His father, Johann, ran the Eckener Brothers tobacco and cigar factory. His mother was from a seafaring Danish family. Rejecting the family business, he headed south to the city of Leipzig, studying psychology and earning a doctorate at Leipzig University. Eckener felt at home at the institution, one of Europe's oldest universities, whose renowned alumni included Goethe, Nietzsche, and Wagner.

Eckener then tried journalism, but found his calling in his early thirties with propaganda, at first doing public relations for the Zeppelin factory. He was a natural propagandist, informed by his deep study of behavioral psychology. He would show little allegiance to truth. He knew how to drill into brains, how to massage the message.

Eckener was so adept at spinning tales and ginning up favorable Zeppelin press that the company took the unusual step of auditioning him for a more visible role, as a Zeppelin pilot. Aviation was so new, there were no formal flight schools. Any candidate merely needed to apprentice on a ship under a captain to learn to fly it, and Eckener turned out to be very talented at operating the treacherous flying machines.

Once on the bridge, he rose quickly in the little company and would eventually earn the nickname "The Pope" because he viewed all of his instincts about operating Zeppelins as infallible. With an enviable record in the sky, he gained wide respect.

Count Zeppelin never lost sight of the goal of weaponizing his ships. When a reporter once tried to interview him about his Zeppelin, the Count dismissed him with contempt: "I am not a circus rider, performing for the public. I am completing a serious task in service of the *Vaterland*."

The Count's military ambition put his scientific team ahead in several new technologies, including aerodynamics, weather tracking, the stress and strength tolerances of aluminum and alloyed metals, and the fabrics and coatings of both outer covers and the gasbags within. His company also had to develop training for pilots and crews to pioneer the aerial transport of passengers and cargo.

In 1909, the Luftschiffbau Zeppelin opened the first airline in the world. Known popularly as *Delag*, the Zeppelin airline shuttled commuters between Friedrichshafen and Staaken, outside Berlin. In suits and ties or long dresses, seated twenty at a time comfortably in wicker chairs, most of the passengers had never flown before. Peering out the windows of the *Bodensee*, and later the *Nordstern*, they marveled at aerial views of church steeples and acres of farmland, cattle stampeding away, frightened by the drone of propellers in the sky.

Count Zeppelin was direct in his feelings about the airline that Alfred Colsman, his longtime associate, had established. When Colsman first proposed an aerial passenger transportation business to tide the company over while it tried to interest the military, the Count replied, "I detest any notion of commercializing my invention!" But Delag was actually an advertisement to persuade the reluctant German military that the Zeppelin was a safe, reliable vehicle. The German army had been interested in the flying machine, but could never really shake the worry that flimsy, slow-moving balloons, filled with flammable hydrogen, were too easy a target for the enemy to shoot down.

That changed when World War I began. The Imperial German Army quickly ordered dozens of them. Unlike battleships with names memorializing heroes, the Zeppelins, with a few exceptions, used numbers. Each had the designation LZ, initials for *Luftschiff Zeppelin*, or airship Zeppelin. Models LZ 26 through LZ 114 were delivered during the war, with machine guns typically affixed to the bridge, or gondola. Bombs were tossed overboard by hand.

The attacks, which struck civilian victims indiscriminately, felt more like terrorism to the British than legitimate war practices. In January of 1915, the first civilians in England killed by Zeppelin bombing were a fifty-three-year-old cobbler, who perished when he left his workshop to investigate a strange hum in the sky, and a seventy-two-year-old woman just returning home from grocery shopping. The next day, newspapers across England decried Germany's "frightfulness" and its Zeppelin pilots as murderous and cowardly.

The Zeppelins, in fact, caused far wider panic and outrage than deaths and destruction. And they became a rallying cry throughout Germany. During the first world war, German schoolchildren would recite this ditty:

*Zeppelin, fly.*
*Help us in the War.*
*Fly to England—*
*England shall be destroyed by fire.*
*Zeppelin, fly!*

Count Zeppelin, winning back some esteem in the military after a humiliating demotion earlier in his career, argued that Germany could quickly vanquish England with squadrons of Zeppelins. If a ton of bombs could be dropped at once into English harbors, one bizarre battle plan had it, powerful resulting waves would crush the hulls of Britain's mighty ships. Another scheme envisioned a great raid with twenty airships dropping 6,000 incendiary bombs all at once onto London. The theory was the vast fire that would erupt would be impossible to control. Count Zeppelin met with one general in late 1915, stared him straight in the eye, and proclaimed, "All England must burn!"

During the war, Eckener was deployed to train Zeppelin pilots for spy and bomb squadrons. One of his assistants in that training was Ernst Lehmann, a young naval officer who had been diverted from his passion for shipbuilding, which he was pursuing at the Imperial Navy shipyard at

Kiel. Recruiting Lehmann from the navy, Eckener began training him to fly Zeppelins in passenger service in 1913.

Eckener was a technical advisor to Peter Strasser, who became a hero in Germany as the chief commander of the daring Zeppelin raids during World War I. Eckener trained more than fifty-eight crews, more than a thousand airmen in all. Lehmann was a short, genial man who would shine far brighter than other Zeppelin commanders—a little too brightly for his teacher, Dr. Eckener.

The war ended. Germany was vanquished. Whatever fury the European capitals felt for Zeppelins, their militaries were desperate to have one of their own. Germany wasn't allowed to keep its handful of flying war machines—they had to be relinquished as war booty to the victors. France acquired the *Nordstern* and the LZ 114, which it renamed the *Dixmude*. England was awarded its own war-reparations ship, the LZ 113. Germany relinquished the *Bodensee* to Italy.

With the peace came flight fever. The race to cross an ocean by air was on. As American, French, and British scientists worked to perfect their own airship models, Britain pulled off a stunner. In early July of 1919, a crew piloted the first airship across the Atlantic. The 3,000-mile crossing was historic, but did not inspire great confidence.

The crew of the ship, called the R 34, slept in hammocks and cooked food on a heating pad welded to the starboard engine. Flying around storms and hitting heavy winds, the airship flew 108 hours and 12 minutes, before landing on fumes on Long Island. It had only forty minutes of engine fuel left. Hours before it landed, the R 34 sent an alarming wireless message to the U.S. Navy: "Rush help, making for Boston. . . . Come quickly. Gasoline giving out. Send ship."

When the R 34 finally did arrive, no one on the ground knew exactly how to land the monster balloon. A British major, a certain J. E. M. Pritchard, had to parachute from the R 34 to the ground to supervise the landing. It made him the first person to arrive in America having flown from Europe.

The world awaited a German design to conquer oceans. The U.S. Navy was eager for its own Zeppelin as war booty, but German crews in the summer of 1919 had destroyed the last seven of their beloved ships rather than release them into enemy hands. So, the United States persuaded its allies to keep open the Count's famed Zeppelin factory in Friedrichshafen, just long enough for it to design and construct a ship for the U.S. Navy. Once the United States got its state-of-the-art flying machine, the Zeppelin works could be dismantled once and for all.

Eckener was elated. He had worked closely with the Count to fly Zeppelins for more than a decade. The Count had died, at seventy-eight years old, just before the war had ended. That left Eckener as the company's guiding spirit. Flight was so new to the U.S. military then that the army, responsible for land, and the navy, soldiers of the seas, squabbled over who exactly would oversee a planned fleet of aircraft. By 1918, they resolved that the navy would be solely responsible for Zeppelin building.

Eckener, happy to have a sanctioned loophole for keeping the Luftschiffbau Zeppelin open, held his breath for U.S. funding. In a bizarre attempt to end-run the navy, an army colonel then tried to order a Zeppelin from the Germans, perhaps operating rogue, perhaps with authorization. William N. Hensley Jr., a balloonist for the U.S. Army, signed a construction contract on Thanksgiving Day of 1919 with the Zeppelin company. The airship order was in direct contradiction to the prior-year agreement between the army and the navy, and the U.S. Secretary of War stepped in days later to kill the contract. Fortunately for Eckener, the navy then followed with its own legitimate order, which would be for model LZ 126.

The LZ 126, along with the next ship soon on the drawing boards, the LZ 127, or the *Graf Zeppelin*, were prototypes for the *Hindenburg*. The first two models strengthened the confidence of Eckener and his German designers that they could safely carry passengers in hydrogen balloons, and that the sky was the limit as to how big they could build them.

Completed in 1924, LZ 126 was the largest ship anyone had ever attempted, 658 feet in length and nearly 91 feet in diameter at its fattest point. The project allowed Dr. Eckener and his engineers to design the first Zeppelin specifically for transoceanic travel, a major advance. The Zeppelin firm needed to learn how to deal with atmospheric forces over oceans and how to staff and operate a ship that could zip along in the air with no land in sight, for nearly four days, flying a stunning 5,000 miles.

It would be the farthest a Zeppelin had ever flown. No one knew, in fact, if it was really possible.

After two years of construction, LZ 126, the project that kept the famed Zeppelin factory from closing, reached a final critical phase: installing the outer covering. As the largest ship ever tried, the LZ 126 would literally stretch the abilities of aeronautical cloth to the breaking point. As with skin on humans, the outer cover needed to be flexible enough to stretch, but strong enough to protect the internal body.

Zeppelins complicated the whole matter by orders of magnitude. Several acres of cloth had to be carefully fitted to extend over the giant cylindrical rings that formed the cigar shape of the ship. It all had to be rugged enough to protect the vehicle from the strong winds that pound an airborne ship, as well as the extremes of tropical heat and freezing weather.

The delicate job of covering the ship fell to the Zeppelin company's wizard of fabric, Karl Hürttle. A trained artist, he worked in textiles, rugs, tapestry, and interior decorating before joining the Luftschiffbau Zeppelin in 1915. By the time he worked on LZ 126, he had supervised the covering of more than fifty Zeppelins. He brought a scientist's mind to the fine points and technology of woven cotton cloth, yet spent his life collecting fine paintings, including a precious Chagall. He knew the cloths of the heavens and their weaves intimately, the twill, rib, mock, leno, basket, sateen.

At the factory, technicians weren't allowed to touch the actual ship until Hürttle had trained them how to properly stretch cloth; coat it with various adhesives and apply coats of dope, an acetone solution with a closely guarded secret recipe that was used to tauten the material; waterproof it; and give it a silver cast to reflect the sun's rays. Hürttle would later form an outer-cover school. Trainees needed to learn the meticulous sequence of tensioning the cloth, lacing the cover, brushing a first coat of dope, then tensioning the cover again and again to make it as streamlined as possible for a smooth flow through the sky.

The operation was like fitting a tight sleeve over the light aluminum framework, which resembled a row of spoked bicycle wheels running from the Zeppelin's nose to its tail. On the factory floor of the immense hangar in Friedrichshafen, two dozen men would spend weeks in the fall of 1924 arranging eighty-five-foot-tall ladders, with rolling and locking wheels, around the curved framework. Scaffoldings were all around. Workers tucked, painted, stretched, re-stretched, repainted, and measured tension again and again, to be sure the cover was snuggly fit to exacting tolerances.

The outer cover was one of the trickiest parts of a Zeppelin, along with the design of an aluminum-alloy hull that had to marry two material attributes that rarely partner: light and strong. The design of the hull and outer cover were trade secrets of the Germans. They did not divulge, for example, that one of its chief designers used bridge structures as an engineering model for Zeppelin frames.

Scientific literature on aeronautical craft was scarce, leaving others in the dark. The occasional captured Zeppelin during the war and other intelligence helped some. But, by and large, scientists outside Germany were completely puzzled by the enigmatic engineering calculations that allowed objects weighing several tons to float in the air and not break apart when winds rose above a strong breeze.

Hürttle inspected and double-checked every inch of the silver covering before the LZ 126 was marched outside the hangar for its first flight. He rode along on board the giant ship as it conducted test flights over Germany that September. The ship was ready to be flown to a naval base in Lakehurst, New Jersey, special delivery by Eckener and Lehmann. The outer cover was perfect. It was October 1924, the chill winds of winter still in the offing.

The fabric wizard was not around when a later Zeppelin model was built and completed in the dead of winter—an unlucky combination that would see that airship arrive at Lakehurst thirteen years later and burst into flame.

LZ 126's takeoff from Germany was set for early the morning of October 11, 1924. In a procedure called "weighing off," the passengers, crew, and cargo were all carefully accounted for, so that the correct volume of hydrogen in the gas cells would be inflated to lift the immense balloon-craft off the ground and into the air.

When the captain felt all systems were go, he would give the lift-off command, shouting, *Luftschiff Hoch!*; in English, "Up, ship!" The ships were typically "walked" out of their enormous hangars, with 200 or more burly ground-crew men holding ropes attached to the levitating Zeppelin to keep it from floating away before the officers were ready to fly. On the command, the ground crew released their grip on the ropes.

That morning, though, the release order was delayed. The ship's meticulously inventoried weight was mysteriously high, by about 300 pounds. Something was wrong. Crewmen began searching the aircraft, and they discovered two stowaways, a reporter and a photographer who had changed into work uniforms and snuck on for a scoop. They were escorted off by police.

At 7:30 in the morning, the "Up, ship!" call came, and LZ 126 left German soil. A crowd had been at the landing field since daybreak. It was a cold morning, a bittersweet one. Count Zeppelin had moved his operation to the little town of Friedrichshafen, on the shores of the Bodensee, the sparkling lake that bordered Germany, Austria, and Switzerland. Many of the people of Friedrichshafen had not seen a Zeppelin come out of the factory in years. They might never see one again, they thought. These floating giants had given them so much pride, and now their newest, largest, most state-of-the-art Zeppelin was leaving the homeland, for America. The ship passed over the Baroque onion-bulb towers of the old Palace Church, a landmark on the Friedrichshafen skyline, and headed off.

On the ground, they began belting out the German national anthem, "*Deutschland, Deutschland, über alles!*" The Zeppelin crew could hear the beloved lyrics, "Germany, Germany, above everything!"

"The last words we heard before leaving our native land," recalled Lehmann. "Our hearts beat faster. It was a solemn moment."

Over France, the first lunch of the voyage was exquisite. Turtle soup to start. Hungarian goulash with peas and carrots. Pudding and coffee. Not only was air service across oceans unheard of, but the menu on board rivaled that of fabulous steamships puffing away below.

A little over three days later, with no problems despite the treacherous air over the North Atlantic in the fall, Lehmann spotted the coast of America. "Now we know how Christopher Columbus and his crew felt," Lehmann told his men, "when the lookout on the *Pinta* sighted land."

His first time to America, Lehmann compared Boston from the sky that evening to "a diamond merchant's showcase, with innumerable lights gleaming below us." In New York, the war-reparations Zeppelin circled the Statue of Liberty as sirens in the harbor sounded their welcome upward. In a flyover of Broadway, factory whistles sounded. People crowded, pointed, and waved on rooftops. Newspapers called the oversize Zeppelin the "Queen of the Air."

President Coolidge sent a congratulatory message to Dr. Eckener. Praising the "trailblazing exploit," he said, "it gives me and the people of the United States great pleasure that the friendly relations between Germany and America are reaffirmed." Karl von Wiegand, a correspondent for the Hearst chain of newspapers, wrote, "Germany has rehabilitated herself in the eyes of the world."

The Zeppelin arrived around 9:00 a.m. on Wednesday, October 15, 1924, at the airfield at Lakehurst, fifty miles southwest of New York City. It had flown one-fifth of the world's circumference in three days, nine hours, and two minutes. Upon delivery of the $860,000 ship, the U.S. Navy handed the Zeppelin men a little slip of paper, a written receipt.

Lakehurst left Eckener stunned. The Americans had cleared more than a thousand acres from the New Jersey pine belt and constructed the single largest room in the world. The steel hangar at Lakehurst was thirteen stories tall and cost over $3.5 million. It was a landmark visible from miles away. A man-made cavern 806 feet long by 263 feet wide, its rolling doors were 177 feet tall, each 1,350 tons. Seeing airships as cutting edge, the military would pour $9 million into Lakehurst, the giant hangar, barracks, helium storage, and mooring masts.

The base began with great hope. In 1919, the acting Secretary of the Navy, Franklin Delano Roosevelt, approved the acquisition of about 1,700 acres near coastal New Jersey. The army had previously used the site, called Camp Kendrick, for chemical warfare research. The navy base, pioneering in aviation, had a pigeon loft, for carrier pigeons to fly messages air to ground, and a parachute school. Graduation required a candidate's packing his own parachute and jumping from an airship 500 feet above ground. Eckener realized the United States was serious about airship development, a thought that haunted him.

Very soon after the Lakehurst base was opened, though, meteorologists noted something puzzling about its location. It was plagued by storms and wind. As one navy book, the *Rigid Airship Manual*, noted, "Practically every storm that passes over this country or along the Atlantic coast exercises for a greater or less time an influence over the winds at Lakehurst," meaning Lakehurst was a port for every storm.

President Coolidge invited Captains Eckener and Lehmann to a meeting at the White House. Navy Secretary Curtis D. Wilbur announced that the LZ 126 would be christened the *Los Angeles* "because it came to us like an angel of peace."

Back up the coast, away from the Zeppelin celebrations, fear gripped Lakehurst, where the LZ 126 was parked in the hangar. The ship was filled with hydrogen, a gas so dangerous it was no longer used in U.S. airships. Hydrogen, the most common element in the universe, was cheap. It provided the lift for a Zeppelin—hydrogen's having one-fourteenth the density of air, and thus much lighter—but it was highly flammable. Hydrogen is what fuels the sun and makes all the stars shine.

Having the tiniest of molecules, hydrogen is also the Houdini of elements—it likes to escape. With a hydrogen gas leak, a single spark could set an entire Zeppelin ablaze.

The ship had to keep the hydrogen in meticulously constructed gasbags that were gastight. For sheer safety reasons, U.S. operators of Zeppelins had switched years earlier to helium, a fireproof gas that had only 93 percent the lifting force of hydrogen. Helium was much costlier and, due to geological quirks, in short supply outside the United States.

The insistence on helium as a lifting gas followed several spectacular fiery crashes, including the *Wingfoot Air Express*, a small hydrogen-filled dirigible owned by the Goodyear company that crashed into a stately bank building in downtown Chicago in 1919, killing thirteen people, most bystanders who were burned to death on the ground.

Inside the hangar at Lakehurst, to prevent sparks or friction, navy crewmen secured every light and motor, every buzzer, every piece of electrical equipment. Men were ordered to wear rubber shoes, and were warned to operate tools gingerly to avoid sparks. And absolutely, positively, no smoking. Cigarettes, whose glowing tips could fatally ignite an entire ship, were *verboten*.

The *Los Angeles* needed to be converted from German to American standards for safety. The ground crew logged when they began to release the hydrogen, a Saturday in October at 1300 navy time. The entire operation was carefully monitored until the gasbags were completely deflated. Then, the men in the big hangar breathed again. The last of the dangerous hydrogen was in storage tanks being driven away.

The day after Eckener and Lehmann, as second in command, delivered the LZ 126 to Lakehurst, they had an extraordinary meeting. It was at two in the afternoon, Thursday, October 16, 1924. In room 331 of the U.S. Navy building in Washington, thirty-six men from all walks of the military and aviation met to discuss the future of flight. One attendee was Orville Wright, who twenty-one years earlier piloted a double-winged contraption above a North Carolina beach in the world's first controlled flight of a plane. He and his brother, Wilbur, gave wing to an industry.

It was a pivotal moment for aviation in the fall of 1924, and the packed room at the navy headquarters was abuzz. No one knew just then if planes could ever be developed large enough to carry dozens of passengers safely and tons of cargo. Eckener and Lehmann had demonstrated that they could do precisely that with a Zeppelin, and over an ocean.

Some of the brightest inventive minds in the world were fascinated with airships. Auto baron Henry Ford thought air travel would inevitably split into two markets, with planes covering short city-to-city routes and airships eating into the steamship business of voyages between continents. In early July 1919, he had witnessed the arrival, landing, and departure of the British airship R 34 at Mineola, Long Island. He was mesmerized. Within a few years, he would bankroll the construction near his auto factory in Dearborn, Michigan, of a half-million-dollar mooring mast, where the *Los Angeles* could park. It was a big gamble, but if Zeppelin travel caught on, Ford wanted thousands of prospective airship flyers connecting through Michigan, making his state a hub for travel across the United States. Ford would eventually meet personally with Lehmann to discuss designs for his new airport.

After the Washington photographers and men with their reels took publicity shots at the navy building, Eckener stepped up to the podium. He was to address members of the National Advisory Committee for

Aeronautics, or NACA. Decades later, the group would change a letter in its acronym and become a futuristic agency called NASA. The committee wanted Eckener's opinion on safety and flight.

They murmured among themselves, wanted to know if he seriously thought passengers could be flown safely in hydrogen-filled aircraft. Eckener spoke in German. Captain Lehmann, who had much better command of English, translated for the audience. Was it safe, Dr. Eckener, to carry passengers on airships floating with hydrogen?

"This is a question which is not so easy to answer," Eckener began, knowing the viability of his company, which barely averted being shut down after the war, rested on his answer. "It is not entirely out of the question to operate commercial airships when inflated with hydrogen.... There must be a crew which is trained and instructed to use the greatest care and caution in handling hydrogen." When the Zeppelin factory began a couple decades earlier, he added, they were building and operating only a few ships at a time, learning and perfecting how to fly them more safely. When Germany was at war, however, production sped up, and it was harder to monitor safety. "When more ships and crews, especially untrained crews, were in operation, the discipline was lost and there were occasions when cigarette butts were found on the decks of hydrogen-inflated airships."

Hydrogen was safe, he said, to the degree that the gas cells, the pouches that held the hydrogen and lifted the ship, were absolutely gastight. "For as soon as the gas cells are leaking in the slightest degree, they will form a mixture of hydrogen-air in the space between the gas cells and the outer covering. The least formation of a spark, for instance when the ship is meeting a cloud electrically charged, might lead to an ignition of the hydrogen-air mixture, which is impossible as long as the gas cells are absolutely tight."

Lehmann, delivering in English the words of Eckener, added that hydrogen could be controlled safely on a small scale. "But soon after the enterprise begins to grow in extent, then it will be more and more difficult, and finally become impossible to keep up the discipline and prevent a disaster which might develop, which, in Dr. Eckener's opinion, would be a deadly blow to airship navigation."

As it turns out, Lehmann heard Eckener's warning louder and clearer than the boss did.

## 3

# "Noble Wine"

FOR AN ENCORE TO THE *LOS ANGELES*, HUGO ECKENER DREAMT UP A new Zeppelin that would be so large, so striking to all who witnessed it float overhead that it would become the wonder of the world in a few short years. It would spark a media furor wherever it passed, making him a global celebrity irresistible to a shifty German nationalist group angling for repute.

The odds were poor that the ship, to be called the *Graf Zeppelin*, would ever materialize in Germany. In Akron, Ohio, the industrial power Goodyear Tire and Rubber was developing its own rubberized airships to compete with Germany's Zeppelins. Other American business interests wanted to fund their own new Zeppelins, trying to bring the ultramodern airship into viable passenger service. Architects sketched the top of the forthcoming Empire State Building, the point of the tall pencil, as a mooring mast, as its builders dreamed futuristic. Many people expected money would flow in once these Zeppelins were filling the sky.

Even Captain Lehmann saw more opportunity in America. He was thirty-seven when he left Germany for a job at Goodyear in 1923, as its vice president for engineering. A dozen other top technicians from the Zeppelin factory steamed across the ocean to work with him. The coveted Zeppelin brain trust came to be called the "Twelve Apostles." Lehmann sailed back the next year to help Eckener fly the LZ 126 to Lakehurst, but then it was back to his desk in Ohio.

Eckener could not keep his men from fleeing. He had done the impossible by keeping the Zeppelin plant going, but Germany was still rebuilding, and government funding had dried up for the big balloons.

Streets and buildings needed repairs, and the last big Zeppelin they had built ended up in America for good. Officially, anyway, the factory was supposed to be closed. Friedrichshafen, the town put on the map by the crazy Count and his flying sausages, looked bleak.

Fingers tapping the keys of his grand piano at home in Akron, Lehmann was flirting with American citizenship. Just over five feet tall and known as the "Little Captain," Lehmann was an ambitious aircraft flyer and builder, torn between countries. He had been whipsawed his entire adult life by politics, which he cared little for. As a boy growing up on the shore of Lake Constance, the *Bodensee* in German, he could see the snow-peaked Alps in the distance. The large lake had a curving shoreline shared by Germany, Austria, and Switzerland. The Bodensee summoned young Ernst to a seagoing life, to worlds beyond his lakeside village of Ludwigshafen.

Lehmann was a bubbly conversationalist and spoke fluent English, though with a trace of his native German. He recited poetry and ballads. He often surprised people he barely knew with thoughtful gifts. And, with all his time in the skies and some cutting-edge patents, the engineer had the brains everyone in aviation wanted.

By the late 1920s, Lehmann and his wife, Susanna, were celebrated society darlings in Akron. Hour on hour, the little German man with the big smile entertained guests in his home, banging out swing hits on his piano, striking the imposing chords of Beethoven, and crooning folk songs from the old country. Lehmann started paperwork to become an American citizen.

Eckener wanted Lehmann back, wanted the Twelve Apostles back. His devotion to Zeppelins at the expense of all else, though, put him on a collision course with one of the top executives of the Luftschiffbau Zeppelin, Alfred Colsman. After the war, with Zeppelin production all but forbidden, Colsman, a close friend of Count Zeppelin's, pushed the Luftschiffbau Zeppelin further into a host of businesses, including light-metal alloys and aluminum consumer products such as stylish pots and pans and elegant hourglass-shaped vases. Its Maybach Motors division made engines and, later, opulent motorcars. The company also produced chemicals and gearboxes and drivetrains. Colsman was prudent, frugal, a *Pfennig*-pincher. Faced with an empty airship hangar, he once briefly turned it into a motion-picture studio.

As Eckener climbed at the company, he and Colsman, who had built the firm as its general manager over twenty years, disagreed over the future prospects of the Zeppelin flight business. Employment had sunk to 550 from its wartime workforce of 13,600. Things came to a head when the Luftschiffbau Zeppelin could not find an insurance company willing to cover any loss of the LZ 126 on its trans-Atlantic delivery trip to America. The ship had cost nearly $1 million, a loss that could sink the company. Eckener took a big gamble that he could pilot the ship there safely. Other attempts had failed. Britain's R 34 itself barely made it, flying 2,000 fewer miles.

Colsman saw Eckener as a fame-seeker and imprudent businessman. Delivering the ship across the treacherous North Atlantic without incident was a stroke of luck, Colsman thought, a stunt that put the company at unneeded risk. But it had, indeed, worked. Insurance didn't matter. And Eckener did become a celebrity. Ends justified means. The Pope prevailed.

The relationship between the two men, both leaders in the company, hit bottom after the *Los Angeles*. They began communicating only through formal, written memos. Eckener's stubborn fixation on Zeppelins at all costs was wearing on Colsman.

Even the Count himself had grown weary of his Zeppelins in his later years. Before his death in 1917, Count Zeppelin had become convinced the future was in planes. He worked tirelessly to develop a class of huge bomber planes, called R-Planes, to fulfill his ambition of German dominance of the air. Into his seventies, the old man with the bushy white mustache routinely climbed ladders to peek with glee into the cockpits as the planes were shaping up in their hangars. He pushed his engineers to pioneer all-metal aircraft, which would become the industry standard decades later.

The Count was curiously visionary. At one point, he hired an inventor named Anton Flettner, who was developing remote-control devices. His first application was to steer circus horses, with radio packs delivering pulses in their saddles. Flettner later turned to a wirelessly controlled miniature tank, but the German army was unmoved by a demonstration. The Count, though, thought the ingenuity of using electronics and radio signals to navigate machinery could be applied to remote control of Zeppelins and aerial weaponry. After the Count's death, Eckener insisted development work focus solely on Zeppelins. It would be many decades later that military scientists would see the full potential in pilotless craft, or drones.

That the Count lost interest in his namesake technology would be surprising, to hear the way Dr. Eckener told the story. Eckener portrayed the Zeppelin as the Count's undying dream, a piece of German national heritage. To keep the flying machine alive, he spun rather fanciful tales about the company's history. The Count, being stodgy and of noble birth in a fading, old aristocratic Germany, hated the idea of Zeppelins ever being used for commerce, transporting commoners being beneath the dignity of him and his mighty machines.

One piece of lore was called the "Miracle of Echterdingen." In 1908, when Count Zeppelin was still struggling to prove the feasibility of his balloons, one crashed as it attempted to meet an army requirement of a twenty-four-hour flight and was destroyed in the southern German town of Echterdingen. According to the story, the Count was crestfallen and defeated, ready to abandon his airships forever. But the public, in a spontaneous outpouring of sympathy and fund-raising, swooped in, with voluntary donations sufficient for the Count to renew his life's work. The German people, according to the tale that Eckener spread, saved the Zeppelin. It is true, schoolchildren did send in their coins to help the old inventor; but, in reality, most of the money to get him back on his feet came from businesses, the government, and wealthy aristocratic friends. It was never the wide groundswell that Eckener made it out to be.

By the summer of 1925, having saved the factory by delivering the LZ 126 to the Americans and then hoping to build the world's largest Zeppelin, Eckener tried to capitalize on this heartwarming myth of a people and their beloved inventor. He and his captains fanned out across Germany, delivering lectures, pleading for donations, and reminding them of Echterdingen, the way they came to the Count's aid nearly twenty years earlier. They passed the hat. They panhandled.

Colsman's variety of businesses under the Luftschiffbau Zeppelin umbrella threw off enough cash to fund much of the *Graf Zeppelin*'s construction cost. But the company would need some government funds, too, and public support. For Eckener, there seemed to be a greater urgency. He had gotten a taste of public adoration in America, mobbed by the thousands, the radio men, the newsmen, a red-carpet welcome at the White House. Eckener now craved that adoration at home and, looking outward, wanted to give downtrodden Germans, vanquished in the war, a genuine vehicle for pride, for celebration of German superiority, for rebirth as a technical superpower.

Translated from the German, the campaign was called the Zeppelin-Eckener Fund of the German People. It was a calculated attempt to link the storied machine, the celebrated pilot, and the concerted will of the German people. It was, in fact, a referendum on Eckener as a national leader, at a time when the postwar Weimar government in Germany was weak, riddled with indecision, and deathly afraid of anything the Allies might construe as warmongering.

Government diplomats were sensitive to the recollection throughout Europe that the Zeppelins had rained terror from the clouds. And the French were shocked to discover that the Zeppelin operation had not been dismantled, as mandated under the Versailles Treaty. The factory had been allowed to stay open to build a Zeppelin for the Americans, and then, slyly, it just never shut its doors.

When government officials complained that the *Graf Zeppelin* campaign might rile the Allies, Eckener simply devised a pretext, calling the new airship a "North Pole Zeppelin," aimed at exploring the mysterious ice cap at the top of the world. It was being designed for a scientific expedition. But it was all a ruse, as Eckener privately confided to the German chancellor in the summer of 1925. The polar-exploration mission, Eckener wrote to Chancellor Hans Luther, is "just a façade." Actually, he wrote, they were trying to save the Luftschiffbau Zeppelin, which after seven years of depression was hanging by a thread. He told Luther he thought there was broad support for his cause, from all parties and corners of society, people who viewed the Zeppelin as a national treasure.

Burying the true origin of the Zeppelin as an aerial terrorist weapon, Eckener appealed to nationalism. No genuine German, as one fundraising leaflet put it, would fail to contribute to save the Luftschiffbau Zeppelin, no matter how small the donation.

Still, the German public didn't buy it. The fund's goal was seven million marks, and early signs suggested it wouldn't reach even half of that. Eckener personally felt the sting of rejection, later remarking privately: "The German people were more interested in throwing their money away on wasteful inessentials than in supporting their Zeppelin heritage." Which is to say, a Zeppelin heritage that was his.

The entire project hit other headwinds. Shortly after the donation campaign began in the summer of 1925, the U.S. Navy suffered a tragedy with its *Shenandoah* airship, the first large airship made in America. The navy, likewise, was trying to stir up public interest in the balloon ships, and it sent its two-year-old *Shenandoah* on barnstorming trips around the country, to state fairs and other gatherings. The navy wanted to demonstrate that the United States, too, was on the cutting edge of aviation. But one evening over the small town of Ava, Ohio, the *Shenandoah* encountered a tremendous storm and broke into three pieces, killing fourteen crew members. In the woods a quarter mile from the tail section, rescuers found an engineer's body, still clutching a piece of girder in his hand.

One of the survivors, Charles E. Rosendahl, the navigator, became a hero and the nation's leading champion of airships. When the *Shenandoah* split up, he and a handful of men were in the nose section of the airship, which had separated from the engines, and began to climb, to nearly two miles high in the sky. With no engines and no steering controls, they were tossed around at the whim of the frenzied winds. By slowly releasing helium, Rosendahl managed to corkscrew downward, crash-land, and save himself and his men, with remarkable bravery and presence of mind. A dozen years later, Rosendahl would be in command of the airship base at Lakehurst, to witness an even greater tragedy.

At a time when people were wary of flying in general, what really gave the world pause was that the *Shenandoah* fragmented chillingly in midair. Why did it break up? Could it happen again? The *Shenandoah* was modeled on a German Zeppelin the French had salvaged in 1917, when the ship was forced to land and the crew couldn't destroy it, as protocol called for, before they were captured. The French copied the exact dimensions and shared the resulting blueprints among the Allies. The *Shenandoah* accident nearly killed airship development in the United States.

In Germany, Eckener pushed ahead for his new airship, unmoved by that tragedy. After three years of fund-raising, ending in 1928, he still had not generated enough funds for construction. Instead, it was the Colsman businesses, the ones Eckener dismissed as "pots and pans," that actually paid for the *Graf Zeppelin*. Casting the fund-raising campaign nonetheless as a success, Eckener set out to raise his renown in Germany by becoming a showman, with all the world his stage.

The *Graf Zeppelin* was a wonder. The first Zeppelin built specifically to fly round-trips over oceans, it was massive, 775 feet long. At a fat 100 feet wide, its circumference alone was as tall as a nine-story building. The hulking men of the ground crew looked like ants by comparison. Eckener once compared the ship in flight to "a fabulous silvery fish, floating quietly in the ocean of air."

The *Graf Zeppelin* had passenger cabins for overnight stays, modeled after ones on ocean liners, but much smaller. It was really an experimental aircraft. For a round-trip between Germany and America, early tickets were so expensive at $7,000 (nearly $50,000 today) that only the super-rich could afford it. Aside from that, only the daring would really fly it.

Ever mindful of publicity, Eckener had radio equipment on board for some of the first broadcasts while in flight. Among notable passengers was Grace Drummond-Hay, the thirty-three-year-old widow of a British diplomat. As the only woman on an inaugural flight, she would draw considerable press attention. She wore stylish cloches and floppy hats, long beaded necklaces, graceful gloves that stretched to her elbows, and tight black dresses. She wrote beautifully, and at times would drop her typewritten stories by parachute to copy boys waiting at a preordained spot below. They called her Lady Zeppelin.

The press had a field day, too, with Hansi, the first canary to fly the entire Atlantic. The little golden warbler was chosen by Eckener's wife, Johanna, as a mascot for the *Graf Zeppelin*. Chirping in its wire cage, the little canary also could serve to warn of any gas leaks.

For a ship intended to show how safe Zeppelins were over oceans, things didn't start well. On its first journey to America, in October 1928, the cotton fabric on the port fin of the *Graf Zeppelin* tore loose in a storm, exposing the ribs of the ship and endangering the entire ship if it ripped any further. The fins were used to stabilize the Zeppelin, like the fletching, or feathers, of an arrow. Because every part of the flight was closely monitored by reporters, word got out quickly that the Zeppelin was in trouble.

Broadcasts followed for hours, leaving millions on edge: They might be attuned to a disaster in real time. Headlines fanned the panic. Blasted across front pages were the headlines:

*Zep Fights for Life*
*Graf Feared Destroyed*
*Zeppelin forced off course; wanders near Bermuda; ignores Navy calls*

Amid the uncertainty, a Catholic priest and Presbyterian minister held a service for the ship over the airwaves on New York's WOR radio station. After reporting the latest bulletins, the air then went dead for a moment of silent prayer for the passengers and crew.

Four volunteers from the crew, including Eckener's son, Knut, tied themselves to the ship and slid onto the fin to make an emergency sewing repair. They slid along the girders like sailors clinging and swaying on a ship's yardarms at sea. They did their needlework as the ship bumped along in the October cold, with nothing but the rippling Atlantic in clear view 200 feet below. If it didn't hold, there was no backup plan.

On board, by special invitation, was Charles Rosendahl, the heroic survivor of the *Shenandoah* disaster. As the premier advocate of airships in the United States, he had been invited along by Dr. Eckener on history's largest Zeppelin. Unsure they would make land, Eckener asked Rosendahl to radio the U.S. Navy and have ships sent just in case, a distress call like that of the R 34 years earlier.

With passengers frightened, the ever-cheerful Captain Lehmann, second in command to Eckener on the flight, began ambling through the halls of the ship, breaking the tension with a serenade on his accordion.

In the end, the daring midair repairs had saved the ship, which, after nearly 112 hours and 6,168 miles, proceeded on to mobbing crowds over New York and then on to the Lakehurst field for landing. Lady Zeppelin provided fawning coverage, despite the misadventure. She wrote that she would travel confidently with Dr. Eckener on his Zeppelin anywhere in the world. "If the airship should come to any harm," she added, "I would weep, because part of my heart would die with it."

But she later confided different feelings in a letter to her mother: "Eckener should never have sent for the ships—it was not necessary and proves that he lost his nerve. The two men who kept their nerve were Knut Eckener and Captain Lehmann."

Riding in open limousines, Eckener, Lehmann, and the crew were celebrated in a ticker-tape parade along Broadway, which looked like a snow globe, with confetti, scrap paper, and torn-up phone books floating in the air. Eckener waved his hat to the cheering crowd. It was as big an outdoor celebration in Manhattan as that of Charles Lindbergh, following his solo New York to Paris flight a year earlier.

The next year, 1929, Eckener would reach his peak of fame. In a publicity masterstroke, the German aviator charted a 21,000-mile course for the *Graf Zeppelin*, to encircle the entire globe. It was imaginative, daring, a made-for-media adventure, complete with newspaper and radio reporters aboard. For a full month, in the late summer of 1929, the *Graf*'s every movement was followed on front pages worldwide. Schoolchildren tracked the Zeppelin on maps in their classrooms. Radio broadcasts were interrupted with bulletins of sightings.

It was, in many ways, a mad, mad, mad idea. In 1924, a team of U.S. Army pilots spent more than six months, with long layovers, circling the globe in planes. But no one had been daring, or foolhardy, enough to try to convey passengers in an orbit of the entire earth. Would the big balloon crash into the ocean? How would it fare over long stretches of barren Siberia? Would it blow up in a thunderstorm, as at least one Zeppelin had in the war? No one knew if the *Graf Zeppelin* would be seen one day and then disappear over the horizon, never to be seen again. It was an imaginative and daredevil exploit that invited macabre voyeurism.

Colsman, the general manager of the Zeppelin company, had little patience for Eckener's theatrics and his willingness to bet the company over and over, barnstorming for publicity. He also found it hard to stomach the $250,000 operating cost for the grand mission. But Eckener had struck a deal to back the incredible trip with the American newspaper baron William Randolph Hearst, who paid $100,000 for the English-language rights to dispatches from the Zeppelin. Stamp collectors, coveting the souvenir of postage carried round the world, ponied up thousands more. Of course, to ensure extra press attention, Lady Zeppelin was on the passenger list, along with the U.S. Navy's Rosendahl.

The truth is, it was a very dangerous mission. When the *Graf* began its world flight, it was the largest airship that had ever been built, the behavior of its rudders in the air could be erratic, and the ship was only a year old. It was reckless to subject passengers to what was in effect a test flight. But Eckener plunged ahead, charting a course for the Zeppelin to fly an average seventy-six miles an hour, over two oceans and three continents, with stops only planned for America, Japan, and Germany.

The world tuned in to broadcasts as the *Graf Zeppelin* took off from its home in Friedrichshafen early the morning of August 15, 1929, with crowds in the thousands cheering and waving handkerchiefs. Eckener shouted the German for "Up, ship!" The *Graf Zeppelin* floated upward, and the engineers started the engines to crank the four propellers, which were arranged outside the enormous round body of the balloon. Most of the twenty passengers aboard were reporters, given that the one-of-a-kind round-trip fare was $9,000. The crew was forty-one men.

As Germany receded into the distance and the *Graf* headed into Russia, the reporters and few guests played cards, chitchatted, and grew a little anxious about the vast Siberian no-man's-land they faced the next day. After dinner, in the dining room with fancy crystal and silverware, a young American millionaire named Bill Leeds, who dressed like a dandy with a fancy suit and straw hat, cranked up a gramophone he had brought aboard, playing swing and dance records out its horn-shaped speaker. He would drink into the night and sleep in late, a habit that would suit him for much of the trip. Some of the reporters grumbled about not being able to smoke, and resorted to sucking on lollipops, unlit menthol cigarettes, and empty pipes.

As the long hours over Siberia passed, it was clear to all looking down from the windows at the endless gray wasteland far below that if anything went wrong, they would be stranded in the wilderness, with little hope of being saved. Just before he boarded, a friend handed Karl von Wiegand, a Hearst newspaper reporter, a revolver and a box of cartridges, saying to him only, "As a last resort."

Tension was in the air. When he came off watch, Captain Lehmann strolled around the lounge and dining room, squeezing on his accordion, playing excerpts from *Die Meistersinger*, a cheery Wagner opera. Moods brightened.

"Russia thrilled us all," recalled Drummond-Hay. "We gazed down in silent awe upon the panorama of Old Russia as never before seen by human beings, pioneering over land closed for centuries, without modern means of communication, whose peasants live the simplest life of almost any people: the Russia of Tolstoy, Turgenev, Dostoevsky." Lady Zeppelin's first world-flight dispatch for the Hearst newspapers in New York, Chicago, and Los Angeles took up half the front page and all of the second.

Louis Lochner, a reporter on board who would become a friend of Eckener's, asked the silver-haired captain how he planned to fly an upcoming leg of the lengthy trip. "I can't tell you now," Eckener replied. "I'll have to determine that when we get there. I'll have to sniff the air; then I'll know how we are to proceed."

Overhearing their talk, Lehmann, first officer on the *Graf Zeppelin* for the historic voyage, took Lochner aside. "Maybe you think Dr. Eckener was joking," he said. "I tell you, he meant it literally. While the rest of us try to figure this thing out scientifically, Dr. Eckener just has a sixth sense."

"It's simply uncanny how he can sniff currents," Lehmann added with his characteristic slow smile. Eckener could also sniff out political currents.

Four days after leaving Friedrichshafen, the *Graf Zeppelin* arrived over Tokyo the evening of August 19 to one-hundred-degree heat and a hero's welcome. City sirens wailed. The cheers of "Bonzai!" rose up from the ground. The crowds massed in the hundreds of thousands, waving from rooftops and from the streets. Over six days in Tokyo, Eckener and other officers of the *Graf* were feted all over the city.

The *Graf Zeppelin* took off from Japan then for a historic, first aerial crossing of the Pacific. Except for some frightening clouds in mountainous coastal areas, and the need to thread two fierce thunderstorms over the ocean, it was an uneventful trip over the 6,000-mile route to southern California.

On Sunday evening, August 25, the American coast came into view, and the *Graf Zeppelin* headed for the San Francisco Bay, about 1,600 feet above ground. Eckener had managed to make the U.S. coast in only sixty-eight hours, the first time anyone in history had flown there from Asia across the Pacific. Several military planes flew up to escort the Zeppelin through the bay, and the ships in the water had flapping celebratory flags and whistles blowing welcome, while thousands of cars blew horns to greet the famous visitor. Pressed by reporters on landing, Lady Drummond-Hay told them, "I want a manicure, a bath and some sleep."

The flight across the continental United States proved the bumpiest of the entire trip, with turbulence so frequent, so rattling, that the dining room served meals on aluminum tableware, sparing the delicate porcelain plates. The arrival over New York was as tumultuous as the one the previous year, and among the thousands cheering on the *Graf Zeppelin*'s arrival at the Lakehurst field was aviation hero Charles Lindbergh, Lucky Lindy himself, with his boyish face, curly hair, and slim body. When he first stepped aboard the *Graf Zeppelin*, Lindbergh was underwhelmed. He couldn't fathom such a colossal vehicle for three or four dozen passengers. He saw no future for the slow-moving Zeppelin.

The trip itself was an unqualified success. The *Graf Zeppelin* had crossed two oceans and three continents, flying around the world in a record time of about twelve days. The total time, including layovers, ran twenty-one days, five hours, and thirty-five minutes.

Dr. Eckener and crew were celebrated with another ticker-tape parade in New York City. *Time* magazine would soon put Eckener on its cover. Eckener and Lehmann flew by plane to Washington, to be greeted at the White House by President Hoover. "The spirit of high adventure still lives," Hoover bellowed. "Its success has been due to the eminent scientific and engineering abilities of the German people, translated by your skill and courage. . . . You have lifted the spirits of men with renewed confidence in human progress."

The ceremony ended, the president and Eckener shook hands, and then Hoover mentioned something personally to Eckener. Gesturing goodwill between the nations, the president made Eckener an extraordinary offer, one that could have saved lives and changed history. The secret proposal would not surface until eight years later, around the time Eckener would be called to the office of a Hitler henchman named Göring, with much explaining to do to.

The *Graf Zeppelin* sat. It was stranded at Lakehurst, wind-bound, in the big hangar. It was all set to return to Germany, and Eckener was going to stay in the United States for meetings with bankers and investors to drum up money for a new, even bigger project, a follow-up to the *Graf Zeppelin*, project LZ 128.

That left Captain Lehmann, Eckener's right-hand man, in charge. The twenty-two passengers were ready, the baggage was stowed away, and the ground crew waited for orders. But a cross-hangar wind had sprung up that evening, and Lehmann was characteristically cautious with passengers on board, with crewmen counting on him. It wasn't safe to take off, and the captain wouldn't budge.

Lehmann, an engineer by training, was different than his boss, Eckener. The older man was willing to take risks, convincing himself they were prudent, but risks nonetheless. As the son of a chemist, Lehmann had grown up amid sulfuric acid and other chemicals and had a scientist's respect for the power, and danger, of chemicals and nature. With the winds threatening, he held up the departure a full eight hours, until he thought it was safe to proceed.

His caution was rewarded as the Zeppelin lifted off without a problem, but it was a staunch reminder that Zeppelins weren't invulnerable and couldn't take off in heavy winds, a serious obstacle to dreams of providing regular passenger service. Knowing that, Dr. Eckener, who worked obsessively for positive press coverage, couldn't have been happy about the long delay, which the evening and morning newspapers dutifully reported. But the ship was in Lehmann's command, and all Eckener could do, standing on the field in his suit and tie, was wave a handkerchief and say good-bye finally to his "baby."

On the flight back to Germany, Lehmann was mortified to catch a passenger smoking, something clearly forbidden on a hydrogen-filled ship. Lehmann and Eckener, along with most of the crew, were smokers themselves—Lehmann, a cigarette and pipe man, and Eckener, a cigar man, his favorite being jet black Brazilian cheroot cigars—but they both had to suffer through the long hours without puffing or risk blowing their ship to smithereens.

Lehmann was particularly sympathetic of passengers' suffering withdrawal on the long flights. On one Germany-to-Brazil trip on the *Graf Zeppelin*, Lehmann met a professional balloonist who was a heavy smoker. Lehmann laid down the law, plainly: "No cigarettes. No exceptions." The captain then handed him a small, wrapped box. "When you get the urge," he said, "open it." Minutes later, the man unwrapped the package and found a shiny harmonica. "My nearly uncontrollable urge to smoke never left me that whole crossing," recalled Ward Van Orman, the grateful smoker. "Before we were halfway across the South Atlantic, I had mastered *Juanita* on my new German harmonica."

Still, it seemed nothing would shake Dr. Eckener from his reliance on dangerous hydrogen. For one thing, most of the helium produced in the world was concentrated in one place, the United States. And two years before the *Graf Zeppelin* rose for its world tour, the U.S. had enacted a law to keep the precious gas out of the hands of foreign powers. Goodyear lobbied for the helium-control law, hoping to protect its developing blimp business.

But there were channels, were ways to apply for exceptions, and Eckener was on friendly terms with Goodyear, with a dozen of his engineers working at the Ohio company to help it develop American airships. He could have purchased helium from the United States. Eckener was never fond of relying on anyone, however, much less the whims of a vanquishing power like the U.S. The powerful country could grant him an exception, release the helium to him, and then yank its approval all over again.

In short, Eckener hesitated. Perhaps as a result, Colsman resigned from the Zeppelin company, the firm he had personally held together through the leanest of lean postwar years. Colsman seemed to know that Eckener wouldn't stop until he took a great fall.

Eckener ignored repeated warnings. As construction began on the LZ 128, a representative for an upstart American Zeppelin operator was aghast to learn that the successor to the *Graf Zeppelin*, intended to carry American passengers in regular service, would use hydrogen. Dr. Jerome Hunsaker of the International Zeppelin Transportation Corporation wrote to Eckener, saying, "Our group would never agree to build a terminal for the use of a hydrogen airship . . . with danger of disaster always present." He argued that they abandon the hydrogen plans. Eckener was unmoved. The LZ 128 would use hydrogen, safely, as all German Zeppelins had for a generation.

Then an event that shook all of England left Eckener second-guessing himself on hydrogen for the new LZ 128. All the major nations had been racing to compete with Germany for dominance of the skies, developing both planes and airships. In 1930, Britain's promising new airship was named the R 101. It had been finished in 1929, the same year the *Graf Zeppelin* circled the globe. The following year, it was lengthened to 777 feet, making it the largest airship around. The R 101 was intended to connect the continents of the British empire, flying passengers from the British Isles to Canada, India, and Australia.

On its first long-distance flight to India, on October 5, 1930, the R 101 crashed and burned in a tremendous ball of hydrogen-fed flame in northern France. The disaster killed forty-eight of the fifty-six aboard, including the British Secretary of State for Air, Lord Thomson of Cardington. Few corpses pulled from the wreckage could be identified.

Not since the *Titanic's* sinking in 1912 had the British public been so heartbroken. Five days after the fiery disaster, hundreds of thousands watched mournfully as the forty-eight flag-draped coffins, led by horsemen, arrived at Westminster Abbey. Walking behind the coffins was Dr. Eckener and others from the Zeppelin company, paying last respects to their airship compatriots.

After the tragedy of Britain's R 101, the Zeppelin company had a change of heart. The forthcoming LZ 128 would be filled only with helium, its annual report for 1931 said, safer but more expensive. Eckener and his design team had already raised money to build a larger hangar. Aside from a shortage of funds, the *Graf Zeppelin* was constrained by the relatively small dimensions of the hangar in Friedrichshafen. A Zeppelin would need much more helium volume for lift than hydrogen, meaning the helium-filled ships were going to have to be much, much larger. They could now easily build a ship for helium. The Zeppelin had finally abandoned dangerous hydrogen, for safer skies.

The new hangar at Friedrichshafen was 820 feet long, 164 feet wide, and 151 feet high. The LZ 128 that had been on the drawing boards would be a monster, nearly twice as fat as the *Graf Zeppelin*. Workmen began assembling the massive aluminum-alloy rings that would form the body of the new ship. And as it began to take shape, Eckener second-guessed himself all over again on hydrogen. He couldn't stomach that helium cost seven times more than hydrogen, couldn't figure out how the company would ever establish profitable passenger air service with helium. And he didn't want to be subordinate to the whims of the United States, which had cornered the market on helium. The company scrapped the helium LZ 128 and began developing a new ship design, Project LZ 129, that would use both hydrogen and helium in the large gasbags.

In December 1930, the Luftschiffbau Zeppelin managed to pick up five and half tons of duralumin, an aluminum and copper alloy that weighed a third what steel did and allowed Zeppelins to be strong as bridges but float like bubbles. The British seller was eager to unload it at any price. The metal came from the charred, three-month-old wreckage of the R 101. And Eckener used the salvage from that tragedy for his new project, the supersized LZ 129, what would eventually be named the *Hindenburg*.

It was confounding, how country after country had tried to fly these balloon machines, with mostly tragic results. All the while, Germany floated the largest objects ever to move through the sky with a near-perfect record of safety all over the earth. It was maddening. How did they do it? Into the early 1930s, airships were the only flying craft that could fly long distances nonstop carrying tons of cargo and people. The airship experiment held the promise of the world's first regular transoceanic air service, so long as the twin perils of flammable lifting gas and structural fragility could be surmounted.

Lindbergh and others were making their hazardous single-engine airplane crossings of the oceans, but the *Graf Zeppelin* seemed easily to transport the famous and the adventurous between continents on a spectacular series of demonstration flights, many between Germany and

Brazil. It carried tons of cargo, and had a dining room with sumptuous meals, wine in crystal goblets, passenger cabins—nearly an ocean-liner experience in the clouds. The *Graf Zeppelin* was on its way to being the first aircraft ever to reach one million miles journeyed, the same as two trips to the moon and back. It never had a single fatality.

For the rest of the world, omens fell from the sky. France had given up its airship ambitions in late 1923 after its war-reparation ship, built by the Germans and surrendered in 1920, blasted into bits in the air in a thunderstorm off the coast of Sicily just before Christmas. The fiery explosion of the *Dixmude* was seen for miles in all directions. Virtually all salvagers found of the fifty persons on board was mutilated human heads and numerous body parts.

The next year, the *Shenandoah*, the first large airship built in America, broke up in midair in 1924, killing fourteen. The British quit developing airships after the R 101 explosion in 1930. Three years later, the United States would nearly walk away from airships altogether, after the *Akron*, built by Goodyear and slightly longer than the *Graf Zeppelin*, crashed at sea, killing seventy-three navy men. Even with safer helium, most of the crew had perished. Franklin Delano Roosevelt, the new president, declared the *Akron*'s fate "a national disaster."

Germany was the glaring exception, and the world's press took note of the growing Eckener legend. When the veteran Zeppelin captain turned sixty-five in August 1933, the *New York Times* caught up with him in Rio de Janeiro, where the *Graf Zeppelin* had arrived for its fourth trip of the year. This time, the *Graf Zeppelin* had a huge swastika on its tail, as required by the new Hitler government. Aircraft were required to carry the black-red-white-striped flag of the Weimar government on the starboard side and the Nazi black, red, and white with the hooked cross on the port. Eventually, both sides would carry the swastika, a symbol of Germany's national resurgence.

The *New York Times* article called Eckener "presidential timber" in Germany. And it noted that Eckener delighted in recounting just how he met the famous Count Zeppelin nearly three decades earlier. After completing his doctoral degree in psychology at Leipzig, Eckener and his wife, Johanna, moved to Friedrichshafen. Johanna was a woman of sturdy build, square-jawed, and had pouchy eyes just like her husband's. At the time, they had a daughter and a son, Hanneliese and Knut. Later, they would have another daughter, Margarethe, whom they would come to call Lotte. Eckener hoped the resort town, with the calming waters of Lake Constance, would inspire him, as he planned to write a book on labor and capital. It was 1904.

"We met during a rowing and sailing contest on Lake Constance," Eckener said of Count Zeppelin, "and our acquaintance soon reached the stage where I felt myself emboldened to express my views on dirigibles and their handling, having acquired some knowledge of nautical science in my old hometown of Flensburg. I bluntly told the Count that his system of navigation was all wrong, that since a dirigible was no different from an ordinary ship, its operation also depended on the simple application of the general laws of navigation." Eckener then explained how the impressed Count hired him for his scientific staff, and he later became the "guiding genius" of the whole operation.

It was a memorable story, how they met. The Count, at that point in 1933, was dead—no way to get his take on the first meeting. Years later, however, Eckener would recount in his memoirs an entirely different set of circumstances for their meeting, and how the Count personally solicited him to work for the Zeppelin factory, going so far as to stalk Eckener at his home.

In that version, Eckener was working in his garden at his house one morning when his housemaid excitedly came up to him and said Count Zeppelin was at the front gate, calling on Eckener. The Count made an impression on Eckener, as the old man was wearing a morning coat, top hat, and, of all things, yellow gloves, Eckener wrote. The Count explained that he had read an article by Eckener in the *Frankfurter Zeitung* and that Eckener had made some technical mistakes he would like to correct. The two got to talking further, and over time the Count was smitten with Eckener and just had to hire him.

Two completely different accounts of a first meeting. And there was a third. That version came more credibly from Colsman, who spelled out the introduction of the Count and Eckener in much less flattering terms. Colsman's version came out in his own memoir, published the same year, 1933.

If Colsman got it right, neither story Eckener told was correct, in an early troubling sign of Eckener's credibility. According to Colsman, Eckener was a struggling news reporter for the *Frankfurter Zeitung*. Colsman himself actually hired Eckener, meeting him in Hamburg and asking him to move south to Friedrichshafen to work on publicity for the upstart Zeppelin company. Only later did Colsman learn that Eckener had been writing to the Count for some time, asking for a job at the company. The Count had lukewarm interest in Eckener, Colsman recalled, and the requests turned to begging. At one point, Colsman continued, Eckener wrote to the Count, pitifully saying, "Does your Excellency not have any use for me?"

Their meeting was brief, by Goebbels's recollection. Goebbels, a top lieutenant in the Third Reich, had risen surprisingly far, for a slight man with a limp. He could command a crowd with a speech, but had something of a pip-squeak voice. He had been a so-so journalist, but found his calling in propaganda. He was a natural-born liar. He adored Hitler, and vice versa. Hitler was like an uncle to Goebbels's small children.

Goebbels worked long hours, fueled by hate. Hatred of Jews, hatred of Communists. Hatred of anyone Hitler wanted him to hate. In the dead of summer, the first Saturday in July 1933, at his office at the Ministry of Propaganda, Goebbels met first with the eminent Swiss psychologist Carl Jung. After a series of supplicants to his office in the months since Hitler elevated him to oversee all media, entertainment, and culture in Germany, Goebbels was puzzled by Jung's visit. "It was rather a strange situation," he reflected the next day in his diary. "Neither one of us wants anything from the other."

But the next guest wanted something indeed. Hugo Eckener calling. Goebbels had read much about him, along with the rest of the world. But at the very height of his celebrity, Eckener picked a miserable time to build a successor to the *Graf Zeppelin*, trying to leapfrog himself in making the largest airship the world had ever seen. No sooner had the designers and engineers finished plans for the LZ 129, and construction begun, than the world sank into the Great Depression. The U.S. stock market had crashed, and vast unemployment struck worldwide. Funds dried up.

Construction of the airship that was to be the *Hindenburg*, the product of a generation of German expertise in aviation, was stuck. Looking something like the ribs of some dead animal, the Zeppelin-in-progress seemed like it might never be completed.

Here Eckener found himself at an impasse. He hated relying on anyone, which is one reason he hesitated to seek helium from the United States, and yet the cost for aviation, whether planes or airships, was so high that anyone hoping to work in the field simply had to have government funding. The *Hindenburg* alone was estimated to cost more than $2 million. One airship.

Eckener needed the government, Nazi or otherwise. And the Nazis, in turn, needed Eckener. Hitler had risen a little too quickly, and the public mostly associated him with his thuggish Brownshirts. They hit the streets, beating opponents and stirring up the occasional international incident, as when they assaulted a man in Berlin for not saluting the Nazi flag and had to apologize to the American embassy when they later realized he was a doctor visiting from New York.

Sending a chill throughout Germany, the Berlin police chief, Heinrich Himmler, told the newspapers in the spring of 1933 that he was opening the Third Reich's first concentration camp, to hold as many as 5,000 political prisoners. It would be housed at an old munitions factory in the Bavarian town of Dachau, a place in which Hugo Eckener would later show special interest.

It was Goebbels's job to twist the image of this oppressive regime to one restoring order for the good of the German people. He had to paper over the terrorism. Right when Eckener came into his office, Goebbels was assembling what he called his "press attachés," German luminaries of high regard from all walks of life, people who could endorse Hitler and make his plans sound right-minded. A world celebrity, Eckener seemed to view Goebbels, this newcomer on the political scene, as he did most government bureaucrats, as inferiors, as gnats.

Grudgingly, he had to ask Goebbels for a stack of cash, about a half-million dollars, to keep the *Hindenburg* alive; Goebbels needed press attachés. Fearing his dream ship would evaporate, Eckener was an easy mark.

Goebbels confided to his diary that the German aviator "seems rather strained" financially.

The Nazi financing paid off quickly. The *Graf Zeppelin* was plugged into immediate service for the Nazi propaganda machine. At the big annual Nazi Party conference in Nuremburg several weeks later, early September 1933, 11,000 flags fluttered in the breeze as the crowd awaited the *Graf Zeppelin* to circle overhead.

Eckener had taken off from Friedrichshafen, with the bells in the onion-bulb towers of the Palace Church ringing, and steered northward to Nuremburg to do a flyover of the thousands of cheering Nazi militants below. The trip was out of his way. Eckener would later have to backtrack, to head south for a scheduled South American trip.

To the shouting throngs, Goebbels addressed one of his favorite topics, "The Jewish Problem." The Propaganda Minister said, "What is happening in Germany is not persecution of the Jews, but restitution of elementary justice for the German people."

When Hitler took the podium, he intoned: "We found the key, which, for all time will close the door to our enemies. This meeting is a visible demonstration of the result of our fourteen-year fight. The party has become a state. Now our duty is to educate every German to be a citizen of this German state. You must form an iron front encompassing every German."

The *Graf Zeppelin* hovering as a symbol of Nazi might, Hitler brought tremendous applause for his Third Reich when he concluded: "We plan that we will meet here two years hence. So, we will meet ten, a hundred and a thousand years hence."

The crowd broke into one of the most beloved Nazi anthems: On one side of the arena, thousands would shout *Sieg!* and the other side would respond *Heil!* Victory. Hail. *Sieg Heil! Sieg Heil! Sieg Heil!* The chant would become so emblematic of the Nazi movement that decades later a vanquished Germany would make it illegal even to utter those two words together.

The next month, Eckener agreed to fly the *Graf Zeppelin* over the 1933 World's Fair, being hosted that October in Chicago. Another chance to align Germany-Hitler-Nazis and the world's utter fascination with the *Graf Zeppelin*. It was Zeppelin fever. Merchandise for sale included Zeppelin candy, Zeppelin cigarettes, Zeppelin harmonicas, and Zeppelin yachting caps.

Chicagoans that fall couldn't help but notice the immense, twisted swastika on its tail, as the *Graf Zeppelin* had become a floating advertisement for the Nazis. Goebbels's plan was working. He was taking the goodwill people felt for the famed Zeppelin, which had visited Chicago during the world tour just four years earlier, and marrying it with Hitler. The association was so clear, the Zeppelin so obviously a servant in the Nazi cause, that it would prompt a bizarre fabrication many years later of how Eckener outfoxed Hitler by hiding the swastika from Chicagoans.

Once he landed, Eckener hosted a banquet in downtown Chicago for the German ambassador, Hans Luther, who had briefly served as Germany's chancellor after World War I. The ambassador was trying to burnish Hitler's image in America. Only six of Chicago's 500 German-American societies supported the dinner; the rest opposed it, opposed Hitler. With the swastika flag on one side of his podium and the American Stars and Stripes on the other, Luther addressed the diners. Germany did not want to "Nazify" other nations, he said, meaning to expand its territory.

"The much-criticized Hitler government has no intention to Germanize anyone," Luther declared. "Hitler literally has said that all this talk of Germanizing has to be stopped once and for all." He concluded, repeating the words of Chancellor Hitler, that "only a madman could believe in the possibility of war" between France and Germany.

Taking questions from reporters, Eckener told them the *Graf Zeppelin* was nearly profitable, though it cost a whopping $300 an hour to operate. Noting that the *Graf Zeppelin* only carried twenty-four passengers on the trip to Chicago, he added, "We have a new Zeppelin under construction that will seat 54."

"What are you going to call the new ship, Dr. Eckener?" a reporter asked.

"Have you any suggestions?" he laughed.

As fall gave way to winter, the unnamed ship, LZ 129, was forming in Friedrichshafen, in the new, larger hangar built to accommodate the colossus. Nearly three-quarters of the duralumin frame was in place, thanks to the cash infusion from Goebbels and the Nazis. With cotton stuffed in their ears to muffle the thunder of machinery, workers installed thousands of rivets, and used pulleys to lift and install the massive gasbags. Carpenters had half the passenger cabins completed.

The chief designer of the ship was Dr. Ludwig Dürr, whose face seemed stuck in a scowl. He had bushy arches for eyebrows. Dürr had been building Zeppelins going back to the early days with Count Zeppelin, and he projected that the largest flying object ever attempted would begin trial flights in early autumn of 1934—an overly optimistic target, it turned out. The press was fascinated with the LZ 129, the successor to the *Graf Zeppelin*, a breakthrough new ship that would be somehow larger, and reporters disclosed every detail they could unearth. The ship would have a novel smoking room, erasing a serious shortcoming at a time when smoking was as natural as wearing hats.

It would be the first German Zeppelin designed to use helium. Passenger quarters would be inside a ship for the first time, not in an isolated compartment below the balloon's main structure, as in the *Graf Zeppelin*. The new location, up within the gasbags, would be safe because passengers wouldn't be surrounded by dangerously flammable hydrogen.

Commander Rosendahl and some of the top brass of the U.S. Navy were eager to tap into the state-of-the-art in Zeppelin design so that they could keep the airship alive in America. After serious accidents, the airship program was hanging by a thread, and the navy begged Eckener for permission to send naval observers, including Rosendahl, to ride the new ship once it was completed.

Goodyear, which was already sharing engineers and patents on airships with the Luftschiffbau Zeppelin, tried to use its history, goodwill, and partnership to ferret out any details it could about the LZ 129. Eckener, Dr. Dürr, Lehmann—they were all tight-lipped. Goodyear's president, Paul Litchfield, finally managed a breakthrough with Eckener. Litchfield proposed sending a young engineer to observe the construction of the LZ 129. That man, Harold Dick, would become the first American to infiltrate the secretive Zeppelin works in Friedrichshafen.

In December 1933, the basic skeleton of LZ 129 was complete, with girders and tension wires woven like spiderwebs. The workers celebrated by attaching a small Christmas tree to the nose of the ship and singing carols, including a relatively new one called "*Stille Nacht*," "Silent Night."

In truth, though, the workforce was exasperated. The Zeppelin company was a large employer in the town of Friedrichshafen, home to 28,000. In the foundry and elsewhere, workers complained of cramped conditions and poor ventilation, making it hard to breathe. Long hours of biting cold aggravated their deft finger work. Eckener simply dismissed the complaints at the Zeppelin factory, making none of their recommended changes, in a troubling sign. He would soon abide much, much worse conditions for workers. In a word, inhuman.

In the summer of 1934, Chancellor Hitler ordered the Night of the Long Knives purge and appointed himself Germany's supreme dictator. To show the world that all of Germany was behind him, he and Goebbels conjured up the referendum to legitimize that power grab. The week before the August 19 vote, Goebbels took to the radio to whip up support for the *Ja*-for-the-Führer campaign. "Who votes against Hitler," Goebbels warned, "is an enemy of the people."

The Propaganda Minister released to the world's press the names of the luminaries who would be heard throughout Germany on the radio, four times a day for three minutes. The "Nazi spellbinders" were popular figures, American newspapers reported, including Winifred Wagner, daughter-in-law of the famed composer; Colonel Oskar von Hindenburg, son of the late president; and Captain Hugo Eckener, commander of the *Graf Zeppelin*.

An impressive list, working to rehabilitate Hitler's reputation. A United Press correspondent in Berlin, Frederick Oechsner, wrote that "Nazi 'three-minute men,' operating as oratorical light artillery, opened a strange six-day speaking campaign" in favor of Hitler. On the first day, Monday, August 13, 1934, he wrote that that artillery included the famed Zeppelin flyer Hugo Eckener. American news articles on the referendum duly noted that enthusiasm for Hitler and Nazism was dying down in Germany, and its economy was flagging. Hitler himself would plead with the German public to "demonstrate to the world, misinformed by lies of the international press, that Hitler governs not as a dictator, but with the full faith and trust of the German people."

Eckener may have figured that his broadcast would not be heard outside Germany. And if he felt any reservations, any misgivings, about throwing his reputation behind the mastermind of the fresh horror of the Night of the Long Knives, it certainly didn't show in his powerful, unflinching endorsement. In the baritone voice of the Zeppelin master that Germans knew well, Eckener spoke into the microphone.

Bemoaning the upheaval Germany was currently in, he began by arguing it was impossible going forward to govern traditionally. Rather, he proclaimed, "One firm will has to command in a dictatorial fashion. Weakness of thought here would be weakness of will, and that would be the more disastrous at a time when it is a matter, in the most bitter earnest, of the survival of our people as a great nation."

On August 19, 1934, Eckener said, the German people must answer the question of whether they wished to confirm their trust in their own Adolf Hitler, with an unlimited authority as their Führer. Following years of desperation, he advised listeners that "stern, indeed drastic interventions and methods are unavoidable in this. Mistakes and excesses may have occurred—how could they be avoided in such times?—pressed grapes are sour and cloudy as they ferment, but a clear and noble wine will one day result."

Eckener continued: "The clever and experienced minds among our people should put themselves at the Führer's disposal and help to solve the dreadful problems. . . . What is at issue now is the conviction that the Führer's will is pure and sincere and that his goals are good and great." The Zeppelin celebrity noted that Hitler's platform was partly to restore the honor and veracity of the German people, treated as a pariah recently. "The goals are set high and broad," Eckener said, "and can arise only from an elevated spirit and a great heart. Who would not want to offer his hand to help make them reality?"

Recently deceased President Hindenburg was a man of sincerity, duty, and patriotism, Eckener said, a man who should be an eternal model for all Germans. And Hindenburg himself bequeathed to Germany Chancellor Adolf Hitler as a model. "Let us honor his memory and follow his example in this fateful question, answering with a clear 'Yes' on Election Day," Eckener concluded. "This is what I have resolved, in my fervent efforts to find what is right, to tell my fellow members of the people."

Eckener's speech likened Hitler and his murderous regime to "noble wine." The official referendum tally released days later showed 89.9 percent of Germany had voted in favor, backing Hitler's consolidation of power. People throughout Germany couldn't recall Eckener's ever having lent his voice to politics, only airships. It would all stick in the memory of an ambitious young law student in Tübingen, near Stuttgart, who would recall it years later at a most inopportune time for Eckener.

Construction of the LZ 129 in Friedrichshafen moved along at a brisk pace for a full year, and by December of 1935, design drawings for the airship began to carry its chosen name, honoring Germany's fallen hero, *Hindenburg*. The cigar-shaped skeleton of the ship was ready to be wrapped in the all-important outer cover, more than six acres of linen and cotton aeronautical cloth that weighed a stunning six tons. The magnitudes on the *Hindenburg* were so great, it put the construction team in uncharted territory. No one knew, once the thing was fully wrapped, how it would actually perform in the sky.

The covering job alone would take longer than a month, with an outer-cover gang of twenty-four men working to position, tighten, lace, retighten with cover pullers, paint with dope, and re-tension again and again. Any sloppiness, any slack, could jeopardize aerodynamics, the very airworthiness of the airship. Vibration bedevils machinery, undermining structure, sturdiness, and safety.

There were two misfortunes that winter. Karl Hürttle, the fabric wizard who had overseen the covering of more than fifty Zeppelins, was not in Friedrichshafen to supervise this one. He had been spirited off to Goodyear years earlier, and was working in Akron, Ohio, that winter. The other issue was noted by George Lewis, one of the men sent by Goodyear to report on the specs and construction of the state-of-the-art *Hindenburg*. He made an astute entry in his notes: "Some concern is felt over the fact that much of the outer cover is being installed in below-freezing weather with high humidity, it being thought that this may result in sections of the cover being not particularly tight."

On January 16, 1936, Dr. Dürr, the chief Zeppelin designer; Captain Lehmann; and an engineer moving up at the company, Rudolf Sauter, had a special meeting to address "safety measures demanded" by aviation authorities in the government. Apparently, those representatives had just inspected the *Hindenburg* in progress and immediately became alarmed by some potential hazards. "Other than the protection provided by the airship's bird-cage form and large mass, it has no lightning protection," they warned.

Dr. Dürr explained that scientific and experimental results first had to be conducted to determine the precise location that voltage would accumulate in a lightning strike. Lehmann, who had encountered lightning while flying before, said that the bow is the most likely place for any lightning strike. As a safety measure, he recommended that they fill the two cells at the bow with helium, creating a buffer that could not be ignited. The three Zeppelin men decided, at Lehmann's suggestion, to hire a high-voltage laboratory and conduct studies with appropriate models to determine the potential for ignition of the gas cells.

The first season for the *Hindenburg* was weeks away.

# 4

# A Quivering Cover

THE CONSTRUCTION CREW BEGAN TO INSTALL THE INNER WALLS OF THE *Hindenburg*, with murals painted by Professor Otto Arpke, a noted graphic illustrator in Germany. The walls of the smoking lounge were sealed for fire safety with an air-lock door and insulated with asbestos. For the lounge, Arpke painted a parade of specific balloons, each one a breakthrough in the history of man's attempts to float ships in the heavens.

It was a 300-year journey in muted pastels. First was the musing of Francesco Lana de Terzi, an Italian mathematician and priest of the seventeenth century, who drew plans of a sailboat levitated by four vacuum balls, pumped out, lighter than air. Since he used sound principles of mathematics and physics, his notion inspired a century of balloon development in Europe. "God would surely never allow such a machine to be successful," de Terzi once wrote. "Fortresses, and cities could thus be destroyed . . . as iron weights, fireballs and bombs could be hurled from a great height." Exactly as Count Zeppelin had always hoped.

Next on the mural came the first aircraft, the famed hot-air balloon of the Montgolfier brothers of France, which in 1783 flew the first creatures recorded: a rooster, a sheep, and a duck. Painted colorfully, the balloon looked like a Christmas tree ornament. The same year, another Frenchman, Jacques Charles, sent human pilots aloft in a pioneering hydrogen balloon, a true forerunner to the Zeppelin.

It wasn't until 1884 that the *La France* balloon managed the breakthrough feat of lifting off, flying, and returning to its starting point; in other words, true navigation. Next on the wall was Count Zeppelin's first airship, the pencil-like LZ 1 of 1900. It was followed by an airship of

Alberto Santos-Dumont, a Brazilian aviator who astounded Parisians with his daring flights in the early twentieth century. Next was Italy's polar-exploring *Italia* airship of 1928, and finally, the world-circling *Graf Zeppelin*.

The *Hindenburg* was in final stages of completion, thanks to a final boost of cash from, of all people, Hermann Göring. An early sidekick to Hitler, the chubby, jovial World War I flying ace was the new Führer's top pick to run the powerful Air Ministry. Hitler had a special appreciation for flight; he was the first politician in Germany to rise to power by campaigning cross-country in an airplane. In one blitz, he visited twenty-one towns in a single week.

Atop the Air Ministry, Göring had already begun his own empire-building, ordering construction of a seven-story fortress in Berlin as headquarters for a German air force he was about to expand enormously. And illegally. The Versailles Treaty severely limited any rearmament by Germany, and it banned military aviation altogether.

The head of the Air Ministry summoned stone from fifty quarries to erect a symbol of Nazi defiance to that agreement. By employing laborers working double shifts and weekends, the monster Air Ministry building was up and running in a year and a half. A Third Reich guidebook pronounced it a "document in stone displaying the reawakened military will and reestablished military readiness of the new Germany." With several sprawling wings, it would have 2,800 offices and 4,000 bureaucrats. It filled several blocks. It was, in 1936, one of the largest buildings in all of Europe. In several grand halls, Göring would receive and intimidate visitors, one soon to be a very nervous Hugo Eckener.

Göring knew there were some limitations to planes, including distances they could fly before needing to refuel, and believed Zeppelins could be better employed for long-range scouting. Pouring fully $2 million into the Zeppelin company, Göring moved to restructure it, separating construction from flight operations. He called the new operating company the Deutsche Zeppelin Reederei, or DZR, and made the government airline, Lufthansa, the dominant partner. This would have unexpected ramifications for Eckener, and, as Göring was a warmonger at heart, it meant Zeppelins were destined somehow for warfare. Just as Count Zeppelin had always hoped.

As final coats of dope were painted on the *Hindenburg*, the ship needed to be pressed into test flights soon to be ready to carry passengers for the opening of its maiden season that spring. Harold Dick, the observer working for Goodyear, and Lieutenant Commander Scott E. Peck, a U.S. Navy observer, were among those intently watching and taking notes from the ground.

On March 4, 1936, the ground crew walked the *Hindenburg* from the construction hangar, and Lehmann and the crew rode it up into the air. On the ground, Peck, Dick, and the others were thunderstruck when the aircraft started propelling forward. In the first moments of the *Hindenburg*'s first flight, smoke was suddenly trailing off the top of the ship. The panic broke, though, when word spread that it was merely dust that had accumulated on the massive upper side of the outer cover while the ship was being built in the hangar.

Lehmann set a course over the Bodensee, where they cruised for nearly three hours, to be sure everything was shipshape. Then, heading out over land, they cranked up the motors and checked the turning radius, how well the colossal rudders steered the hulk, and how quickly they could bring the *Hindenburg* to a stop in midair. It could come to a halt within an impressive one-and-a-half ship lengths, it turned out.

Flight tests were essential to determine how the aircraft would actually behave in the sky; estimates based on scale-model wind-tunnel tests proved unreliable again and again when the full-size ships took to the air. Judging the performance of the outer cover was one of the critical assessments. In flight, the outer cover absorbed the brunt of wind resistance, nearly half, which was far more than any other part of the Zeppelin. The control surfaces of the fins were second in creating aerodynamic drag, but only one-fifth of it.

From the ground, Dick spotted something the crew on board could not. "The outer cover is not satisfactory, but the additional coats of dope may help," he scribbled into his notepad. He knew that a vibrating outer cover was a hazard, and he thought the Zeppelin designers were going to have to add extra supports to keep the cover steady. "It appears that flutter girders or flutter wires will have to be added in several panels in the after section of the ship."

After a short second test flight, Lehmann undertook a lengthy third one, a full thirty hours. He insisted on subjecting the new Daimler-Benz engines to a prolonged test before he dared fly the experimental new *Hindenburg* over an ocean. For the important engine trials, Lehmann flew the *Hindenburg* east nearly to Salzburg, north one hundred miles past Frankfurt, and back south to Friedrichshafen. Running nonstop over thirty hours, the engines performed well.

A fourth flight test turned up a problem: The outer cover remained somewhat loose. On the morning of March 17, Dick noted: "The outer cover still has a very bad flutter just forward of engine number one. This is particularly noticeable at low speeds."

It was a vexing problem, the quivering cover. But at least the motors were not acting up.

Sniffing the changing currents, Eckener would continue to oblige Nazi interests again and again. For the forthcoming maiden flight of the *Hindenburg* to America, Eckener invited aboard Dr. Theodore Lewald, the president of the German Olympic Association, who was trying to thwart a proposed American boycott of the Olympics, set for Berlin in the summer of 1936. "The Olympics without America simply would not be the Olympics," said Lewald. "It is unthinkable. Dr. Eckener will arrange for me to make a broadcast from the ship when we reach America."

Dr. Lewald made his position clear, saying, "Believe me, we wish more than anybody in America that we had some Jewish athletes of Olympic caliber. But we have none, and I believe no one in America would want us to put a second-rate athlete on our team just because he was Jewish. That certainly isn't the Olympic spirit."

It wasn't just internationally that the Nazis were unpopular. Public surveys revealed that Hitler's popularity in Germany had been fading since the fall of 1935. Nazi assaults on the clergy and shortages caused by the government's preferring imports of raw materials for a rearmament over food were among the troubles. To divert attention from the worsening home front, Hitler started looking outward, eyeing Germany's borders for a bold move that would electrify the nation.

The first week of March 1936, Hitler ordered thousands of troops into the demilitarized Rhineland area, bordering France. The pretext was that France had recently violated a particular treaty. And then, Hitler waited. He forecast that France was still battle-weary from the Great War and would not attack, but he took a huge gamble by marching into the forbidden border territory.

Hitler would reflect later that it was the most nerve-wracking forty-eight hours of his life. "If the French had invaded the Rhineland, we would have had to retreat in humiliation and shame since the military forces at our disposal would not at all have been equal to even moderate resistance," he would recall. It was a moment that might have stopped World War II from ever happening. But the French merely conceded the territory.

Again, Hitler wanted to show the world that he was exercising not the will of a dictator, but the will of a nation. He called for a referendum on whether the public approved of the Rhineland remilitarization. Despite tension in the streets from the constant shouts of "Heil, Hitler!" and the all-day marching of Brownshirts, the continual clicking of heels, and the menace of the frightening camp at Dachau, the German people really did support the military move. William Shirer, an American correspondent working in Berlin, wrote, "I think that a substantial majority of the people applaud the Rhineland move regardless of whether they're Nazis or not."

To ensure that that sentiment showed clearly in the polls, Goebbels turned to his trusted endorsement team again, Hugo Eckener being a top player. Eckener agreed to give a speech on March 29, election day. But then, one week before the big election, he changed his mind. It might have been that he felt some regret for his glowing review of Hitler, right after the Night of the Long Knives: the three-minute recorded speech in the summer of 1934 in which he equated Hitler with "noble wine." It might have been that he felt nothing but contempt for Goebbels, a bureaucrat about whom he told occasional jokes in private.

Whatever the case, Goebbels wasn't angry, just befuddled. Nearly everyone in Germany thought defending the territory that was theirs anyway was a smart, gutsy move. Why not Eckener? Was he not a German patriot? To Goebbels, Eckener seemed ungrateful for the half-million dollars the Propaganda Ministry provided him to jump-start the stalled *Hindenburg* project. Accustomed to temperamental celebrities, musicians, and artists, Goebbels wrote sarcastically in his diary, on Sunday, March 22, 1936, "Dr. Eckener canceled the speech on March 29th. A true patriot!"

Annoyed at the flip-flop, Goebbels apparently gave some instructions to the German press corps to downplay references to Eckener in their stories, or to ignore him altogether. The American press, smelling a juicy scandal, tried to sort out exactly what Goebbels had ordered. It seemed like Eckener was blacklisted somehow. Whatever action Goebbels took, it did not concern him enough to discuss it in his diary, which was an exhaustive inventory of every gripe or perceived slight, of every insult, private or public, to him or the Nazi Party.

Leaving the hangar for its seventh flight on the morning of March 26, the *Hindenburg* had its first accident. Minor, but embarrassing. The *Hindenburg* had been chartered by the Nazis (at a considerable profit of nearly 90,000 Reichsmarks) to fly for three days with the *Graf Zeppelin* over all the major cities of Germany to get out the vote in support of Hitler's Rhineland move. Just after the more than one hundred men of the ground crew walked the massive ship out of the hangar, part of the apparatus attached to the critical lines they were holding split. The *Hindenburg* was on the verge of slipping perilously out of their control.

"The ship then began to walk the men across the field, instead of the men walking the ship," wrote Commander Peck, in a letter later that day to Admiral Ernst King, the U.S. Navy's top aviation officer. Danger brewing, Captain Lehmann needed to get the ship into the air quickly. After the men released their hold at the order of "Up, ship," a gust of wind apparently spilled off the hangar's roof, forcing the *Hindenburg*'s tail down quickly. It was surprising, as Peck noted the wind speed on the field that morning was only six to eight knots, ranked a "gentle breeze."

The bottom fin crunched on the ground, but further damage was averted because Lehmann managed to get the ship into the air quickly.

The accident proved awkward, as the *Hindenburg*, along with the *Graf Zeppelin*, was orchestrated to be in the public spotlight just then, with photographers clicking away. The ships had been chartered by the Nazis to drop leaflets and to broadcast speeches. Some party dignitaries were aboard the *Hindenburg*, which was being portrayed as a futuristic symbol of Nazi technical prowess. And now it had an obviously bent tail.

After checking on the damage in the air, Captain Lehmann landed at the field shortly thereafter and had the *Hindenburg* walked back into the hangar for repairs. When they were ready to take off again, the wind had picked up and Lehmann ended up delaying departure by three full hours, even sending the ground crew home until the wind conditions were optimal. In reporting on the accident, the *New York Times* praised Lehmann's prudence and caution, landing the *Hindenburg* for repairs "rather than take a chance" by rushing off on the campaign tour.

Yet, twisting those facts around, Eckener years later would tell a different tale of the accident. In it, he made himself a hero and Lehmann a Nazi puppet. And that version stuck. Another strand in Eckener's looming web of deceit.

Shortly after the Rhineland referendum, the *Hindenburg* took off on its first flight across the Atlantic. Thirty-five passengers. Two tons of freight. Destination, Brazil. News reached Eckener en route that Goebbels had ordered reporters to downplay or dismiss him in their stories about the *Hindenburg*'s first adventure. And Eckener suddenly understood that Goebbels was not a man to cross. He would have to go on the offensive, even before he returned to Germany, to restore his good name.

As the *Hindenburg* neared Rio de Janeiro on April 5, 1936, Eckener radioed a statement to the press, explaining why he declined to speak before the Rhineland voting: "Without direct news from Germany, the inquiry surprises me as a bad joke. My attitude in the election was that of a voter. Therefore, I refused to participate in propaganda when invited."

Eckener had to have understood that any fall from grace with the Nazis jeopardized his command of the *Hindenburg*. So, he sought to clarify, once and for all, reports that he had objected to the new ship's being used to promote the Nazis. "I never protested against the use of the airship in the election propaganda," he stated emphatically. "I expect to return to Germany with the *Hindenburg* and retain my position as long as I can."

His position was precarious. Other reports had it that Goebbels blacklisted Eckener because he refused to name the new ship the *Hitler*, instead of the *Hindenburg*, suggesting he had a problem with the Führer. So Eckener arranged an interview with Louis Lochner, a friend of his who was a reporter on board the *Hindenburg*. "I always say 'Heil, Hitler!' when the occasion demands it, contrary to certain reports," Eckener told him. "I have always served Germany well and will continue to do so."

The Zeppelin company really wanted to wow the world with the new *Hindenburg*. Instead, the first arrival in Brazil was, in a word, ugly. The *Hindenburg* approached the airfield at Pernambuco, having traveled over 5,900 miles. The *Graf Zeppelin* had regularly landed there, at the field lined with palm trees waving in muggy winds. But on this day, the ground crew on hand for the landing was new.

Looking out the window, at the hundred or so men who didn't seem to know how to handle the landing lines, Commander Peck got nervous. "They wandered about the field like cattle, apparently not having the slightest idea of what was required of them," he recalled. The field was muddy, and the *Hindenburg* was nearing the ground. Peck, a veteran airship man, asked permission to hop out and help direct the landing crew. Captain Lehmann joined him.

There, in the muck, Lehmann and Peck pulled on the lines along with the Brazilians, hauling down the ultramodern *Hindenburg*. "The mud was over our shoes," Peck recalled, "but after much shouting . . . the ship was docked a few minutes later."

The U.S. Navy was champing at the bit to learn everything it could about the new German super-Zeppelin. Admiral King had written to the Zeppelin company and to Eckener, begging to put naval observers aboard the *Hindenburg*. When he got permission to send two, he repeatedly requested three instead, with assurances two men would share a single bed.

While the Germans eventually acquiesced on allowing navy observers, access was frustrating. In reporting to Admiral King on the *Hindenburg*'s first major flight, Peck had to admit: "The officers are quite free with information . . . while everything is going smoothly, but when trouble brews, they become incommunicable, and logs and other sources of information are tactfully secreted."

Peck wrote his notes in the *Hindenburg*'s writing lounge, a calm area with chairs and desks, where passengers scribbled out postcards and letters and looked out the large slanted windows at the ocean below. Peck had a nose for trouble. At one point, a valve used to release hydrogen in one cell stuck open and it lost about half its volume, creating a real hazard. "The matter was kept entirely secret in order to prevent worry to the passengers. I found out about it only by my own observations. The ship flew extremely heavy all night."

So as not to jeopardize his future access, Peck asked the admiral to be discreet with the revelation. "I would not want the Zeppelin people to think that I had passed this information to anyone outside our service so I would therefore request that the information be handled accordingly," he wrote.

Peck also reported another serious matter: engine trouble near the Cape Verde Islands, 350 miles off the coast of Africa. "The engines are a military secret and very little authentic information is being circulated. I hear through the grapevine route that several pistons broke at the top at the point where the piston pin is fitted." His information was spot-on. When they arrived back in Germany, all the engines were sent back to the manufacturer for repairs.

The breakdown over the ocean was surprising because Lehmann had fully tested the engines, running them continuously for thirty hours during one test flight, and he felt confident they were good to go. And if they weren't for any reason, if the *Hindenburg* wasn't ready for its first over-ocean flight, Lehmann had backup plans to send the *Graf Zeppelin* to carry the thirty-five passengers booked for the first flight to Brazil. Then the *Hindenburg* could simply make the next scheduled trip, two weeks later. Lehmann was, if anything, a cautious engineer.

Peck was anxious on the flight. "The situation looked quite serious at times when two engines would be stopped and the other two running at reduced speed," he wrote.

Years later, Eckener himself would reflect dramatically on the peril faced on the bridge at that moment on the *Hindenburg*'s first over-ocean trip, when engines were crippled far from the African coast. His memoir recounted the open ocean below, the Sahara Desert lying off the starboard side. There were seventy-five people on board. The situation was perilous. He quickly considered trying to rush back to Brazil. Then he considered diverting the *Hindenburg* to a quick landing in the African desert, in case, say, another engine failed. He imagined a scene in his mind: a crash in the desert. Seventy-five people, shouldering water and provisions from the *Hindenburg*'s wreckage, making their way to a remote village for help. "I admit that I have hardly ever felt myself in such great spiritual need as in these hours of vacillation and perplexity," he wrote.

One big problem with Eckener's heartfelt confession is that Lehmann was the captain at the time. In the control room, it was Lehmann who managed to avert a disaster. Eckener was on board solely as a passenger. He was never in command of the *Hindenburg* on that flight.

By this point, Eckener had lost command entirely of the *Hindenburg*, the ship he more than anyone had brought to life. When Göring and the Nazi Air Ministry plowed $2 million into the Zeppelin operation and split off flight operations into its own company, the DZR, the man put in charge was Lehmann. Airship construction would remain the responsibility of the old Luftschiffbau Zeppelin, under Eckener.

A confidential government memo in March 1934 apparently spelled out some of the reasoning, as it contemplated how to form a national airship company that could enhance the prestige of Germany. Basically, it said, Eckener wasn't a competent businessman. The strategy would require "expert financial management on the part of the management of the airship enterprise . . . not something Dr. Eckener could provide. An exceptionally devoted supporter of the Zeppelin cause and an outstanding airship captain, he was no financial expert."

The new government overseers of the Zeppelin business knew that it was Colsman who, despite Eckener's resistance, kept the operation alive through the lean years after the war by diversifying beyond airships. And Colsman had just published his memoir the year before, making it clear the legendary Count himself had doubts about Eckener: "Count Zeppelin could not ignore Eckener's remarkable aptitude for solving the problems of airship travel, but . . . I had not noticed that he had endeavored to promote Eckener's advancement in the range of functions of airship construction. To the contrary, as the navigation issues moved more to the forefront, Count Zeppelin—as well as the leader of DELAG—made greater efforts to bring in other advisors for the development of airship travel."

Colsman added that after the war, curtailed by treaty from building large airships, Eckener nearly walked away from the company and contemplated a newspaper job back in his hometown of Flensburg. During those very years, Lehmann was gaining valuable experience at a large American corporation, as vice president of engineering at Goodyear. Their age gap favored Lehmann as well. He was fifty; Eckener, nearing seventy.

Lehmann had also amassed considerably more flight hours. Between 1928 and 1935, he commanded the *Graf Zeppelin* on 272 of its trips, nearly two-thirds of the total. Eckener was captain for 133 flights. While Eckener was aloof with his crews, Lehmann was like a father to them. Lehmann once reflected on how the narrow confines of the airship bound the fates of the crew together. He felt intimately acquainted with his men, even beyond the line of duty. "The commander on board is not merely a superior, he is also a comrade, friend, and adviser, father, doctor, and pastor in one," he reflected.

With Lehmann in charge of flight operations under the reorganized Zeppelin operation, he became commander of the latest, greatest airship on earth, the *Hindenburg*. And that set off enmity that Eckener, long known as "The Pope," would never, ever get over. But he would get even.

## 5

# Begging for Helium

THEY CALLED IT THE SUPER-ZEPPELIN, THE FASCINATING *HINDENBURG*, A ship of firsts. Even before it was constructed in its hangar, American newspaper syndicates had already reserved spots on its first flight to the United States, effectively its world debut. Eight reporters were on board that first week of May 1936 to chronicle the first piano concert on an airship, the first stewardess, the first Catholic mass. A record 106 people for a transoceanic flight. An announcer from National Broadcasting Corp. would transmit dispatches aboard, melding the craze in radio with the latest in aviation.

It was so futuristic, a hundred people hurled over the ocean in a capsule. The *Hindenburg* itself was an experimental German aircraft, with its German engines an oil-burning diesel type never tried. Its windows were composed of a German chemical advance called Plexiglas. For an exhibit, the transparent plastic was shaped into a see-through violin that would soon be a hit at an international exposition in Paris. The Germans appeared to be at the cutting edge of everything.

The *Hindenburg* seemed to convey to the New World a newer world.

"I wanted to pinch myself during the voyage to make sure I was not dreaming," Lady Drummond-Hay recalled. "I looked out of the windows up to the sky, down to the sea. Even to me, one of the veteran Zeppelin travelers, it did not seem easy to realize that these beautiful rooms and all they contained—carpets, modern electric fittings, chairs, tables with vases of flowers upon them—could really be 'flying' through the air at more than a mile a minute."

After visiting their bedrooms, passengers on the *Hindenburg* amused themselves with a whole new thought. Late Victorian Agers who witnessed cars replace horses, who lived through the dawn of radio and the recent discovery of a new planet named Pluto, joked that the world had come to this, that babies could now be conceived in the clouds. Webb Miller, a reporter, suggested that the first baby boy be named *He-lium* and the first girl, *She-lium*.

Captain Lehmann bounced about the *Hindenburg* like a child. He was perfectly giddy. He loved giving passengers personal tours of the colossal new ship, describing its technical wonders. As he led Miller through the *Hindenburg*, a sixth of a mile long, neither man knew that every inch they walked, over one hundred tons of fabric, girders, and machinery, in exactly one year would lay in ashes. Soon, though, Lehmann would have an inkling.

They slinked through the narrow, triangular catwalk that ran the length of the ship. Miller was impressed by the immense aluminum-alloy rings, the ribs that formed the *Hindenburg*'s rounded shape. They were reinforced by an intricate arrangement of trusty girders and wires thick as fingers. The girders were punched with holes, like Swiss cheese, to make them lighter. And all around them puffy gas cells, pumped full of hydrogen.

Clutching anxiously at struts as he walked along, Miller felt vertigo. He kept eyeing the outer cover below his feet, worried a single misstep would fling him through the skinny fabric. Then it would be a fatal free-fall, a half mile into the chilly ocean.

"You needn't be so concerned," Lehmann said, noticing his anxiety. "That fabric is strong enough to bear the weight of a man. You wouldn't go through if you slipped off on it." But the captain could tell he wasn't getting through.

"Here, I'll show you," Lehmann said. He hopped off the catwalk right onto the outer cover, bouncing like a trampolinist. Lehmann did not explain that the specially treated cotton aeronautical covering was of different widths, at various points in the ship, and he had vaulted onto one of the thickest spots.

The *Hindenburg*, slightly longer than the *Graf Zeppelin* but a good deal fatter, at 135 feet in diameter, contained nearly double the amount of buoyant hydrogen. It was extraordinary, the amount of lift, the cargo that could be carried. As Lehmann liked to point out, 1,750 locomotives could be shipped inside the airship, which, when empty, weighed no more than one of them. With the powerful, new 1,200-horsepower engines, classified a military secret, and riveting engineers around the world, the flying time to North America was cut by one-third. To steer this monster, the tail fins were 105 feet long and 49 feet wide. To drive it through the air, four sets of propellers.

Lehmann showed Webb the dials and gauges used for meteorology and navigation that filled the instrument boards in the control car, a little windowed bubble near the nose of the ship. There on the *Hindenburg's* bridge, Lehmann demonstrated how wired instruments could valve out hydrogen or water ballast to elevate and lower the ship, and how he could give orders by telegraph or telephone to fourteen points on the *Hindenburg*. He showed Webb the weather charts, updated continuously via wireless reports from ships passing below.

While in the control car for a tour, Captain Lehmann introduced two of the most valuable crew members, the elevator men. One was charged with operating the vertical rudder; the other, the horizontal. They were used to steer and to adjust altitude, and had to be handled nimbly or the vast ship could veer violently. There were about fifty crewmen on the *Hindenburg*, including the steward and kitchen staff.

The smoking room had sealed doors, along with a steward on duty to ensure that no one left with a lit cigarette. At a time when nearly everyone smoked, the room, which could seat eight people, removed a major aggravation of air voyages on hydrogen-filled ships. Another technical sleight of hand, thanks to fireproof materials and German ingenuity.

Caution was stowed on board as well. There were four emergency boats, each capable of carrying twenty-five people, inflatable when they hit water. There were life jackets for each passenger and buoyant pillows for each of the crew.

On Sunday evening, Father Paul Schulte celebrated the first Catholic mass on an aircraft, boarding with a papal document authorizing the service. Pope Pius XI decided that the passenger salon of the *Hindenburg* was a place of dignity and history, and that the large ship was sturdy enough that the sacred wine wouldn't be in danger of spilling. The Flying Priest, as he came to be called, was an aviation buff, a pilot who flew planes for church missionary work. He loved the trip. "It was all quiet up there and one seemed near heaven," he would recall.

In his white gown, with a makeshift altar with flowers and unlit candles, Father Schulte began the Sunday mass, invoking the name of God the Father, Son, and Holy Spirit in the Latin, saying: *In nomine Patris, et Filii, et Spiritus Sancti.*

Later, passengers attended a piano concert, with Professor Franz Wagner of Dresden playing works of Chopin, Beethoven, and Brahms, broadcast to radio listeners around the world. The piano was built with aluminum instead of wood, making it a featherweight of only 112 pounds, important on an airship where every pound mattered. On the wall behind the piano was a head-and-shoulders photograph of Adolf Hitler.

In the dining room, which could seat fifty passengers at once, diners gazed out the windows at clouds as waiters in dapper suits served them. On elegant blue-and-gold-rimmed china, the five-course dinner one evening was celery cream soup, Strasbourg goose liver in aspic, carrots in butter, chanterelles, croquette potatoes, a mixed cheese platter, and coffee. The food arrived piping hot, conveyed via a dumbwaiter from the kitchen. Forks and glasses clinked, amid hushed conversation in English and German. The bar menu: Martini, Manhattan, Bronx Side Car, sherry, champagne, whiskey, gin, and brandy, each from 1.50 to 1.80 Reichsmarks (RM). The wine list included a 1921 Curé Bon La Madeleine, Bordeaux, at 5 RM a bottle, and a 1929 Kessler Riesling for 9 RM.

The fare for the *Hindenburg* was set at $400 one-way between Frankfurt and Lakehurst and $720 round-trip. Over the two-and-a-half-day voyage, passengers strolled on the 200 feet of walking space on the promenade deck, looking down at the ocean out the large Plexiglas windows, angled outward, and occasionally sticking their arms out to feel the wind pass at seventy miles an hour. At one point, Captain Lehmann ordered the ship lowered so passengers could get a better view of icebergs floating in the ocean. With their Kodaks, the passengers snapped photos of the sparkling spectacles as well as the cigar-shadow of the *Hindenburg* moving across the water below.

In the writing room, the newspaper reporters clacked out stories on typewriters, *rat-a-tat, rat-a-tat*, while others wrote out postcards and letters, which they could deposit in a tube fired straight to the mailroom. Some were there passing time, waiting for their turn after putting their name on the sign-up sheet for the shower.

Few people spent much time in their cabins, small rooms only five and a half by six and a half feet, with two little bunks, a wash basin and mirror, and a dim, forty-watt bulb. A small closet was large enough to hang six suits or so; otherwise, clothing had to be kept in one's suitcase. Passenger space was larger on the *Hindenburg* than on the *Graf Zeppelin*, however, because all the rooms were moved fully inside the hull. But moving the passenger quarters inside the *Hindenburg* did put them in closer proximity to the potentially explosive hydrogen.

Louis Lochner, the Berlin correspondent, spoke at length with Commander Peck, on board as an American naval observer. Looking forward, Peck forecast that a successful series of transoceanic flights by the *Hindenburg* would surely drum up interest again in America, deflated by airship tragedy after tragedy, and the United States would soon have its own airship fleet. There was so much riding on the *Hindenburg*.

At one point, Lochner noticed something odd on the guest list, similar to the snooty Who's Who of passengers given out on ocean liners. In the crew portion of the pamphlet, Hugo Eckener was at the top, but without any duties listed, while listed next was Captain Lehmann, titled "Commander" of the *Hindenburg*. His watch officers, all men he'd flown hours and hours with, were Max Pruss, Albert Sammt, Heinrich Bauer, and Knut Eckener.

When Lochner showed the officer list to the older and more celebrated captain, who hadn't previously seen it, Eckener laughed it off, saying something about being happy to be at the top of the list. But Lochner later reflected, "I had the impression nevertheless that he felt hurt."

The *Hindenburg* arrived on Saturday, May 9, 1936, at Lakehurst, after flying before dawn over slumbering New York City. Early in the trip, the airship had passed the luxury French ocean liner *Normandie*, which had left the coast of Europe hours earlier than the *Hindenburg*. The *Hindenburg* averaged over sixty miles an hour, while the *Normandie* lumbered along closer to thirty-five. It beat the steamship, expected in New York Monday, by two days.

When the *Hindenburg* arrived at the naval base, the ground crew was stunned to see how large the airship was. Even those who had pulled on the cables to haul giants like the *Macon* and the *Akron*, those who had seen the entire two-decade history of airships in the United States, were astonished by the size of the *Hindenburg*. There were 100,000 spectators ringing the pineland field in New Jersey.

Through the cheering crowd, an escort of sailors led Dr. Eckener and Captain Lehmann from the ship to a room in the giant hangar. There they stood side by side at a podium while movie cameras cranked and flashbulbs popped, and a hundred reporters fired off questions. Eckener was clearly the larger celebrity, the number of camera lenses pointed his way in evidence. Immediately, questions rose about Eckener's tiff with the Nazi government.

"Ah!" said Eckener, raising a dismissive hand. To some, he looked old and tired at that moment. But he stood upright in his civilian suit, sticking out his jaw as if pointing to the reporters with his goatee.

"There was a slight misunderstanding, which was not the fault of anybody," he said. "But the whole question has been settled satisfactorily." He said it in a way that it was clear he wouldn't entertain a follow-up question.

A reporter then shouted to both men: "There has been some question as to who was in command of the *Hindenburg*."

"I was," Lehmann fired back, without hesitation. The Little Captain looked snappy and fresh in his navy blue, gold-braided uniform. "Dr. Eckener was aboard in the capacity of advisor." Lehmann added with pride that he was also in command on the *Hindenburg*'s first flight, to South America.

"But there was never any conflict over authority," Lehmann added, diplomatically, sensitive to the feelings of the senior pilot at his side who trained him years earlier. "There was always close cooperation."

Eckener said nothing.

As reporters then directed more questions to Lehmann, their relationship undoubtedly curdled.

"Who's got a smoke?" Lehmann said. "That's what I want now." A dozen packs of cigarettes were suddenly thrust at him. Between puffs, Lehmann answered questions in impeccable English. And as he drew in on his cigarette, a thought suddenly occurred to him. He told them helium wasn't available in Germany currently, but he hoped on a future trip to America to replace the hydrogen in the *Hindenburg* with the vastly safer gas. What he did not add was that Eckener had resisted helium again and again.

Over the next two days, the two men, fates tied together, were whisked all over official Washington and New York. President Roosevelt met with Eckener and Lehmann at the White House, where they entertained the political legend over fifteen minutes with tales from the flight. Admiral King personally groveled to them, begging that they allow three naval observers on the return flight, promising again that his officers would "double up" on beds. Usually one was on watch and one off, anyway.

The next day, at a banquet at the elegant Waldorf-Astoria in honor of Eckener, Lehmann, and the other *Hindenburg* officers, the orchestra opened the dinner playing both "*Deutschland über Alles*" and the "Horst Wessel" song, the marching-music anthem of the Nazi Party. About half the diners cocked their arms up in the Nazi salute. Dr. Eckener was among them. He beamed with pleasure when informed of reports that a big reception awaited his return to the Frankfurt airport. District Nazi Party leaders would honor him by presenting a silver cup.

Eckener could no longer stand Lehmann's being captain of the *Hindenburg*. The day after the ship returned to Germany, he wrote a letter resigning from the bridge of the *Hindenburg*. Noting that it was nonsense to fly with two leaders, he informed Lehmann that he decided not to take part in the next trip to North America. He told Lehman that he would make other trips, though, when it suited him. He signed it, "Eckener."

The following day, a Saturday afternoon, May 16, 1936, Captain Lehmann replied that he did not at all appreciate being notified that Eckener wouldn't show up for a flight just two hours before departure. Clearly annoyed, Lehmann said he deplored Eckener's decision and found his reasoning "disgraceful." He signed it, "Your devoted E. A. Lehmann."

Just as with Alfred Colsman, the relationship with another trusty Eckener colleague had sunk to the point that they would speak mostly in writing. It was at this point that Eckener found new comrades. He began showing up at the regular beer evenings of the Army Weapons Office, or the *Heereswaffenamt*, where he drank with leaders of his nation's armaments companies and other industrialists. The nightly discussions involved rearming Germany.

As Captain Lehmann undertook that next flight in late May, he ordered the engines slowed over England one Friday evening and the *Hindenburg* hovered over the town of Keighley. Father Schulte, the Flying Priest, then dropped a wreath of fresh carnations, with instructions to the finder to deliver them to the town cemetery at the cross of the grave of his brother, Lieutenant Franz Schulte, buried there as a prisoner of the Great War. A few boys scrambled to pick up the parcel, which also had *Hindenburg* souvenirs, and headed off to the cemetery. Lehmann personally arranged the memorial stop as a favor to Father Schulte.

The rest of the *Hindenburg*'s maiden season, 1936, went off magically. There were fifty-six trips in all, from Germany to North and South America and other locales. The shiny, new *Hindenburg* flew 191,592 miles over nearly 2,800 hours. Its average speed was a breakneck sixty-eight miles per hour. It carried nearly 2,800 passengers and nineteen tons of mail and cargo.

Freight was all over the map. Monkeys, gorillas, and chimpanzees for research and zoos. Guinea pigs, pedigree dogs, queen bees, canaries, and carrier pigeons. Parts for machines and automobiles, radio tubes, and lamps. Exotic orchids and roses, children's clothing, and rabbit skins. A one-ton airplane. Captain Lehmann did, however, politely decline the request to ship a grown elephant from India to England.

The *Hindenburg* was a star at the Olympics in Berlin that summer. She arrived over Olympic Stadium around two in the afternoon on opening day, with the five interlocking rings painted on her belly. Goebbels and his Propaganda Ministry paid 3,500 RM for the Olympic rings to be painted on the hulls of the *Hindenburg* and the *Graf Zeppelin*. More than two million people crowded the stadium and the surrounding streets in Berlin. The orchestra, horns blasting, drums thundering, was drowned out by the cheering of thousands as they waved handkerchiefs at the *Hindenburg*.

Looking up was the African-American track-and-field man Jesse Owens, who would soon run off with four gold medals, spoiling the grand plan of the Nazis to demonstrate the supposed supremacy of the Aryan race at the games. When the *Hindenburg* left and passed over Selb, a porcelain company had arranged hundreds of cups and saucers on its flat, black roof into enormous letters spelling out *Heil, LS Hindenburg.* The factory workers waved up to the *Hindenburg* as it dipped its nose in appreciation.

Weeks later, the *Hindenburg* arrived with a squadron of seventeen aircraft flying in a swastika formation at Nuremburg, proceeding to the tribune to dip in salute to Hitler and Göring. On the Zeppelinfield, thousands of uniformed troops goose-stepped in phalanxes and formations. Swastika flags waved. It was the annual Nazi Party celebration at Nuremburg.

"It is the miracle of our age that you found me . . . among so many millions," Hitler proclaimed, to shouts and applause. "And that I found you is Germany's great fortune."

The drone of the *Hindenburg's* engines, her enormous size—everywhere she went, she called attention to herself, inspiring awe. During one flight over New Jersey that first season, a seven-year-old boy in downtown Princeton looked up, mesmerized by the colossus, the name *Hindenburg* written along the side in odd German script, the mysterious swastikas on its tail. Mark Heald had never seen anything like it, except in the newsreels in theaters. He was attuned to worldly events, as his father was a history professor at Rutgers. Within a few months, the two would see the *Hindenburg* again, in Lakehurst. Briefly.

The urgent warning came at Göring's fortress, the Nazi Ministry of Aviation in Berlin, as eighteen men assembled on November 20, 1936, to discuss the future of airships in Germany. They represented the Luftwaffe, the Ministry of Finance, local airport officials, and the men who brought the world the *Hindenburg.* They were in meeting room 2379/81. It was 11:10 Friday morning.

The *Hindenburg* performed so well its first season, the Air Ministry wanted to hear plans for a fleet of new ships. As head of the Luftschiffbau Zeppelin, the old construction company, Dr. Eckener explained that there was a great deal of interest from leading business circles and the U.S.

government in buying or chartering German dirigibles. Captain Lehmann, representing the DZR, the new flight operations firm, described negotiations with interested British companies.

They discussed progress on a new ship, the LZ 130, whose construction began around the time of the Olympics. It was a sister ship to the *Hindenburg*, with the exact same dimensions. Eckener said the LZ 130 could be completed by August 1937. Dr. Dürr, the firm's longtime designer, and Dr. Eckener then discussed building two new large dirigibles, the LZ 131 and LZ 132.

The plan was the LZ 130 would be made available to America, the LZ 131 would be used for North Atlantic traffic, and the LZ 132 would be available for special trips. That would leave the *Hindenburg* for trips to South America.

The meeting closed with a note of dread from Air Ministry director Willy Fisch. He had been a fighter pilot in the war and helped develop radio communications for aviation. He was tall, heavy, and imposing, a bear of a man with a moon face and thick black eyebrows over round glasses.

Fisch pleaded with the men, as he had before, that by all means helium, which cannot catch fire, must be used as the lifting gas for the new dirigibles. It seemed the Nazi air leadership was terrified that a deadly airship catastrophe would be a blow to their image on the world stage, that a hydrogen ship was obviously a ticking bomb.

It was not at all what Eckener wanted to hear, given his plans for the *Hindenburg*. He and Dr. Dürr raised objections immediately. To begin with, the high price of helium would increase construction costs, they argued. Since helium is less buoyant than hydrogen, they would probably have to stretch the size of the Zeppelins, add two additional sections. Even with that, Eckener added, a helium ship would reduce the number of passengers and the amount of cargo it could carry, a loss of twenty tons. Higher costs, lower revenue.

To address the Nazis' concerns about hydrogen, Eckener promised to study the issue. At one point, the Zeppelin company had considered using combined helium and hydrogen in the *Hindenburg*. Plans were drawn up for double-skinned gas cells. The inner gas cell would be filled with hydrogen, then surrounding it for protection would be a fireproof helium outer bag. The arrangement resembled an egg, with the helium the egg white and the hydrogen the yolk. That way, the Hindenburg could economize on its use of more-expensive helium. But helium's price had been falling for several years. Increasing supplies of helium had narrowed the price gap with hydrogen from seven times more expensive to only triple the price.

Whatever the case, within two weeks, Eckener would move forward with plans to pack more people onto the *Hindenburg*. As part of a winter overhaul, workers began constructing cabins for additional passengers. All the extra weight ended any hope that the *Hindenburg* could operate profitably with helium.

When he wasn't flying, Lehmann quickly grew restless. He had just arrived at the landmark age of fifty as the *Hindenburg's* first season began, and he decided the time was ripe for his memoirs. Helping him as editor was a kindred spirit, Leonhard Adelt, who was a little older at fifty-five. Both men were on their second marriages, and each had a young son. Adelt, a tall man with round glasses, had worked as a newspaper reporter and magazine editor for years. He had also written several books romanticizing aviation and had even experimented with airships on his own. Flying brought Lehmann and him together in Munich and Leipzig. Over time, they became good friends.

By the winter of 1936, the two had finished drafts of the memoir, whose title in English is *The German Air Patrol and World Voyages*. Even with Adelt's help, Lehmann had mostly assembled a mishmash of memories from the war, reflections on the grandeur of the *Hindenburg*, and technical musings about safety. In truth, Lehmann's life was fascinating. He was the most experienced Zeppelin pilot who had ever lived, knew where all the skeletons were buried in a generation of airship history, and had had several brushes with death.

Lehmann reflected poetically about something entirely new to the human race, living in the clouds. "Over the blue Atlantic, the heavens curved off into infinity," Lehmann recalled, piloting the *Graf Zeppelin* between Germany and Brazil two years earlier. "If I were not an aviator, I would like to travel once as a passenger, to indulge myself completely in the contemplation of the thousand-fold colors and forms that nature creates out of nothing but air and water." Even the tall, curving girders that formed the top of a Zeppelin, he described as "a cathedral."

He came to love the water early, as a boy growing up on the shores of Lake Constance, the Bodensee, in Ludwigshafen. Surrounded by fruit orchards, the town emerged from an enchanting countryside at the foot of wooded hills. Little Ernst would spend his days watching nightingales, grebes, and kingfishers fly over the lake. On clear days, he could see the Alps off in the distance. Voyage beckoned.

At fourteen years of age, he decided to become a shipbuilder. He would later enroll in college to study shipbuilding and marine engineering. In 1912, after several years of voyages on sailboats, he became a navy engineer at the Imperial Dockyards at Kiel. He quickly figured out he didn't like government work, and just then Dr. Eckener reached out to him, looking for a pilot of the commuter airship *Saschen*, owned by Delag, the world's first airline. Lehmann signed on. He was so talented that by the winter of 1913–14, he was helping Dr. Eckener train the first officers and crews of the navy's new airship division.

In 1914, Lehmann commanded the *Saschen* as an army airship, flying raids and scouting missions over Belgium, England, France, Russia, the North Sea, and the Baltic. He flew other Zeppelins to war through 1918. It was always perilous. Large spotlights shined cones of light from the ground onto the slow-moving, bomb-carrying airships in the dark of night, making them easy targets. Anti-aircraft weaponry was constantly improving, blowing Zeppelins out of the sky. Even frostbite was a hazard, as onboard heaters were too heavy given weight limitations. To try to keep warm, men wore thick, woolen underwear, fur overcoats, and leather helmets, and stuffed layers of newspapers under their flying suits.

Lehmann worked on a Zeppelin mission that was to become legend. In late 1917, his assignment was to prepare for a long-distance flight from Friedrichshafen to resupply a struggling army garrison in German East Africa, more than 4,000 miles away. The ship chosen was the LZ 59, nicknamed *Das Afrika-Schiff*, the Africa ship. Knowing they could never refill the ship with hydrogen once it arrived in the remote corner of the Dark Continent, the army garrison was instructed to cannibalize the

Zeppelin for supplies. The cotton outer cover was to be used for tents and tropical uniforms; the gas cells were to be cut up for sleeping bags; and the Duralumin girders and struts were to be repurposed into a wireless tower and collapsible barracks.

The ship nearly made it all the way to its destination, but the Germans aborted the mission after learning that the German army on the ground there was unable to secure the intended landing spot for the *Afrika-Schiff*. It was one of the most audacious missions of World War I. The aim of the expedition, to bring relief to the German outpost in Africa, had failed, Lehmann would later relate: "But the moral effect of a bold act is not tied to success and time."

Lehmann was also an eyewitness to the dawn of aerial warfare. Worse, he was an accomplice. Weaponry in the skies raised new moral issues. Lehmann must have known that some of his previous Zeppelin raids had killed civilians. Even if military targets were the objective, accuracy was poor for hand-dropped projectiles. Still, he completely opposed intentionally targeting the public, as in the plan to drop 6,000 firebombs to set all London afire. "Asked for my technical opinion," he wrote in the memoir, "I admitted that the idea itself was feasible. But the thought of delivering all the horrors of bombing down upon a defenseless civilian population outside the actual war zone and destroying irreplaceable cultural prizes was reason enough for us to dismiss the plan."

After delivering the *Los Angeles* to the Americans in 1924, Lehmann joined Goodyear as an engineering executive, since it looked like building large airships in Germany would be forbidden forever. During the Great Depression, Eckener lured him back, however, to fly with him on the *Graf Zeppelin* on the world tour. There were promises of piloting the yet-to-be-completed *Hindenburg*. Meantime, Lehmann commanded the *Graf* until 1935, on nearly 300 of its 500 flights, more than double the flights Eckener piloted. He was captain on most of the flights of the *Hindenburg* to South America and ten round-trips to Lakehurst in the summer of 1936.

It is notable the way Lehmann discussed the propaganda flights for the national referendum on remilitarizing the Rhineland the previous summer. In his memoir, he had no praise whatsoever for Hitler or the Nazi Party, omissions that could have hurt him. Instead, he viewed the four-day flyover of nearly every inch of Germany, more than 4,000 miles, like a wide-eyed boy who got to see the entire nation he grew up in from the air, always to the cheers of his fellow Germans. The ship, emblazoned with the name of the national hero Hindenburg, along with the *Graf Zeppelin* dropped election pamphlets and broadcast speeches over loudspeakers.

Instead, Lehmann reserved his praise for his countrymen. "The appearance of our airship was always the signal for a spontaneous outburst of enthusiasm, for the ship was a symbol of freedom to the German people," he marveled. The cheering below drowned out the sound of the *Hindenburg*'s motors.

Lehmann was apolitical, aware that the Nazi Party was the government to be reckoned with. He mostly steered clear, preferring to stay in the private sector. His colleagues at the Luftschiffbau Zeppelin and DZR began closing correspondence with "Heil, Hitler!" but Lehmann maintained the old standard signoff, ending letters with "With German greetings."

For the memoir, Lehmann and his friend and editor, Adelt, spent considerable time talking about Zeppelin safety. Lehmann had been at the state funeral for the victims of Britain's R 101. Based on the official final report on the disaster, he told Adelt that the gas cells weren't properly arranged to prevent friction and chafing against the framework. The airship, headed for India, encountered a rain squall and one of its gasbags in the bow of the ship, damaged by earlier chafing, apparently burst open from the gas pressure, exposing the flammable gas to electrical charges in the sky. For a Zeppelin, it was a doomsday scenario.

In 1916, Lehmann was flying a Zeppelin that was struck on the nose by lightning. Piloting the LZ 98 over Hanover, he and the crew suddenly saw a blinding flash. They immediately landed and inspected the ship. They found small burns and holes in the bow marking precisely where the lightning struck. To a layman, Lehmann would write, it might seem incredible that an airship, filled with flammable hydrogen, could survive such a strike. But research and careful investigation of dozens of strikes showed that the metal framework of the airship acts like a lightning rod, keeping the electricity separate from the gas cells.

Only a leak would be catastrophic. "Lightning . . . obeys the laws of nature," Lehmann reflected. "As long as the airship pilot himself—and this is perfectly within his power—ensures that no gas seeps between the cells and the outer cover, lightning means no danger whatsoever for a Zeppelin."

A captain of the most famous Zeppelin around, Lehmann was enjoying a second career personally. He had divorced his first wife and was recently remarried. He and his new wife, Marie, had a son together. Captain Lehmann played a grand piano at their home, which had a garden and a boat shed on the banks of the Bodensee. Marie's pet name for her husband was Luv, the same name they chose for their baby boy. Having a first child, at middle age, was sobering. It made Lehmann more cautious, as he was providing for a child for the first time.

On shore leave, he was happy to be back with the wines he knew, the strong-flavored Müller-Thurgau and the wonderful late Burgundies, including Weißherbst, a fragrant rosé. And he got to enjoy again all the local fish he had grown up eating on Lake Constance: salmon, locally called *Rheinsalm*, and catfish, grayling, and trout. Thaws in the Alps flowed into Lake Constance via the Rhine.

Both Lehmann and Adelt knew the local ballads and folk songs of the Bodensee area of southern Germany. They had grown up learning about bygone figures like Dr. Mesmer, who used magnets to treat patients, and the miraculous healer Gaßner, who viewed illnesses as devils, which had to be forced out of the afflicted by inducing flatulence.

The friends also knew well the chilling tale of the poet Gustav Schwab, who wrote the legendary ballad "The Rider of Lake Constance." In the poem, a horseman gets lost in fog and gallops across the frozen-over lake. On stopping, and suddenly realizing he had clip-clopped for miles perilously over thawing ice, the Rider of Lake Constance drops dead from horror.

That winter, after months of work together, Lehmann confessed something else to Adelt, something not for publication. He couldn't hold it in. The veteran Zeppelin man was anxious, very worried about a structural problem just discovered during the overhaul of the *Hindenburg*. Lehmann was so terrified to learn of the problem—and only after the *Hindenburg* completed its entire maiden season—that he looked Adelt in the eyes and said he felt as if he himself was *Der Reiter am Bodensee*, the Rider of Lake Constance.

# 6

# Twine and Tape

THE DISCOVERY WOULD SHOCK CAPTAIN LEHMANN, BUT THE WORKMEN didn't seem to understand the danger. After the *Hindenburg's* successful first year, ticket reservations picked up. Dr. Eckener had plans drawn up to install ten new cabins in Bay 11 of the ship, behind the current passenger quarters for fifty, enough for twenty-two more passengers. Nine were standard two-bed rooms; the tenth could accommodate a family of four. The new cabins, though, had a big upgrade: Each had four-foot-wide windows that for the first time allowed outside views from within private rooms.

The gas cell in a Zeppelin is the balloon that lifts it up. Basically, the *Hindenburg* was like sixteen balloons inside a ribbed barrel levitating it all. The gas cell located in Bay 11, where the new rooms would be located, would have to be removed, cut smaller, and retailored to fit around the new passenger quarters. As the men deflated gas cell #11 and packed it to ship off, they noticed the very top was severely scraped, damaged somehow.

They made a note of it, and continued down the checklist. It was the first week of December 1936, and the *Hindenburg's* winter overhaul was taking place in Frankfurt. Shortly after splitting from the Luftschiffbau Zeppelin, the DZR, the flight operations firm, moved the *Hindenburg's* flight and repair base from Friedrichshafen, in deep southern Germany, to Frankfurt, which was more centrally located and therefore easier for passengers to get to and from.

The lengthy worklist for the *Überholung*, or overhaul, was signed by Rudolf Sauter, the *Hindenburg's* chief engineer. The *Hindenburg* had a very busy first year, fifty-six flights in all, nearly 200,000 miles, much of it through the turbulence and tempest over the North Atlantic. The overhaul was part of 403,000 Reichsmarks in spending for maintenance on the *Hindenburg* in its maiden season.

The overhaul men checked the bulkhead wiring, and cleaned the rudder wiring and re-greased. They pulled power units from the four engines and sent them to Daimler-Benz for rehabbing. They installed a new RPM indicator, and reinforced the brake drum. They dissembled the rudder wheel and drive, then cleaned and packed them with new grease. They shipped out the starting batteries for refurbishing. They sawed and hammered the new passenger quarters into place, following the blueprints. They replaced the sizable portion of the outer cover painted with the interlocking Olympic rings, paid for by Goebbels.

The wear and tear on the *Hindenburg* was obvious in the worklist, which read, in part:

- Wash carpets.
- Replace dishes.
- Polish washbasins "like new."
- Repair the table in the crew mess.
- Double-check to be sure all items were in place for any forced water landing: rescue boats, drinking-water jugs, emergency provisions, and radio equipment.
- Test all fire extinguishers.

Christmas had just passed, and the balloon-making factory at Tempelhof was getting antsy. They had gas cell #11 on hand, but still needed technical drawings from the DZR to cut the gasbag into shape to fit around the new passenger quarters. The sailing season was just a few months away, and gasbag work required methodical cutting, stitching, and testing.

Word of the delay reached Albert Sammt, a rising captain at the DZR, who was on vacation. In thick, looping black ink, he handwrote his exasperation on the stationery of the Spa Hotel and Winter Sports Field. It was a fabulous resort in Freudenstadt, on a high plateau at the edge of the Black Forest, known for its fresh air. Internationally known, visitors over the years had included George V of England and Mark Twain. Sammt told the factory to step on it.

Awaiting the specifications, the balloon experts had a larger problem. They were puzzled by the chafing at the top of the gas cell. If it was a fault with the fabric, then why in that location and nowhere else? Could it be repaired, or did it need to be replaced? Sections of the gasbag where it had chafed were cut out and tested. The strength of the textile had been compromised, the tests found, nearly by a third. Any degradation, any weak point, could burst when inflated at high pressure. It was the very scenario Lehmann believed destroyed the R 101 in a fiery blast.

At the laboratories of the Luftschiffbau Zeppelin in Friedrichshafen, they decided to try a simulation. They constructed a test segment the size of a single outer-cover panel on the *Hindenburg*, roughly twelve by fifty feet, with all the supportive wiring and netting. They then inflated a gas cell underneath it with air.

Karl Hürttle, the fabric wizard, was on hand to investigate. He joined the newly formed DZR in 1936, after spending eleven years at Goodyear, working mostly under Lehmann. Hürttle was still in Ohio when the *Hindenburg* outer cover was installed, in the deep of a German winter. He would spend weeks puzzling over the cover.

After observing the interaction of all the elements, the scientists at the Luftschiffbau Zeppelin discovered that the *Hindenburg* had a peculiar and harmful side-effect. It was acting something like a snare drum. When a drummer strikes a drumhead, it sends a vibration down to a "snare" of wires, which resonate and rattle. The *Hindenburg*'s outer cover had an unwanted flutter, like drumsticks tapping out a roll, and that vibration set the gas-cell wires rattling, destructively. As one engineer's memo put it, "The conclusion drawn was that the flutter from the outer cover was transmitted to the wiring, which picked up the vibration and caused a chafing of the cell."

But the connection was apparently kept under tight wraps. Some within the company were aware of excessive flutter from the outer cover, but very few seemed to know about the damage to gas cell #11. Individually, they might seem like simple maintenance matters, harmless. Together, they were toxic.

Fixing the gasbag abrasion problem promised to be expensive. After some debate about who was at fault, the balloon maker or the *Hindenburg* factory, Karl Rösch, lead engineer for the technical department, weighed in. "We recommend reporting damage to the gas cell of 129 just as any other warranty-covered damage that occurred during airship construction," he wrote to Captain Lehmann on January 20, 1937. "This is a matter of design flaw."

In the one-sentence telegram, the technical leader put two words together that were an explosive combination. *Zellenschaden. Konstruktionsfehler.* Gas-cell damage. Design flaw.

Captain Lehmann knew better than anyone what it meant. The engineers were going to have to stop the *Hindenburg's* destructive flutter. Time was running out.

The balloon factory completed the alterations on gas cell #11, one of the largest on the ship, holding one-tenth of the *Hindenburg's* hydrogen. It was reinstalled back in Frankfurt. As the overhaul progressed, the workmen tore the entire top cover of the *Hindenburg* off, from the nose to the tail, and inspected the top of each of the sixteen gas cells for any damage.

The outer cover posed a curious problem. After a quarter century of making Zeppelins, these were hardly amateurs in airship design, but the *Hindenburg* was a much larger, much fatter vehicle than ever tried before. Wind tunnel tests can help predict aerodynamic stresses and vibration in novel aircraft. As an aircraft is scaled up, though, pilots know flight tests are the only way to determine the actual behavior of the vehicle in the elements. In some places, the outer-cover panels of the *Hindenburg* were twelve by fifty feet, fully 15 percent larger than the largest on the *Graf Zeppelin*. That's a colossal sheet of cloth to restrain in the wind.

It might just be that the *Hindenburg*, the largest aircraft ever made, was simply too big to fly.

While the engineers wrestled with the cover flutter, they devised a makeshift solution for the gas-cell damage. With the outer cover gone on top—the *Hindenburg* scalped—factory hands went to work securing the wiring that held the gasbags in place. The wiring was designed as a barrier between the gas cell and the hull, or outer cover of the ship. It was there to protect the gas-cell fabric from puncturing on the hull's structural metal rings. Each gas cell in its netting looked like a ham in its meat netting, except with the ham pressing upward.

To eliminate the vibration of the wires, the workers painstakingly tied off each of the hundreds of spots where the wiring crossed. The idea was that when the tied-up wires resonated with the outer cover flutter, they would act as one large grid, thus dampening tremors that could tear fabric. They tied the wiring crossings together with cord and then taped them. Wherever they spotted abrasions on a cell from the wires rattling, they glued one-and-a-half-inch reinforcing strips over them. The *Hindenburg* would start its second season held together, it turned out, with twine and tape.

As an anti-flutter step, the engineering department quietly added one more step to the winter overhaul: painting the entire top half of the *Hindenburg* with two new coats of dope, a lacquer. It must have puzzled the painters, hung from scaffolding on the ceiling and perched on dizzying fire ladders. The extra dope, from the equator of the ship up, added considerable weight, each coat covering more than three and a half acres of fabric.

Finally out of its hangar in Frankfurt, the *Hindenburg* was cleared to test the overhaul. And there were other tests. For some time, Lehmann had grand hopes of connecting Zeppelins with fast-advancing planes. He foresaw planes docking on his Zeppelins, delivering mail from a city they were flying over, or maybe passengers who wanted to connect mid-voyage.

It was 1937. Modern times. Who knew where things could go? Lehmann even lined up a plane to deliver two customs agents to the *Hindenburg* on its next flight to the United States. That way, the agents could clear passengers to enter the country before they even landed.

To flight-test the docking operation, the Zeppelin company hired quite a colorful flyer. Colonel Ernst Udet, a World War I ace who became a stunt flyer, buzzed around the *Hindenburg* for hours in his Focke-Wulf biplane on a Thursday in early March. With thousands cheering from the ground, the biplane, which looked like a fly by comparison, tried to land on a little trapeze hanging below the *Hindenburg*. But Udet kept crashing into the trapeze. Twice, he had to make emergency landings when his propeller was damaged.

Udet and Goodyear engineer Harold Dick puzzled over the bungled test. U.S. Navy pilots had mastered such docking maneuvers on the American-built *Akron* and *Macon* airships. Udet told Dick he was buffeted around by some mysterious turbulence each time he neared the *Hindenburg*. Dick told him the probable cause of the turbulence, something he had seen near the docking point Udet struggled with: a loose section of outer cover. When Lehmann heard the test results, he cancelled his big plans to airlift the customs agents to the *Hindenburg* in May.

The first long-distance voyage since the overhaul would be handled by Captain Max Pruss, flying to Brazil on March 16, 1937. The Zeppelin company began serving the South American country to accommodate the middle-class Germans who fled to Brazil after being hurt by the hyperinflation and unemployment that ruined many in Germany after the first world war.

Lehmann, trying to run a company with plans for a fleet of four Zeppelins by 1940, had already turned over the bridge of the *Hindenburg* to Pruss halfway through its first season. The two men had crewed together, delivering the war-reparations Zeppelin, LZ 126, to America years earlier. They had flown together tens of thousands of miles since, and were good friends.

Blindsided by the gasbag damage and repairs, the workmen in Frankfurt couldn't complete the new passenger cabins before the first scheduled flight of the 1937 season. The *Hindenburg* took off for Rio with only the old cabins in working order. The new staterooms would be expedited when the ship returned, to be ready for the looming first North American flight, leaving May 3. On the way over the South Atlantic, passengers were entertained by the twenty chattering apes in the cargo hold, being shipped to a zoo in Rio de Janeiro.

On the return trip, the *Hindenburg* arrived in a blustery German snowstorm at the end of the month. Immediately, Captains Pruss and Sammt received letters from DZR headquarters. Had they noticed the outer cover being excessively loose?

They replied that the *Hindenburg* cover was always very loose following a major flight. Their reply suggested they hadn't been told there was anxiety over the outer cover, merely a question of improvement. They suggested some additional light rods positioned within the structural rings might steady the cover.

It was a miserable week for the Lehmanns. Suddenly ill, their two-year-old died, on Easter Sunday. The Little Captain and his wife had to bury their only child, Luv. Lehmann had a dangerous job, on a Nazi-sponsored Zeppelin, neither a blessing. Should anything happen to him, he told Marie, he wanted to be buried with his son.

With Marie still distraught, Lehmann faced an agonizing decision. Knowing what he did about the gasbag damage found at the overhaul, knowing that they were still unsure if the twine-and-tape repair would hold, he felt he just had to be on the *Hindenburg's* next flight. No one knew better how to handle a Zeppelin in an emergency than he. No one.

He could help eagle-eye the gas-pressure board. If any gasbag should develop a leak, it would definitely register there. He knew best when to call for emergency procedures: Deflate any faulty bag rapidly. Redistribute as much of the hydrogen as possible into the remaining, good gasbags. Reduce altitude and fly slowly to reduce the stress on the hull. All the way, maintain poise, for the passengers' sake.

With an engineer's mind for precision, he knew the *Hindenburg's* exact structural breaking point. It was designed so that the hull could stay intact, and continue to fly, even on the very remote chance that two adjacent gasbags completely deflated.

Lehmann hadn't been on the *Hindenburg* for its last sixteen flights. But duty prevailed on him to return, to leave his heartbroken wife, for the season's first crossing to America. Pruss would still be the official captain. Lehmann fully suspected his reappearance on board, after so long an absence, would draw press attention, particularly given that there were four captains already scheduled to fly. He would be described with the unusual title of "observer."

Margaret Mather sat anxiously on the bus Monday evening, May 3, as it motored through the beech woods to the airfield at Frankfurt. A woman of sixty, she was an American who lived in Rome, and was eager to visit her brother, an art professor at Princeton. She could take an ocean liner, but ships made her seasick. The idea of traveling across the ocean on the *Hindenburg* left her feeling a different kind of queasy.

When she arrived at the airport and saw the silvery *Hindenburg*, sturdy as a bank building, her fear melted. As she and the other thirty-five passengers stepped up the retractable stairway, feet clanging step to step, they first arrived at the B deck, with the galley, restrooms, shower, and smoking lounge. Continuing up an interior stairwell toward the A deck, they passed a statue, a bronze bust of the late, great Paul von Hindenburg, the namesake of the ship. The A deck, above the B, had all the sleeping quarters and public spaces, including the dining and writing rooms.

Some boys in Nazi uniforms surrounded the *Hindenburg* just before takeoff. A brass band in blue-and-yellow uniforms filled the evening air with upbeat marching music, the band leader thrashing his baton. In the bright glass bubble of the control car at the bottom of the *Hindenburg*, the captains busied themselves with charts and last-minute checks of gauges and controls. They conveyed orders by phones in the control car. The ground crew held the mighty *Hindenburg* to the ground with their ropes, Lilliputians fastening Gulliver.

The 1937 season was going to be busy. The *Hindenburg* had scheduled eighteen round-trips across the Atlantic, and the U.S. Postal Service had signed a contract for the ship to carry American airmail on those trips. On the current trip, there were 238 pounds of mail, and cargo including a supply of tobacco leaves, partridge eggs, newsreel films, and two dogs.

The new cabins were finally in place for the flight to America, allow-ing for seventy passengers, but the ship was only half-booked for this trip. For the return flight to Germany, the *Hindenburg* had sold out. Many of the passengers planned to travel in grand style to England to see the social event of the spring, the May 12 coronation of George VI. In a scandal that was a sensation around the world, his brother, Edward, had abdicated the throne so he could marry an American socialite named Wallis Simpson.

The band on the Frankfurt airfield struck up its last number, the rous-ing church hymn *"Ein feste Burg ist unser Gott,"* "A Mighty Fortress Is Our God." The ground crew cast off the lines, and just after 8:15 in the evening, the *Hindenburg* lifted off. The ship was insured for six million Reichsmarks, and the passengers as well as crew were also covered.

The passengers settled into their rooms. Some ventured to the promenade deck and fogged the windows, leaning in to watch the glittering metropolis of Cologne emerge from the dark German countryside. As the only unaccompanied woman on board, Margaret Mather was seated at the captain's table at dinner. Captain Pruss, whose officer's coat and pants were saggy, smiled through pursed lips when he arrived late for the 10:00 p.m. seating and apologetically shook hands with Mather and his other tablemates. He ate lightly, drank some mineral water, and rushed back to the bridge.

Seated at a nearby table was the Doehner family. The children were well-behaved in the dining room. Werner was eight; Walter, ten. Both blond, they wore matching collared shirts, ties, and dress pants. Their teenage sister, Irene, sat politely in her short-sleeve blouse with floral print and dark pleated skirt. Her hair in a tight bun, Mathilde Doehner and her husband, Hermann, were returning with the children from a business trip in Europe. Home was Mexico City, where Mr. Doehner was a chemical executive.

After dinner, as the *Hindenburg* progressed in the dark, Mather and the Doehners retired to their staterooms. They were the first passengers to stay in the fancy new cabins, with window views. The original staterooms on the *Hindenburg* did not have windows, leading some passengers to complain the rooms felt dark and cramped, like coffins. Above some of the staterooms was gas cell #11, the previously damaged gasbag.

The following day, Tuesday, May 4, Karl Hürttle was at headquarters in Frankfurt, looking over the letter from Captains Pruss and Sammt about the fluttering outer cover. The fabric expert, whose light-colored suits and huge pinkie ring were remnants of his artist days, realized things still weren't right on the *Hindenburg*, the technological wonder of the Third Reich.

He wrote an urgent letter to Karl Rösch, the leader of the technical department. The additional two coats of doping solution applied to the top half of the ship clearly did not fix the flutter problem. Given the alarming reports from the captains after the South America trip, he wrote, "the desire to correct the stability of the hull becomes obvious. . . . Based on our observations, we concur with the view of Mr. Sammt that the hull is much more stable in the places where [reinforcing] spars are built into the *L. S. Hindenburg* than in other places."

Maybe more reinforcing bars had to be added. Hürttle had already begun using the LZ 130, the ship under construction, as a model to fix the *Hindenburg*. It made sense. They were identical twins. Fix the outer cover on the LZ 130, being completed in the hangar, then apply the solution to the *Hindenburg*.

Hürttle thought the gap between the *Hindenburg's* fabric cover and the skeletal metal rings was too great. He ordered them "to stretch the test panels of the LZ 130 more—that is, to substantially reduce the distance between the longitudinal girder [beam] and the panel of fabric compared to the present width." And he told them to stretch the test fabric only under relatively dry conditions and to schedule appropriate rest periods between the stretching.

He seemed to be taking shots in the dark: Even the top Zeppelin fabric man was stumped. Maybe the Cellon, the water-repellant solution painted on the cover, needed to be retested to see if it met stress requirements, he added. "We believe that it would be of particular advantage if a chemical-technical expert were available for guidance on these important issues," he wrote.

None of this was immediately urgent for the *Hindenburg*, soaring hundreds of miles away over the Atlantic, so long as the winds stayed mild.

# FIRE

*The day will come when, after mastering space, the winds, the tides and gravity, we shall harness for God the energies of love. And on that day, for the second time in the history of the world, man will have discovered fire.*

—Pierre Teilhard de Chardin

# 7

# Headwinds

,

SIX HUNDRED MILES OFF THE COAST OF FRANCE, THE *HINDENBURG* HIT stiff headwinds. They slowed the powerful ship from its normal cruising speed, close to seventy miles an hour, to only fifty-five. The skies over the North Atlantic could be frightening. Winds at gale force. Icy rain. Passing weather fronts churning turbulence. It was a hostile place for aircraft.

The passengers on the *Hindenburg* felt none of this Tuesday, the first full day. In fact, shipboard banter had turned to how smooth and uneventful the flight was so far, with little sensation of any movement at all. "It was like riding on clouds," Joseph Spah, a Vaudeville actor and acrobat, would recall. "There was no pitching or jerking."

The outer cover was, a little too effectively, absorbing the brunt of the headwinds. Hidden from view, the gas-cell wiring rattled and rattled and rattled, straining the tape-and-twine repairs.

After breakfast, Margaret Mather pulled the sliding door of her room closed and latched it. She spent much her time in her bunk on Tuesday, luxuriating in the nice bed linens. Her stateroom walls were pearl-colored, the blankets a modish burnt orange. A slight woman who had dark hair in younger days, she watched the ocean toss and turn angrily below. Even with airplane travel still novel, she was from a wealthy family on the East Coast and flew on planes often. She had flown all over the Mediterranean, from her home in Rome to the Greek Isles, among other locales. She was also familiar with ocean-liner travel, the thought of which made her feel queasy.

At dinner that night, she told Captain Pruss that she was enjoying the trip, and that she was a "wretched sailor on the sea." While pleased, the captain confided to her that it was one of his worst trips ever.

The writing room, where reporters during the first season clanked out their *Hindenburg* adventures on typewriters, was more sedate. The Doehner children played games together, while their mother crocheted. Passengers were charmed by the three siblings and their playfulness. Stewardess Emilie Imhof, not yet fifty, helped with the boys. Dressed like a nurse in her white uniform, she sometimes sported a white headband in her dark hair with *Hindenburg* written across it.

Leonhard Adelt was on board, with his wife, Gertrud. He and Captain Lehmann were trying to wrap up a new edition of the memoir. Though the new Zeppelin company had barely gotten off the ground, Lehmann seemed unusually driven to finish the book.

Adelt was technically impressed with the *Hindenburg*, but felt the trip so far rather dull. Visibility was poor. He spent hours in the smoking lounge, talking with others about aviation and Germany's many problems. He had not forgotten about Lehmann's anxiety over the damaged gas cell. But his friend, the most experienced Zeppelin pilot in the world, was on the bridge, keeping vigil.

Passengers barely saw the usually jovial Captain Lehmann. Walking through the passenger lounges here and there, exchanging pleasantries, he wore a fur-lined leather jacket with the collar turned up, his face partly hid. The piano wasn't on board. He did not play his accordion. Lehmann wasn't himself.

The winds grew stronger, and the second night, Tuesday, May 4, Captain Pruss did not go to bed all night. Bucking heavier gusts, the *Hindenburg* was creeping along at thirty-seven miles per hour. "One felt no motion, though the wind beat like waves against the sides of the ship," Mather would recall. "It was almost uncanny." Inside the ship, rattling gas-cell wires tortured the gasbag fabric.

Checking his weather maps, his charts, and the slow progress, Pruss radioed ahead to the Zeppelin office in New York. They were going to be twelve hours late. Rather than arriving Thursday morning just after sunup, the *Hindenburg* was on course to make Lakehurst by six in the evening.

By Wednesday, the third day, they spotted Newfoundland. Passengers pointed binoculars and cameras. Little white specks appeared near the coast. Knowing they were icebergs, Captain Pruss ordered the *Hindenburg* to descend and veer toward them, to give passengers a thrill. Joseph Spah pointed his Bell & Howell movie camera through the slanted windows at the icebergs. He had been filming for the past three days. Little did he know, his footage would soon be of great interest to investigators in the United States. The sun came out, and a double rainbow curled in the sky.

At the landing field at Lakehurst the next morning, Rosendahl received the latest weather report:

*U.S. Naval Air Station*
*Lakehurst, N.J.*
*Weather Bulletin*
*May 6, 1937 11:30 ES (Local time)*
*PRESSURE SYNOPSIS The disturbance that remained almost*
*stationary over the Middle West Monday and Tuesday is now mov-*
*ing eastward over the lower Lake Region, the northern Appalachian*
*Region, and the middle Atlantic and north Atlantic States.*

*Forecast for this Locality: Today until 1800*
*Flying Conditions: Average to Undesirable*
*State of Weather: Thundershowers*

Just before noon, the *Hindenburg* was nearing Boston. The thrill of arriving, after the long delay, was electric. Everyone began packing their luggage. No one wanted to miss the flyover of New York City. As the *Hindenburg* approached in a mist, Adelt found that the skyscrapers looked like "a board full of nails," the Statue of Liberty a tiny "porcelain figure." When the sun burned off the fog, passengers could see photographers lined with tripods on the roof of the Empire State Building.

Looking down, Mathilde Doehner felt edgy. She had been nervous about the trip from the beginning. A steamship seemed safer to her. She had the three children to think about. Just then, Mr. Doehner pointed to the buildings and said to his wife: "Now, aren't you glad we took the *Hindenburg* and saved two days? We might still be at sea."

"I'll be glad when we're on the ground," she replied.

The *Hindenburg* glided over New York for the next hour. The cigar shadow of the ship darkened spots of the Bronx and Harlem, then Fifth Avenue, Central Park, the East River, and Times Square. After a while, everyone collected their papers and passports, and lined their baggage in the hallways. The stewards removed the bedclothes and piled them at the end of the corridors.

Captain Pruss ordered the ship to steer toward the airfield at Lakehurst, fifty miles to the south. As they arrived over the field a little after four in the afternoon, Mather looked down and saw that there were no crowds of men on the field to greet the *Hindenburg*, to grab hold of its landing lines. The sky was clear.

Out over the Atlantic more than a day earlier, Pruss had forecast a twelve-hour delay, putting the arrival around 6:00 p.m. They made up some time at the end, though, putting them over Lakehurst two hours earlier than that. He was hoping to land, as he had a fully booked return flight, with passengers eager to make the coronation in England the next week.

Pruss took the ship out east to the coast, about twelve miles away, to await the 6:00 p.m. landing hour. Over the next ninety minutes, the skies over Lakehurst were clear. There was a radio announcer on the field impatiently awaiting the *Hindenburg*'s arrival. Had the landing crew been in place, he would have had a perfectly forgettable broadcast.

Anton Wittemann, a *Graf Zeppelin* captain on board as a passenger, entered the control car as the ship cruised along the New Jersey coastline. At its cruising altitude, the *Hindenburg* was still being struck by winds of forty to fifty miles an hour. Worn and threadbare, some of the gas-cell fabric inside the ship was apparently near a breaking point.

As the landing hour approached, Lakehurst sounded a siren, summoning the ground handlers, 92 U.S. Navy men, supplemented by 139 civilians paid $1 an hour. But then rain arrived in Lakehurst. The *Hindenburg* had passed through some drizzle itself, farther south.

At 5:43 p.m., Rosendahl messaged the *Hindenburg*, "Condition still unsettled. Recommend delay landing until further word from station. Advise your decision."

The captains in the control car had a conference. Even a half day delayed, no one wanted to land unless clear weather was reported. The landing maneuver for an airship involved purposely valving hydrogen out so that the ship would reduce altitude. Fortunately, the hydrogen quickly dissipated. But if lightning or other atmospheric electrical charges were present, it could be fatal to release hydrogen. The smallest charge could immediately ignite the whole ship. There was a long-standing rule not to valve gas in a thunderstorm. In other words, never land in one.

With sunset approaching, Rosendahl believed the weather conditions were rapidly improving. He sent another message just moments later, around 6:00 p.m., saying, "Recommend landing now." The *Hindenburg* headed north to Lakehurst.

Around 6:30, stewards began handing out sandwiches, aware that the delays were making passengers grumbly. Mather spoke to a woman, Emma Pannes, who she had gotten acquainted with over the last three days. Emma's husband, John, who was on board with her, was a steamship executive. As the *Hindenburg* approached the landing field, the woman told Mather she was heading to her cabin for her coat.

Mather, the Adelts, the Doehners, and the rest of the passengers were amassing in the public areas on both sides of the A deck, peering out the windows at the field. The naval base, cleared out of a pine forest, was completely surrounded by a fence. They could see the immense hangar, a rectangular building with a bright *L* light on top, signifying Lakehurst.

On the field near the large hangar, Herb Morrison, a radio reporter visiting from Chicago, began narrating into his boxy microphone his report on the first *Hindenburg* flight of the 1937 season to America. With slicked-back hair and dark eyebrows, Morrison had been waiting for hours for the ship, along with some film camera men and photographers. His wool suit was glistening with raindrops.

"The ship is riding majestically toward us like some great feather," Morrison said, "riding as though it was mighty proud of the place it's playing in the world's aviation."

The local radio stations in New Jersey had announced the new landing time, and hundreds of cars had already arrived outside the naval base, jockeying for spots to see the German marvel. Margaret Mather's New

Jersey relatives fought the traffic to pick her up in Lakehurst. Outside the base's fence, little Mark Heald and his parents were in from Princeton. They were parked in their new 1937 Willys four-door sedan. Mark's father, the history professor at Rutgers, and his wife were in the front seat, peering out the rain-speckled windshield. Sitting on a graham cracker can for extra height to see out the window, eight-year-old Mark looked on in awe.

The *Hindenburg*, arriving from the south, glided past its landing spot, about 600 feet from the ground. Below, the *Los Angeles*, the ship that saved the Zeppelin factory, was parked on the field. Circling west, the *Hindenburg* passed over the children's playground, with an octagon-shaped pool and swing sets, and passed over the officers' quarters. It curled in a large loop back toward its landing spot, passing over the rifle range. Its only sound, the low buzz of its motors.

As it circled the field, slowing its speed for a landing, the *Hindenburg* valved hydrogen three times, reducing its altitude to about 300 feet. It nosed toward its mooring mast, a metal tower on the ground.

Suddenly, the men in the control car—Pruss, Lehmann, Sammt—all felt something off. The tail of the Hindenburg felt "heavy," as if it were losing some of its lift. The back of the ship acted like it had lost some hydrogen. Puzzling. Watch officer Sammt quickly checked the pressure gauges for the stern gasbags. Nothing suspicious there. Gasbag fabric worn through would allow a small seepage of hydrogen, dangerous to the ship but undetectable by the pressure gauges.

Not sure what was going on, the men in the control car, the brains of the operation, issued a couple quick orders. One, release stored water, called ballast, immediately. Lessening the weight of the ship in the stern should correct the strange tail-heaviness they sensed. Over the next minute, in three discharges, the *Hindenburg* dropped more than a ton of water. The second call ordered six men back in the stern of the ship to run forward, as a further weight-correction maneuver.

About 200 feet from the ground and nearing the mooring mast, the *Hindenburg* dropped its manila landing lines. The ground crew ran to grab hold. Some looking up could see the smiling faces lined up at the lit windows of the lounge.

The skies darkened, 7:25 at night.

"It's practically standing still now," Morrison said, continuing his running commentary. "They've dropped ropes out of the nose of the ship, and it's been taken a hold of down on the field by a number of men. It's starting to rain again. The rain had slacked up a little bit."

Outside the fence, with a panoramic view of the field, Professor Heald blurted to his wife that he saw a thin line of flame on the very top of the *Hindenburg*, just in front of its rear tail fin. Looking there, his son, Mark, saw it, too.

A woman on the grounds of the base also saw it, a saw-toothed orange fire flickering. Near the mooring mast, Commander Rosendahl saw it, too. A brilliant burst of fire like a flower blooming in an instant. It snapped Rosendahl from his thoughts, the details of the busy season he wanted to go over with Captain Lehmann. Right then, Rosendahl thought: The ship is doomed.

*Frwump. POOF.*

A blinding flash.

"It burst into flames!" Morrison yelped.

The tail of the *Hindenburg* erupted like a pumpkin burst open. A churning cloud, forks of flame. Smoke, fire, and fragments. A giant fireworks show.

"It's burning, and it's crashing! It's crashing terrible!" Morrison hyperventilated into the microphone, his suit toasted from the heat.

*It's a terrific crash, ladies and gentlemen.*

*The smoke and the flames now . . .*

*Oh—*

*the humanity!*

# 8

# "This Is the End"

LEONHARD ADELT NOTICES THE OTHER PASSENGERS STIFFEN. HE SEES a rosy glow. He suddenly knows: The *Hindenburg* is on fire. The only way out, to jump. But—too high up. Bed linens, he thinks: Grab some to soften the landing.

The *Hindenburg* rapidly pivots. Nose still floating, the tail smashes to the ground. A sickening slant.

The floor angling up, Eugene Nunnenmacher, a steward near the dining-room windows, falls between a woman's legs. Margaret Mather hurls downward fifteen feet, smacking a wall. Several others land on her, piled bodies, pinning her to a banquette. She can't breathe, fears she'll suffocate. Arms and legs untangle. She is free.

Flames geyser out the *Hindenburg*'s nose. The bow of the ship sags and starts to drop. Men leap from open windows. Joseph Spah dangles from a window frame, lets go.

The bow crashes to the ground, intact. Its tail is gone, just a churning of black smoke and jutting flames.

Inside, an ocean of fire rushes at the trapped passengers. They see-feel-see flames blue, green, red, yellow. Screams gurgle out.

Margaret Mather shields her face with her fur-coat lapels. She feels the flames, a flickering up her back, onto her hat, her hair. She bats at her head with delicate hands. Sees horrified looks on faces.

Tables and chairs tumble and crash, barricading the Adelts in the writing room. "Through the window!" Leonhard shouts. Gertrud, Leonhard, and others hop to a window frame and leap.

A passenger waits for John Pannes to join him and jump.

"Come on, Mr. Pannes, jump!" he yells.

"Wait until I get my wife," he replies. He disappears to save her.

Mathilde Doehner looks for her husband, Hermann. She grabs daughter Irene, tries to lift the teenager to the window. Too heavy. Losing time, she drops Walter out the window, then Werner. Matilde looks around again for her husband. He must be fighting the smoke and fire to join them. Her back on fire, she jumps head first from the window ledge. Irene leaps.

Nunnemacher tosses off his white jacket and catches Irene. They tumble together. The *Hindenburg* steward burns his hands slapping down the fire on her back and hair.

One man leaps out, hits the ground. Another jumper lands right on his back.

Philip Lenz is stuck in his electric-control room. No windows. The only door jams in the fall. The heat builds. He shields his face with a sheet of metal. The heat surges. He thinks, "This is the end." The door burns through. He escapes.

Cabin boy Werner Franz jumps out a hatch near the smoking room. The teenager hits the ground, dazed, choking in flames. A water tank suddenly bursts above him, dousing the fire, bringing him to his senses. He jumps to his feet, finds an opening in the flaming wreckage, and slips through. He runs against the wind, wisely.

Running the other way, others are overtaken by flames.

Along the bow, a line of fire eats steadily, toward the nose, quickly reaching the giant *Hindenburg* lettering. Letter by letter vanishes.

The control car crashes. Windows burst.

The captains spill out the front window. The rest of the hulk, a skeleton of girders in a whirlwind of black smoke, crashes around the command center, the glass bubble they ran the entire ship from not thirty seconds before. Lehmann, Sammt, and Pruss dash from the flames across the sandy field.

Fred Tobin, a bull of a man with a high forehead, roars: "Navy men, stand fast! There are people inside that ship and we got to get them out!" Navy rescuers charge into the churning smoke.

The Adelts stumble from the wreckage. Leonhard bends hot metal wires apart, burning his hands. Running away, he trips over a motionless body on the ground.

Harry Bruno runs toward the control car to find his friend, Captain Lehmann. When he spots him, Lehmann's white dress shirt is on fire. Bruno smothers the flames with his hands. "I can't believe it," Lehmann utters, and then asks the Zeppelin publicist, "How many of my passengers and crew are saved?"

In black bowtie, Lehmann leans on the arms of Bruno and a sailor. They totter toward help. Lehmann is staggering. Bruno looks at his friend's back. Neck to waist, it is black.

## 9

# Sincere Regrets

SIRENS BLARED. FIRE TRUCK BELLS CLANGED.

"I can't talk, ladies and gentlemen," said Morrison, shaken, in his rambling radio report. "Honest, it's completely a mass of smoking wreckage. And everybody can't hardly breathe. It's hard, it's crazy. I—I—I'm sorry. Honestly, I—I can hardly breathe."

The anguished screams from the ship stopped.

Murray Becker couldn't believe his eyes. He had just shot a photo of the blazing *Hindenburg* still in the air, then changed his camera plate and took another. Then the press photographer had to dash from the fiery wreckage. He saw a man half-naked, clothes burned off, stumbling from the ship. "A moment of spectacular madness," he recalled.

One man ran out from the bent girders, shouted "I'm alright," and fell dead. A few blackened figures emerged from the vast cloud of smoke billowing across the field. Rescuers grabbed them, laid them on stretchers, and stacked them in ambulances. One man's legs looked like charred logs. Someone found Captain Pruss. He was alive, but his lips had swollen grotesquely, looking like roasted sausages.

Harry Wellbrook and his ground-crew companions found three bodies in the stern wreckage, all burned beyond recognition. One man was so horribly burned, they couldn't make out his features. But they could hear him breathing.

Headlights from ambulances and fire trucks beamed. Margaret Mather's relatives, waiting to meet her after the flight arrived, turned and drove away horrified by the explosion. They just knew poor Margaret—no one—could have survived.

An ambulance with the Adelts arrived at the naval base's small hospital. In the corridors, the seriously wounded were moaning on tables and stretchers. In one room, a dying mechanic called for his wife in Germany and a priest. Captain Sammt's face was bandaged like a mummy, with holes for his nostrils and eyes. Margaret Mather's burned hands were being treated.

In another room, Leonhard Adelt, his hands burned, spotted Captain Lehmann, in worse condition, stooped over on a table. Happy he had survived, that he was alive, Adelt walked in and couldn't help but ask, "What caused it?"

"Lightning," Lehmann said.

The Doehners arrived at another hospital. The bun on Mathilde Doehner's head was burned off, and she had third-degree burns on three-quarters of her body. Both her sons' faces were burned. They were screaming in pain. There was still no word on Hermann, their father. Irene was in dire shape. Doctors examining the blackened body of the slight girl, not yet fifteen, could tell the fire burnt her blue eyes blind. One doctor, leaving her room, said, "The best she can hope for is to die fast."

In the hours since a telephone call shook him with news of the *Hindenburg* disaster, Hugo Eckener must have recalled his meeting with President Hoover. It was at the White House eight years earlier. After congratulating Eckener on his fabulous voyage around the world in the *Graf Zeppelin*, Hoover made an extraordinary offer.

He told Eckener he would crack open the American monopoly on helium, a gas so safe it would later fill children's balloons. Eckener could have all he wanted, said the president, offering him, in the name of safety, a legal loophole to the ban on U.S. helium exports.

Eckener refused. The Germans, he felt, had perfected construction, flight procedures, and safety equipment to such a degree that they had tamed the hydrogen dragon. Helium, while safer, would have cost seven times more and would have reduced how much payload they could carry.

Now Eckener, pulled from business in Austria, was on his way to Göring's fortress in Berlin, the imposing gray stone Reich Air Ministry.

It was 4:00 p.m. on Friday, May 7. Hours earlier, the colossal *Hindenburg* was destroyed in less than a minute. Göring wanted answers.

"A higher power in a few seconds destroyed what human hands by infinite care had constructed," Göring said, in a statement to the press. "We bow to God's will, and at the same time we face the future with an unbending will and passionate hearts to continue the work for the conquest of the air."

The news sent a jolt through official Nazi Germany. Goebbels, the propaganda minister, was reading a book of essays when his home phone rang. The *Hindenburg* was completely destroyed at Lakehurst by a devastating fire. Many dead, many injured. "A horrific accident, one that affects us all deeply," he wrote in his diary. "I am filled with dismay and couldn't sleep the rest of the night. The press is full of this bad news, and everyone in the nation senses the gravity of this blow. But we must overcome it."

At Göring's office, it was surely impressed upon Eckener that the Air Ministry had pleaded with him just six months earlier to pursue helium for his Zeppelins as a safety measure. Did he need to be reminded that he resisted that call? Now a world-renowned symbol of Nazi superiority, heavily financed by the Reich, lay smoldering in ashes in America. Apparently, cameramen had captured horrifying footage. A radioman had made a chilling recording.

After dealing with him, Göring handpicked a team of six German experts, including Eckener, to take a steamship to America to help investigators determine the cause of the tragedy. Before they left, Eckener spoke to reporters and, looking at them through his tired, blue eyes, said something bizarre.

"I always insisted airships are safe only with helium, ever since the English dirigible crashed in France five years ago," he told them. He hinted the *Hindenburg* may have been sabotaged. He did not say that he had had previous assurances from U.S. officials that Germany could have the safe lifting gas if he wanted it.

Rather, he began spinning a new narrative: Germany had been a victim of American hoarding. He could only hope, he said, that the *Hindenburg*'s sister ship, the LZ 130, wouldn't become another casualty of the unjust helium ban. "The new German Zeppelin will be filled with helium," he said, adding a dramatic caveat, "if we can get it from America."

As the German investigative team, including Eckener, prepared to board the *Europa* for a four-day cruise to America, Lakehurst remained a hive of activity. Nineteen bodies were initially recovered from the wreckage, and navy men later pulled out fourteen more.

"We could still smell the odor of burnt flesh," recalled William Chapman, a government inspector. Sifting through debris, salvagers found false teeth, jewelry, and watches black as charcoal. The galley refrigerator was lying on its side. When they opened it, the meat was in fine condition, as if nothing had happened.

The toll was distressing. Captain Lehmann survived only one day after the fire. In a New Jersey hospital, he told a priest, bending close to hear his faint voice, to bid adieu to his wife. He breathed his last at 6:10 Friday evening, May 7.

On learning of Lehmann's death hours later, Dr. Eckener spoke to reporters. "He was my oldest and ablest collaborator," he said. "For nearly 30 years we worked together, always in perfect harmony and as close friends." He suggested that Captain Lehmann's expert knowledge would've helped greatly in understanding the cause of the disaster.

Irene Doehner died in another hospital. Her father's body was in the wreckage. He was only identifiable by the wedding ring on his left hand. Gone, too, was Emma Pannes and her husband, John, who perished looking for her.

A ground-crew man burned to death. Twenty-two members of the ship's crew were gone. Captain Pruss, who had disfiguring burns on his face and hands, was fighting for his life.

In Berlin, Goebbels met with Hitler at noon on Saturday. "He is deeply shaken by the accident in Lakehurst," Goebbels wrote in his diary. "But he has always anticipated and seen this coming. He is not a fan of airships at all. Airplanes are the future. He's right about that." Later that night they met again. "There is some suspicion that the Lakehurst catastrophe was a result of sabotage. But no one will be able to determine that.

Göring and Eckener had received threatening letters. The whole world has expressed sympathy over our disaster."

The next day, the Nazis were still trying to process their shock. "Captain Lehmann has succumbed to his injuries," Goebbels wrote in his diary. "Göring is making a powerful appeal for reconstruction of the Zeppelin. It is more of a question of prestige than a question of practicality at this point."

It is true, Göring crossed Hitler in keeping the airship program alive, but the Luftwaffe leader had a different plan for the *Hindenburg's* surviving sister.

The U.S. Navy's official logbook for Lakehurst was sparing in details.

*U.S. Naval Air Station*
*Lakehurst, N.J.*
*Log Book*
*6 May, 1937*
*U.S.S. Los Angeles docked on the north side of hangar #1.*
*1700 Sounded assembly for ground crew for landing Airship HIN-*
*DENBURG. During the landing operation, the Airship HIN-*
*DENBURG burst into flame at an altitude of about 200 feet and*
*was burned to destruction by hydrogen fire originating at or near the*
*stern. The ship fell to the ground on the north side of Number One*
*mooring-out circle approximately 232 yards from the mooring mast.*

*Out of ninety-seven persons aboard about twelve passengers*
*are known to be saved and thirty-seven of the crew are alive, some*
*injured to various degrees. . . . The fire in the wreck was put out as*
*soon as possible by the Naval Air Station and several nearby city fire*
*departments. Rescue work was commenced immediately, with ambu-*
*lances and doctors from several nearby hospitals answering the call for*
*first-aid assistance. Sentry posts were established and manned to keep*
*all visitors and unauthorized persons clear of the HINDENBURG*
*wreckage.*

The log entry was signed, "Rosendahl."

As commanding officer of the base at Lakehurst, Charles Rosendahl had hoped to steer the investigation. He was heartened to hear the news that Göring was accelerating the construction of the LZ 130. Everyone banking on airships had held their breath the last few days. Did the *Hindenburg* spell doom for the airship dream? There was no greater advocate for airships in America than Rosendahl, who was nicknamed "Rosie." He was a fanatic. In private, he referred to the navy's airship program as "The Cause."

After the crashes of the *Akron* and the *Macon*, the U.S. military lost all faith in airships. They were too costly, too big, too slow, too easy for enemies to shoot down. The airbase at Lakehurst was nearly abandoned. The *Los Angeles*, the ship that all of America had cheered when the Germans delivered it, sat in the gargantuan hangar in New Jersey, decommissioned since 1932. Staffing fell in half, to 250. To land the *Hindenburg*, Lakehurst had to pay over a hundred civilians to help man the handling ropes.

When the *Hindenburg* began landing at Lakehurst in 1936, there remained a slim hope that airships could be revived for aerial reconnaissance—for spotting submarines, for example—and for commercial travel. Rosendahl would never give up on them. He had staked his entire career on airships. His dramatic brush with death on the *Shenandoah* made him a celebrity the world over in 1925.

The acclaim gave him clout at the navy. He eventually became friends with Hugo Eckener when he flew on the *Graf Zeppelin* as a navy observer. He helped Eckener to secure Lakehurst as an airport for the *Hindenburg*, breaking down considerable resistance and upending policies against using military facilities for business. Rosendahl and Lehmann, on the other hand, were only acquainted. When Rosendahl married in 1934, Lehmann sent him a congratulatory note on *Graf Zeppelin* stationery two months later, apologizing as he had just heard the "glad news."

Rosie was consumed with keeping the airship alive, against an obsolescence assured by advances in the airplane. He was competitive and a self-promoter. On his passport application, he typed his height as 5 foot 10 *and 1/2 inches*. To counter charges that airships were becoming a waste of taxpayer money, he worked tirelessly to wow all corners of

America with publicity flights of the *Shenandoah* and the *Los Angeles*. Critics decried them as circus flights.

Rosendahl was blustery, ruthless. He worked back channels in Washington to bypass and undercut his boss, the man who preceded him as the Lakehurst base commander. He would dress down officers in public, normally taboo. Rosie was not above lying, and he repeatedly hid the dangers of airships.

With funding uncertain for a new generation of airships, he censored photos of a bizarre mishap on the *Los Angeles* back in August of 1927. Lashed to its mooring mast at Lakehurst, a sea-breeze whipped in, and the tail of the *Los Angeles* suddenly began lifting. The whole ship looked as if it were in a nosedive, pointing straight down, still attached to the mast. The nose of the ship nearly impaled itself on the mast in a head-on collision, as loose equipment and dinner plates inside crashed and tumbled forward.

Endangered crewmen were clutching whatever they could to keep from sliding down what looked like an open elevator shaft inside the ship. Outside, the winds subsided, and the ship's tail slowly dropped onto an even keel again. But the *Los Angeles* could have been destroyed, its gasoline already spilling in the sickening nose-stand.

Someone on the base snapped photos of the death-defying scene. The images would have alarmed a public still wary of flying. For damage control, Rosendahl had them sent to navy headquarters in Washington. Kept under wraps, the censored photos wouldn't be published for decades.

In the passenger waiting area of the large hangar at Lakehurst, hearings were set to begin, four days after the *Hindenburg* exploded into history. The final reckoning on the *Hindenburg* was grim, but, astonishingly, there were more survivors than fatalities. In all, thirteen passengers and twenty-two crew died, along with one ground handler. When the *Hindenburg* left Frankfurt, it had thirty-six passengers and a crew of sixty-one. Fate helped with survival. The ship was relatively close to the ground at the time of the accident. The fire erupted in the stern, near the tail; the passengers and much of the crew were in the bow.

The Commerce Department, responsible for overseeing the nation's business activity, would attempt to solve the mystery. The man heading the hearings was attorney South Trimble Jr., the solicitor of the Commerce Department. To get to the bottom of the *Hindenburg* disaster, Trimble needed someone technically versed to rely on, someone to walk investigators through the science, the jargon. The man he chose as lead technical advisor was Charles Rosendahl, the undying apologist for a dying cause.

In the hangar, which days earlier had twenty-six bodies awaiting identification, several large tables were arranged together. There was a makeshift witness stand. A large bulletin board had the words *ZERO HOUR*. On blueprint paper, a large map showed the *Hindenburg*'s final flight path, a circle over the base. Nearby, the American flag with its forty-eight stars hung like a drapery. The three-dozen men placed their hats on the tables, near glass pitchers of drinking water. Military police lined the walls, pistols holstered.

A stack of folders under his left arm, Commander Rosendahl cocked his right arm and was sworn in. He was the first witness. *Hindenburg* theories ran all directions: lightning, sabotage, sparks from an engine. Rosendahl was determined to work back channels to steer the investigators toward a finding of sabotage. Such a conclusion would preserve his beloved airships. Any structural or mechanical cause, he knew, spelled doom for "The Cause."

Trimble allowed Rosendahl to narrate a statement, his report as the commanding officer of the base. He was barely interrupted by investigators. He described the weather that evening, the *Hindenburg*'s late arrival, the ground-crew arrangements. He calmly explained how he saw the flame at the stern, knew in an instant the ship was doomed. He gave no explanation and, aware he was under oath, did not even suggest sabotage.

"Obviously," he said, "I have no knowledge of what was the origin of the fire."

Stepping from the stand, Rosendahl did not know he was about to be blindsided by the very next witness. Frederick W. von Meister was vice president of American Zeppelin Transport, a U.S. affiliate of the *Hindenburg*'s operating company. He addressed why the *Hindenburg* didn't land when it first appeared Thursday afternoon, though Captain Pruss was very eager to, given that they were ten hours late at that point.

"The ship appeared over the station, if I remember correctly, about 4 o'clock or 3:30 in the afternoon, and proceeded to the southeast of the station. At that time, we could've landed the ship if all necessary personnel had been on the station, but since they had been ordered for six in the evening, the ship had to wait until six."

It was a bombshell. Rosendahl, reduced to a skeleton staff at the base, didn't have enough hands to land the *Hindenburg* in clear weather. The official report of weather conditions, to be introduced later as Exhibit 74 L, showed that there were thunderstorms in the area between 3:30 and 4:30 and between 5:30 and 6:30, but there was a clear, hour-long window for the *Hindenburg* to land, between 4:30 and 5:30.

The base, Rosendahl's responsibility, was undermanned. By the time the temporary workers arrived to help, storms had moved into the area, endangering the ship. Any leak of gas, combined with electrical activity from passing storm fronts, spelled disaster. It was Rosendahl who summoned the ship back at 6:00 p.m., assuring them it was safe. Rosie couldn't have liked the direction things were going.

As the *Europa* steamed its way to America with Hugo Eckener and the other five experts chosen by Göring, Hitler issued surprise orders. He grounded both the *Graf Zeppelin* and the LZ 130 until they could obtain helium. He told the Air Ministry he would not resume Zeppelin flights until he knew that they weren't gambling with passenger lives. Still, Knut Eckener told reporters he was certain that the LZ 130 would be off to the United States in a matter of months.

Knut, who was thirty-five years old, had been in his father's shadow his entire life. Yet he appeared in the press here and there, as when he was cited as a "Zep Hero" back in 1928 for risking his life to repair the busted tail fin on the *Graf Zeppelin* over the open ocean. Handsome and blond, he reminded people of Charles Lindbergh. Knut had a master's degree in engineering, more technical education than his famous father, and he had risen at the Zeppelin company to oversee construction, most recently of the *Hindenburg*. Very shortly, he would be looking over an application for the Nazi Party.

At the Hamburg-American pier at West 46th Street in New York, 10,000 people showed to pay last respects to the *Hindenburg* dead. The Nazi flag was draped over the coffin of each crew member, with Captain Lehmann's also having a funeral spray. A navy blimp circled overhead.

Paul Schulte, the Flying Priest, eulogized, recalling the mass he said aboard the *Hindenburg* on its first flight to America a year earlier. He offered a fond and personal farewell to Captain Lehmann, revealing to the crowd how the Little Captain had allowed him to drop a wreath from the *Hindenburg* to commemorate his brother buried as a war prisoner in England.

Commander Rosendahl took the podium, offering his assurances for the future. "From the ashes of the *Hindenburg* will arise much more efficient and much greater airships," he promised.

Captain Lehmann's body was to be held for the arrival of his wife the next day on the *Europa*, and the widow and the coffin were to return to Germany on the steamship. Marie Lehmann, heartbroken, was also headed to America to speak with her husband's colleagues, hoping to glean anything someone might have seen, or heard, from Luv in the hours before his death.

On the *Europa*, Hugo Eckener wrote a revealing letter to his wife, Johanna. She rarely traveled with him, preferring to keep well in the shadow of her famous husband. He spoke about the *Hindenburg* and mentioned that he had spent days trying to come between the coffin of his fallen adversary, Lehmann, and his grieving widow.

Eckener first said that he had tried to prevent Marie Lehmann from even boarding the ship. He told Johanna that he and others attempted to talk Marie out of it since the coffins were set to be shipped soon, and she and her husband's coffin would pass each other in transit. But she had given the order to leave the coffin in America until she arrived. She apparently wanted to see her husband one more time, Eckener wrote to his wife.

Planning a large memorial service in Germany, the Nazi government had apparently ordered that Lehmann's coffin be shipped with the others, Eckener wrote. But they would allow, if Mrs. Lehmann absolutely insisted, the coffin to be held for her arrival and then shipped a day or two later to catch up with the others. Under no circumstances will she be permitted to see the body, he wrote, since the coffin was already soldered shut for the voyage.

Eckener complained that Marie Lehmann was allowing her own sentimentality, and desire for her husband to be singled out, to subvert the memorial plans the Nazi government had prepared. Moving on, Eckener noted that he bought a few shirts on board and would pick up more in America, and he reported that his stomach and bowels were in excellent order and that he was no longer depressed.

And then a confession: "I sincerely regret that . . . I let myself go on using hydrogen, although we had already designed the *Hindenburg* for helium. Now the situation forces us to get it—and the Reich will foot the bill."

Aware that he had misled the press by suggesting that America had purposely withheld helium from Germany, causing the *Hindenburg* disaster, he advised Johanna that what she might have read about America's helium-export embargo was only formally correct. "In actuality, we have always been able to have helium if we had had an apparatus for it. . . . So perhaps the accident, which could have been worse, will help advance us quickly." He signed it, "That's all for now, warmest regards, Your Hugo."

The next day, Thursday, May 13, one week to the day after the *Hindenburg* was destroyed, Eckener was at Lakehurst. He stayed at Rosendahl's officer quarters on the base, as he had in the past. They reminisced together: On the arrival of the *Los Angeles*, in October 1924. On the quarter-million people four years later who showed up for the landing of the damaged *Graf Zeppelin*, after its precarious fate made headlines. On the flight around the world, and meeting President Hoover at the White House. The Glory Days.

The two biggest airship fanatics in the world were together, for a funeral for the *Hindenburg* and their lives' work. Marie Lehmann, there for her dead husband, would try to meet with any passengers or crew she could, hanging on every word of their recollections. She would be comforted by Jean Rosendahl, Rosie's wife.

Word of Mrs. Rosendahl's magnanimity, visiting and consoling the victims of the disaster, made its way all the way to the top echelons in Berlin. Soon a letter was on her way from Hermann Göring himself. "You cared for my fellow countrymen with unending kindness and love," he wrote to her in the June 8 letter. "You have helped them through not only the first difficult hours to recover from the frightful experience but also lightened the burden of their pain and suffering through your ever-repeated visits and your exemplary Good Samaritan work."

The press was electrified by the *Hindenburg* disaster, and now the dean of Zeppelins was on American soil to solve the mystery. The pot was boiling. But even as Eckener's ocean liner was making its way across the Atlantic, the newspapers had begun pushing back against the story line that an American helium ban was responsible for the tragedy. Reporters apparently found people in the U.S. Navy and the government who swore Germany had never applied to buy helium.

At Lakehurst, the spotlight fell on Hugo Eckener. Did he ask for helium or not? Cornered, Eckener had to come clean. "Discussions concerning the availability of helium were had, but no formal application was made," he said. Later, before a U.S. congressional panel, he would elaborate: "As long as eight years ago, I had the opportunity of discussing this question . . . in Washington with the government authorities. At that time . . . it was indicated to me that as much helium could be made available for our use as we might need." He did not pursue it, he said, because he lacked necessary facilities to transport, store, and re-purify the precious gas.

Eckener still faced questioning by the Commerce Department investigators. They had taken a full week of testimony from eyewitnesses, cabin stewards, mechanics, cooks, engineers, ground handlers, and naval officers. He wanted to inspect the wreckage. Since the press was amassing evidence that he had never asked for helium, he was forced to tell the truth. He had made a blunder that embarrassed Germany in front of the world.

It was a lesson he would take further into life with much grimmer results. Lie, until trapped by evidence.

For now, he needed to see what evidence the corpse of the *Hinden-burg* offered. For an hour under overcast skies at Lakehurst, he and the

German team stooped over bent metal girders and charred remains. He dwelt at the stern of the ship, where the fire had broken out.

Eckener and his colleagues spent a long time inspecting the tail, stepping through the muddy field, with marine guards posted around the perimeter of the wreckage. Two of the German experts climbed and picked through the heap of blackened girders to study more closely, but Eckener remained always outside. Nothing he saw at Lakehurst apparently disturbed him. The real answers sat in the maintenance records in Germany.

The FBI had been snooping around Lakehurst the past week. Director J. Edgar Hoover was already a legend, having been credited for recent operations that captured or killed bank robbers and outlaws including John Dillinger and Machine Gun Kelly. On Hoover's orders, the agents were to assist the Commerce Department, but they would only step in to formally investigate if there were reasonable suspicion of a crime.

Rosendahl asked to meet with the FBI agents when they arrived at the base just after the crash. He suggested the FBI search the field for evidence of sabotage—firearm shells, bomb fragments, suspicious chemical traces—but E. J. Connelly, an agent in the Newark office, told Rosendahl the FBI had no jurisdiction yet.

In truth, the FBI was dying to move in on the drama. One of the G-men who accompanied Connelly at Lakehurst was Reed Vetterli, an agent who had previously been shot in a gunfight with Pretty Boy Floyd. Who knew what headlines they could make, what professional trophies awaited if they arrested the culprit behind the *Hindenburg*? In previous days, Rosendahl had ordered members of his staff to not speak to the press, and he quashed discussions to broadcast the highly sensational proceedings, which would end up being held in radio silence.

That left agent Connelly sitting in on the hearings, every single word of them, taking notes. At the end of the first week, after twenty-one witnesses, he sent a telegram to Hoover: "Testimony to date indicates accident apparently caused by some structural defect. No evidence of sabotage as yet."

Testimony continued. Investigators heard from a crewman called a "rigger," responsible for fabric repairs, then four naval officers who were on the field. Then passengers. The investigative board walked through the wreckage. They went to a movie theater, and with a special projector, watched footage of the tragedy frozen frame by frame. Nothing was adding up.

On Tuesday evening, May 18, the hearing ten days old, Rosendahl called agent William Devereaux, asking him to come to his office the next day to discuss a matter too sensitive for the phone. At the meeting, Rosendahl told the FBI agent he was a personal friend of Hugo Eckener, who told him privately and repeatedly that the ship had to have been sabotaged, either by Communists or anti-Nazis. He said that Dr. Eckener had personally interviewed every member of the German crew since his arrival, the crew naturally speaking more freely to Eckener in private than they would at the public hearing.

Then Rosendahl spun a sensational tale: The crew told Eckener that they were suspicious of one passenger, Joseph Spah. He had repeatedly gone back into the ship, ignoring rules to the contrary, to a cargo area to feed and check on his dog, they said. Rosendahl noted that the man was a professional acrobat, capable of climbing high up into the rigging in the *Hindenburg* to plant a time bomb.

He knew little else about Spah. He was an American citizen; was treated at Fitkin Memorial Hospital in Asbury Park, New Jersey; and "remained aloof from the other passengers." Rosendahl recommended the FBI investigate Spah. Agents would eventually interview neighbors, sift through Spah's personal papers found in the wreckage, and review footage on his Bell & Howell camera. Nothing.

In a final bold stroke to build suspicion, Rosendahl pointed to Captain Lehmann. In the hours before Lehmann died, Rosendahl told the FBI man, he visited him in the hospital. On his deathbed, Lehmann told him an "infernal machine," perhaps a firebomb of some sort, caused the disaster, Rosendahl said.

Finally, Rosendahl told Devereaux that both he and his wife were recently told confidentially by Marie Lehmann that her husband's life had frequently been threatened, along with the Zeppelins themselves. Since Mrs. Lehmann stepped foot in America, Rosendahl seemed eager to keep a close eye on her, figure out what she knew. He had left the *Hindenburg* inquiry right after he testified, in fact, and went straight down to the *Europa* to meet her when she arrived from Germany. He told the FBI agent he had qualms about violating the widow's confidence, but he felt it was "absolutely necessary."

Of course, Rosendahl made this all up. Captain Lehmann died three days before Rosendahl took the stand as first witness at the *Hindenburg* hearing. If Lehmann had just divulged a sensational bomb theory, on his deathbed, Rosendahl forgot to mention it in his sworn testimony. In fact, he said, "I have no knowledge of what was the origin of the fire." Also, Lehmann, by then deceased, was unable to corroborate any of this.

The surprising deathbed confession of Lehmann surfaced exactly one week after Eckener arrived from Germany and became Rosendahl's house-guest. The two airship veterans had had hours to discuss matters privately.

# "Noticeable Fluttering"

HIS TURN WAS COMING, AND REPORTERS WOULD HANG ON HIS EVERY word. But for now, Hugo Eckener just listened at the hearing on Friday morning, May 21. Face pale and drawn, he sat with his head sunk on his chest, blue eyes focused, a silver pencil in his hand.

The hearing was drawing to a close. After wearying testimony from dozens of witnesses, just when no one expected a new bombshell, Reginald "Ducky" Ward took the stand. Ward was a navy boatswain's mate, in charge of crew and equipment. One of the most experienced airship men in the U.S. Navy, he had flown more than 5,000 hours over seventeen years. He was in the control car of the *Los Angeles* during the perilous nose-stand, staring in fear out the front window at the ground 200 feet below. The prior year, he had flown on the *Hindenburg*, taking the controls for an hour over Baltimore and Washington.

During the doomed arrival of the *Hindenburg*, Ward was on the airfield, directing the crew in charge of the landing line on the port bow side. From his vantage point, he had seen something that few others had. His eyes were drawn to the top of the *Hindenburg* settling in to land. Just after the landing, or trail, ropes uncurled to the ground, he looked at a specific spot near the tail, technically, he knew, in between frames 62 and 72.

"About four or five minutes after the trail rope had been dropped," he began, "I noticed the cover on top, between frame 62 and 72, there was a noticeable fluttering of the cover, followed by a ball of flame, approximately ten feet or so in diameter, followed by an explosion." He explained that the ship began to drop by the stern, and then the fire raged rapidly forward.

One of the investigators, Major R. W. Schroeder, assistant director of the Bureau of Air Commerce, Commerce Department, found this a fascinating revelation. A bizarre fluttering of the outer cover. Schroeder handed Ward a diagram of the ship and asked him to draw where he saw the fire. "Will you take the diagram you just made and show with the black pencil the general area of the cloth that was fluttering?" he asked. Schroeder marked the drawing as Exhibit Number 57.

"Was the cloth fluttering like a flag, in the form of a wave, or was it in and out, as a curtain?" Schroeder asked.

"More of a wave motion," Ward replied. "The cloth of ships will more or less flutter, particularly around the wake of the propeller, and it was more like that."

Schroeder continued: "Would your opinion be that the flutter was caused by airflow resonance between the cloth and the propeller?

"The motion of the cloth had nothing to do with the airstream off the propeller. It was entirely too high from the propeller," Ward replied.

It was a tantalizing clue. The *Hindenburg* engineers were back in Germany still trying to resolve an outer cover that stubbornly fluttered. Their effort couldn't help the *Hindenburg* at this point, but the LZ 130 had to be revised to avoid a disaster on it. They knew that when an airship encounters wind resistance in flight, the outer cover bears the brunt of it, 45 percent, to be precise, more than any other part.

Eckener, set to take the stand the next morning, was going to have to explain it away.

The testimony would move slowly, over two hours, as Eckener chose to speak in German, while an interpreter translated. South Trimble, leading the investigation, swore Eckener in. It was Saturday morning, May 22.

"Doctor, at this time, if you have any statement or observation that you would like to make, we would be very happy to receive it," Trimble said.

"The whole occurrence is extremely mysterious," Eckener began. "The fire first appeared in the upper part of the ship, in the upper stern section of the ship. From this we may conclude . . . there must have been free gas in the rear section of the ship."

Reporters scribbled as Eckener reviewed the thunderstorm conditions that meteorological experts had previously discussed. Given the shifting of air masses as storms moved around, he said it was likely there were static sparks in the air.

"How did gas get into the after part of the ship?" Trimble asked, referring to the aft, or stern, of a ship.

"I can only assume that by a process still unexplained to myself a leak must've occurred in one of the after gas cells," Eckener replied, not noting the gasbag damage they discovered months earlier at the winter overhaul. "I am convinced because of some occurrence, still unexplained in my own mind, a leak must've originated in the after part of the ship by which gas could escape and accumulate" in the stern. Perhaps because he was ultimately in charge of design, while his own son, Knut, oversaw construction of the *Hindenburg*, he did not broach any structural flaws.

He called "Ducky" Ward's spotting of the fluttering outer cover "remarkable."

"A peculiar flutter of the outer cover, and that it looked exactly as if gas was escaping or rising at that point," Eckener said. "I consider this observation, which was made by a very reliable and competent witness, to be one that has to be given the most serious consideration."

What caused the leak, Eckener asked of himself, in the rear of the ship? "I really could only make to myself the following explanation: The ship proceeded in a sharp turn to approach for its landing. That generates extremely high tension in the after part of the ship, and especially in the center sections close to the stabilizing fins, which are braced by shear wires. I can imagine that one of the shear wires parted and caused a rent in a gas cell. . . . As gas escaped from the torn cell upwards and filled up the space between the outer cover and the cells in the rear part of the ship—then this quantity of gas . . . was ignited by a static spark."

Eckener continued: "I would like to state this appears to me to be a possible explanation, based on weighing all the testimony that I have heard so far."

No one had considered that a torn wire, snapped in a sharp turn, would tear into a gasbag, destroying the *Hindenburg*. It was a novel idea.

Trimble had to take it all in. "Recess," he said.

It was remarkable, what Eckener had done. Since the winter overhaul, the company had been working to repair the gas-cell wiring that had endangered the gasbags. It certainly had a ring of truth, a wire tearing a gasbag. In his testimony, though, the wiring he implicated instead blamed his captain—for pilot error—and not the structural flaw that alarmed Lehmann, the design flaw that took his life.

Credibility comes from authority, and the middle-aged men of the inquiry, and the reporters around them, had heard of Hugo Eckener most of their adult lives. He was a legend, a star. He had flown the *Graf Zeppelin* all the way around the world, and lived to talk about it. They were star struck.

When they resumed, Trimble, who still seemed to have doubts, asked gingerly, "Were there any other possibilities that you considered?"

Eckener stepped in the sabotage direction. "I am not expert concerning the possibility of parts or packages or the like that might've been put into the airship intentionally. I therefore can only take notice of such theories and hypotheses that are brought to my attention, but I myself cannot judge or talk about them."

But then he did. "From a purely theoretical standpoint, one can think of a lot of things. One could, for instance, imagine that somebody put an infernal machine somewhere in the ship and brought it to destruction in that manner. . . . There are not only no definitive clues that point to such possibility, but it is also a theoretical consideration to which I myself cannot assent."

Another investigator from the Commerce Department, Denis Mulligan, chimed in. He remained puzzled by the flutter of the outer cover. Aside from an escape of gas below it, he asked, were there any other explanations?

Would Eckener mention that two technical experts back in Germany had been working to repair a design flaw that left the outer cover vibrating dangerously? No. Instead, he offered that the cover can loosen when it is wet, as it was on the day of the accident. Mulligan then noted that another witness, a lieutenant who had been high up on the mooring mast, also saw an outer cover flutter. "But we did not press him at that time because we had been advised that that was probably due to the rain on the ship that had just come through," Mulligan said. The investigator sensed he was onto something. He decided to challenge Eckener's explanation for the leak.

"Do you know of any occasion in the previous operation of the *Hindenburg* where a shear wire has broken?"

Eckener looked at him, as Mulligan's question was translated. He would answer, but then quickly change the subject. "No, sir—," Eckener said. "I would like to add something to my statement concerning the possible cause of the accident." Out of left field, he then suggested that a gas-level sensor in the rear of the ship might have triggered an explosion, though he considered it "an extremely remote possibility."

Mulligan steered him right back on track. "Returning to the possibility that you have spoken of, of a shear wire having been broken, what would occur if such did take place," permitting gas to leak out?

Eckener replied that gas-level indicators in the control car would sense it quickly or the man operating the elevators, which control altitude, would notice it. His following remarks highlighted just how resilient Zeppelins were and the daredevil tactics sometimes used for midair repairs. In essence, it would all show why Lehmann, anxious about the gas cells, still thought the ship could be kept in the air even if one or two gasbags tore through and emptied.

"We have had such experiences on a few occasions, that rents in the gas cell have to be repaired, whilst the ship was underway," Eckener said. Returning once from Moscow, a sentry at the frontier fired six to eight shots at them, which they heard. They didn't notice anything for six hours or more, as bullet holes produce very small leaks. They then detected the tail was sinking. Inspecting, they found that the bullet had ricocheted and split a wire, which then tore a triangular hole into a gas cell near the middle, or equator, of the ship. They slowed the ship down and lowered a man tethered to the top along the ship outside, where he patched the tear in thirty minutes.

On another trip, to South America, a crewman making a repair on top of the ship accidentally stepped through the outer cover and gas cell, setting hydrogen loose rapidly. Again, they slowed the speed, and in two hours, a fabric specialist, called a rigger, repaired the hole. Even if two adjacent gasbags were to empty completely, Eckener said, his Zeppelins were designed to stay intact structurally so long as they flew at reduced speed. "Even in this very remote case, there is no danger of loss of the airship," he said.

He explained how miniscule leaks can be. On average, the cells hold 10,000 to 12,000 cubic meters of hydrogen. A small leak of only fifty cubic meters of gas a second would be sufficient to cause the outer cover to flutter above it, he said, while still being too small for the gas-cell gauges in the control car to register it.

Trimble, retaking the questioning, asked: "Doctor, is there anything further you would like to say at this time?"

"I do not know of anything further now," Eckener replied, "but you may rest assured that everything or anything that may come to my attention, I'll be glad and anxious to communicate because I am so much concerned in clearing up the reasons for this accident."

Trimble seemed to want something more. It dawned on him that only a few passengers had been summoned to testify. Why hadn't they asked for testimony from all of them? After the hearing, he dictated a letter that would be mailed to each passenger on the *Hindenburg*, asking where they were at the time of the fire, what they saw, and if they had any knowledge of what had caused it.

In a sense, it was a fishing expedition. All the passengers were inside and in the front of the ship; the fire broke out in the rear. What could they really add?

When Trimble's Commerce Department letter arrived in Mays Landing, New Jersey, Leonhard Adelt read it, then put it down. He took out a black pen and began to write a reply that stood to crack the case wide open.

In extraordinary defiance, two captains on the *Hindenburg* took the stand and rejected Eckener's conclusion about a sharp turn and a broken wire. Albert Sammt, an experienced airship man, said Eckener was wrong. Sammt said Eckener wasn't even on the field to judge whether there was an unusually sharp turn. And, anyway, Sammt added, the shear wires had been punished with far greater stress when he and others had to maneuver quickly to escape storms over the ocean.

Clearly alleging that he and the other officers might have been left in the dark about a structural defect on the *Hindenburg*, Sammt said: "I would be very happy to know whether the ship was damaged before the fire broke out—or vice versa."

The death toll would have been higher, he also told the inquiry board, if not for quick thinking in the control car. When the ship's tail quickly sank as the fire broke out, every impulse in them was to dump ballast water quickly, an emergency discharge to return the *Hindenburg* to an even keel, to keep it floating. In a split second, though, it dawned on them not to order the water released.

"That probably brought the ship down faster and let the people escape," he added.

Captain Heinrich Bauer was recalled to the stand, and he rejected Eckener's explanation for the same reasons as Captain Sammt.

The testimony seemed to indicate that atmospheric electrical charges probably ignited the leaking gas, but C. E. Earle, a navy hydrogen expert, offered another provocative explanation. Schroeder, from the inquiry board, asked Earle if a tear in the fabric of a gas cell itself could generate enough static or frictional spark to cause ignition.

Yes, indeed, Earle replied. "There have been ignitions due to valving or letting it out of a bag, and there have been ignitions due to rips and tears, which were undoubtedly due to static set off by the tearing of the fabric." In other words, the ripping of a cell, as gas rapidly escaped, could in and of itself ignite the hydrogen.

Earle reinforced the idea: "Where the hydrogen is passed through small orifices at high velocity, there is a possibility of sufficient friction to raise your temperature to the ignition temperature of the mixture, and the result is fire."

As the investigators wound down the three-week hearing, they recalled Rosendahl, asking him if he had learned anything substantially new. Mentioning nothing of a deathbed "confession" of Captain Lehmann, Rosendahl assured them he had not.

The FBI had laboratories examine two pieces of Duralumin girders found 4,000 feet from the *Hindenburg* crash site, looking for traces of explosives. They inspected footprints on the field someone thought questionable, making plaster of Paris casts for identification. They sent a valve with a "suspicious" yellow substance to a lab. They ran down everything agents could unearth about Spah, the acrobat, and even dusted for fingerprints on letters mailed after the crash. With no leads whatsoever, the FBI would close the case for good months later.

The crank mail arrived by sack loads to the *Hindenburg* investigators. One man wrote that the disaster was connected to a slave trade and narcotics ring. Many suggested Jews had blown up the ship, in opposition to Hitler. A writer in Los Angeles said the Hitler government, short on funds, sabotaged the *Hindenburg* to collect an insurance settlement.

The replies from the *Hindenburg* passengers to chief investigator Trimble also began to arrive. Mostly, unhelpful. Mrs. Doehner's sister replied for her, saying she knew nothing useful about the cause. One man's hands were still too injured to sign his letter himself. One, written in German, had to be translated. It was dated May 30, 1937, and was addressed simply to Department of Commerce, Investigation Board, Lakehurst. It was from the hand of Leonhard Adelt.

In the three-page letter, in cursive, he told how he saw the last lightning some time before the fire, so it was probably unrelated. He and his wife were at a window on the starboard side watching the landing operation.

> *A soft, muffled thud came from the direction of the front of the airship, and a bright red glow appeared outside. Almost simultaneously with the second thud, which was audible near us, the airship struck the ground hard. . . . I shouted to the passengers, "Through the window!" and jumped through the observation window closest to the gangway with my wife, as the burning frame broke apart above us.*
>
> *The fact that we first noticed the fire only when it had already raced above our heads from the stern to the front of the airship indicates how quickly it spread.*

Then he wrote about Captain Lehmann. Adelt did not mention in his letter that he was friends with Lehmann, that they had spent months going over intimate details of his life and were in the final stages of completing his memoir.

Minus that context, he just reported facts. He had seen Lehmann after the accident at the Lakehurst naval hospital, he wrote. "I asked him briefly, 'What was that?' He answered just as briefly, 'Lightning strike.'"

Then Adelt disclosed that Lehmann had confided to him about the damaged gasbag found at the winter overhaul, and how anxious it made him. "He was worried . . . since a gas cell had been found to have worn through on the upper hanging side when the *Hindenburg* was overhauled over the winter."

Adelt even included how Lehmann had resorted to poetry, to a German ballad, to express how terrified he was about the discovery of the damaged gas cell.

> *"It occurs to me as if I actually was the 'REITER AM BODENSEE' ["The Rider on Lake Constance"]he said to me, "What if the damage had happened during a trip or were to happen again to another gas cell!" His concern was increased by the fact that the young next generation lacked the decades of practical experience that the older people had in fixing things, and it was primarily for this reason that he came along on the trip, in order to keep an eye on them.*

Concluding, Adelt even used the technical term *oxyhydrogen*, which refers to a flammable combination of oxygen and hydrogen—a flash point possible only by a hydrogen leak.

> *In the light of these things that he said, I understood and understand Lehmann's answer, "Lightning strike," as meaning that he conjectured that ignition of an oxyhydrogen mixture by an electric spark was the cause of the catastrophe.*

At the end of the letter, the translator added a note: "'DER REITER AM BODENSEE' ("The Rider over Lake Constance") is the title of a poem. The same describes a rider on horseback, who, having lost his way, rides over the hard, frozen Lake Constance without even knowing it.

When he had reached the opposite shore, and on learning that he had just crossed the great lake and passed a very great danger, he dies from shock."

On reading the revelations, a stunned Trimble immediately forwarded Adelt's letter to Rosendahl, as he did much of the consequential evidence, for evaluation by the panel's trusted technical advisor.

"You, no doubt, will be very much interested in his letter," Trimble wrote, "and would perhaps like to follow it up with Mr. Adelt, as you may want to use him as a witness."

Rosendahl did not respond that knowledge of prior damage on the *Hindenburg*, from a technical genius and insider like Lehmann, was certainly revelatory and must be followed up immediately with Adelt, Eckener, and others from the Zeppelin company. A structural flaw on the *Hindenburg*, he knew, could spell the end of airships, the end of his career.

On U.S. Naval Air Station stationery, Rosendahl quickly set out to smear Adelt's character, to cover up the truth. The day after the letter reached him, Rosendahl fired back a response to Trimble, on June 11: "With regard to the letter from Mr. Adelt, I doubt the advisability of calling him. There were so many stories in the press attributable or connected to him that he must have used his imagination very freely." Then, swiping at journalists for systemically hyping their stories, Rosendahl said:

> *Throughout Mr. Adelt's letter, I cannot help but sense the newspaperman's touch. . . .*
>
> *Furthermore, with Mr. Adelt's lack of technical knowledge of airships, I cannot help but doubt the accuracy of his recollections of the various things that Captain Lehmann is said to have told him. . . .*
>
> *With regard to Captain Lehmann having told him that it was a "flash of lightning," I am inclined to doubt Mr. Adelt's understanding of what Captain Lehmann actually said. I talked with Captain Lehmann in the hospital the next day and discussed the matter with him; Lehmann at no time even mentioned lightning as a possibility, and I know from my conversation with him that he did not in any way believe lightning had anything to do with the casualty. . . .*
>
> *I hesitate to put down into writing what Captain Lehmann gave me on practically his death bed as his reason for the disaster. I can say*

*definitely, however, that it was not a flash of lightning or an explosion of an oxyhydrogen gas mixture by an electric shock. I shall discuss this further with you when I see you in Washington.*

On Rosendahl's recommendation, the panel dismissed the critical Adelt evidence. Adelt was not called to testify, and none of the Zeppelin officers, crew, or engineers was questioned about worrisome gasbag damage or any wintertime repairs. They weren't questioned about the fact that, even with cheaper hydrogen, the *Graf Zeppelin* and *Hindenburg* rang up considerable losses of 2.45 million Reichsmarks in the 1936 season.

After the Commerce Department closed its investigation in the summer of 1937, the official report blamed atmospheric electricity, crackling in the night sky near the New Jersey coast, which ignited hydrogen wafting from a gas cell perhaps torn by a wire busted in a sharp turn during its landing procedure.

In other words, Eckener's words.

# 11

# Broken Water

Wickedness always finds partners.

In the winter of 1937, Knut Eckener joined the Nazi Party. His father, Hugo Eckener, would not become a card-carrying member, but, after the *Hindenburg* fire, he quietly acted like he was theirs.

Through the first four decades of his life, Hugo Eckener had achieved little. Being born into comfortable circumstances in Flensburg, a northern port city, he really didn't work at much through early middle age. He married and started a family. He earned a PhD in experimental psychology, and took odd jobs as a reporter and commentator.

In his forties, Eckener discovered the Zeppelin. Developing into one of the most skilled pilots around, he hijacked it and managed to ride it all over the globe, to Asia, to America, to the White House. To two ticker-tape parades in New York City. He was single-minded in his zeal for the Zeppelin, forcing opponents out of his way at every step, keeping alive an outdated technology. His name surfaced as a possible candidate for president of Germany.

In thirty seconds over an airfield in New Jersey, that all disappeared. Now sixty-nine, Eckener needed to resurrect his life's work. That meant working closer and closer with the ruling party, and its hunger for dominance of Europe and beyond. Through the Nazis, and a growing trove of armaments money, there was a path back into the limelight.

The twin sister of the *Hindenburg* would be his vehicle. Czechoslovakia, the initial target. After four years of social and political uproar in Germany and the rest of the world, most people forgot about Eckener's 1934 radio broadcast, the one in which he forecast that Hitler's Reich would ferment into "noble wine." On March 12, 1938, not a year after the *Hindenburg* tragedy, Hitler invaded and annexed Austria, his native country. It was a stunning act of aggression. Americans were aghast. Propaganda Minister Goebbels rounded up his endorsers. Eckener proclaimed Hitler's swallowing of Austria "a stroke of genius."

Within days of the takeover, termed the *Anschluss*, Hitler looked for his second act. "Now it's the Czechs' turn," he told Goebbels. "At the next opportunity."

Hitler and his generals correctly figured that future warfare would be determined largely by aerial power, by the lords of the air. Fending off airplane attacks on the home front became paramount. All the major nations, especially the United States and Great Britain, were simultaneously racing to develop electronic, early-alert systems to warn them as planes approached their borders. It was all so state-of-the-art, they didn't even have a name for it. Eventually, the technology would be called Radio Detection and Ranging, abbreviated as *radar*.

To figure out how advanced the defenses were for Germany's neighbors, Göring's Luftwaffe packed UHF receivers into trimotor Junkers transport planes. Pilots flew them along Germany's borders to retrieve radio signals for surveillance. They picked up little, though, because the engines were too loud and the planes couldn't fly slowly enough.

Göring began to think about the LZ 130, a quiet, graceful, floating ship. It was the very snooping weapon he needed to help Hitler with his planned invasions. Suddenly, the outdated Zeppelin figured into cutting-edge military planning. Best of all, a Zeppelin could hover, like a hummingbird.

Hitler had Franklin Delano Roosevelt fooled.

After the *Hindenburg* fire, Hitler himself had grounded Zeppelins in Germany until they could be inflated with helium. Pitying Germany, the U.S. Congress moved to ease its long-standing restrictions on exporting the fireproof gas. Those in favor argued it was simply humanitarian to share a safer gas; those opposed felt it could help budding militarism around the world. The Japanese military was so interested in helium, it was trying to extract it from volcano fumes. When Congress changed the law, helium could be exported more readily, but there was a caveat: Any given order could not pose a military threat to the United States.

The door was fully open for Germany. Eckener quickly ordered nearly eighteen million cubic feet of helium, far in excess of its needs for the LZ 130. And alarms rang. Then, when Germany annexed Austria, the United States hesitated all over again, sensing some brewing military threat. With Hitler demanding helium and the U.S. balking, Göring saw his grand plan for spy flights with the LZ 130 evaporating.

He took matters into his own hands. On April 29, 1938, Göring spoke to Hugh Wilson, the American ambassador, in Berlin. He was blunt, undiplomatic, virtually pleading for helium. "I cannot understand what leads a nation to earn the enmity of another over such a little thing," Göring said. A chief lieutenant of Hitler, he gave his word of honor, solemnly swearing helium would not be used for war purposes. It would be stupid to send an airship into battle, he reassured, given that it could be shot down immediately.

If refused helium, the German people would not forget America's "deliberate unfriendliness," Göring warned. He threatened: "Relations between Germany and the United States have been brought to the lowest possible point."

Knowing Roosevelt was concerned about passenger safety, Göring further stated that Germany would continue flying its airships, with hydrogen if need be. Any blood, going forward, would be on America's hands.

Göring failed to make his case. Then Eckener took up the cause, and boarded a steamship to Washington. His efforts to help Göring's campaign would not escape the notice of Hitler. "I cannot believe for a moment that the United States will now let me down on the helium question," Eckener told reporters in Washington. His visit was of great interest, as he had not been in America since the *Hindenburg* investigation.

Eckener said his Zeppelin firm had already spent $400,000 to rebuild the LZ 130 for helium. He sharply rejected suspicions that the helium order was really to make airships safer for military operations. "Perfectly absurd," he replied. "I have already cabled Mr. Roosevelt that the kind of gas used in inflating dirigibles is of no military use whatsoever."

But Eckener apparently knew otherwise. He had previously confided to a U.S. diplomat about how a Zeppelin could actually be weaponized, in an aerial terror attack—specifically on New York City.

As Eckener's helium request was being weighed in Washington, George Messersmith, who headed the U.S. consulate in Germany in the early 1930s, weighed in with a "strictly confidential" letter to Secretary of State Cordell Hull and other officials. Messersmith had left Germany in February of 1934, six months before the Eckener speech endorsing Hitler, and in his experience believed that Eckener had been privately opposed to the Nazis.

In his letter of May 9, 1938, he wrote: "One such Zeppelin might be able to wreak untold damage in a section of New York, which they know well from flights over it, and before this Zeppelin could be destroyed. No one knows this better than Dr. Eckener, who has referred to it in private conversation."

Even after Austria, Roosevelt saw no danger in selling helium to Hitler's Germany. Zeppelins were useless in battle, the old navy man knew. Standing in the way, however, was Roosevelt's Secretary of the Interior, Harold Ickes. A Chicagoan best known for overseeing much of Roosevelt's "New Deal" relief program, he was one of the six cabinet members who needed to unanimously approve a sale of helium to an overseas customer for it to go forward. While the other five were willing, Ickes single-handedly held up the Nazis.

More than once in recent months, Roosevelt had lectured Ickes that the United States had a moral duty to sell Germany helium, but Ickes couldn't shake a sneaking suspicion that Hitler and Göring were up to something. They just seemed a little too interested in a lifting gas for a has-been passenger air service. Ickes even went so far as to meet with Eckener, who struck him as trustworthy enough but probably a Hitler puppet, intentional or not.

That May, Ickes and Roosevelt had a dustup over it all. The president, trying to negotiate, offered: "We would not ship the helium unless we had a guarantee from Hitler that it would not be used for military purposes." To which Ickes replied, "Who would take Hitler's word?"

The tug-of-war over helium then added Commander Rosendahl, pulling for the Germans. In July, Rosendahl visited Friedrichshafen as an honored guest at the July centennial celebration of Count Zeppelin's birth—a stretch of an anniversary—to try to campaign further for American helium. When he returned from Germany, he told reporters that no European country foresaw Zeppelins having a role in any future war.

"If those governments thought so, they would be building airships like they are building all other armaments," Rosendahl said. "Germany is carrying on her plans for airship construction only for peacetime commercial purposes. In America, things are entirely different because we have vast coastlines and we can use airships for patrol purposes. I am still as enthusiastic about an airship program as I ever was. Don't forget the airship is the only aircraft of any kind that has ever carried a payload across the Atlantic and around the world."

That summer, still awaiting American helium, Hitler reversed himself, allowing the LZ 130 to fly with hydrogen, but without passengers. For several years, the Germans produced their huge quantities of hydrogen through an electrical process that decomposed water, splitting $H_2O$ into $H$s and $O$s. Zeppelins had been flying on broken water.

The LZ 130 would be pumped full of hydrogen after all, and Eckener formally gave his approval to the Air Ministry to outfit the *Hindenburg*'s sister ship with espionage equipment to snoop on bordering countries. Göring finally had an invaluable eye in the sky.

In August, still weighing an invasion of Czechoslovakia, Hitler gave Eckener an extraordinary government honor. On Eckener's seventieth birthday, the Führer bestowed on him the rare and venerated title of Professor. Not many Germans received a birthday present from Hitler.

The next month, Eckener stepped to the podium for the inauguration of the LZ 130, the evil twin of the *Hindenburg*. He wanted to evoke the strong and safe service record of his previous ship, the *Graf Zeppelin*. The new craft, he said, would also be called the *Graf Zeppelin*, the second generation.

At the factory in Friedrichshafen, Göring was at the christening. In front of the ambitious architect of the German air force, Eckener addressed the crowd, sounding all the notes of a military rally.

"I wish this ship to carry forth the honor of German technology to all the world as a symbol of unshakable German will! To gain for the German people the place in the world to which they are entitled!"

Cheers welled up.

"To the German people and their leader!"

He then shouted the two-word Nazi chant.

"*Sieg Heil!*"

For the first flight since the *Hindenburg* tragedy, Eckener stepped into the control cabin and ordered the new Zeppelin off to Nuremburg, consecrating the ship at the Nazi Party's hallowed grounds. Hydrogen was on board. The crew was nervous. Everyone personally knew someone who died in the fire the year before. It did not help that there were new precautions, including parachutes on board for each man.

Almost no one knew they were riding in an airship built differently, using lessons from the *Hindenburg* tragedy. The outer cover was constructed in a new way, the gas cells received extra protection. Upon returning home from the Lakehurst inquiry, Eckener personally oversaw the modifications to the LZ 130. The revisions speak volumes about the cause of the disaster.

Karl Hürttle, the fabric wizard, and his team carefully studied the behavior of the LZ 130's outer cover to fix it. For one thing, workers re-tensioned the fabric inch by inch after applying the first coat of dope. The outer-cover panels on the *Hindenburg* and LZ 130 were much larger than anything tried before. So, they adopted the new procedure after discovering that the fabric loosened and softened a bit after the dope initially penetrated into the fibers. They found that the new procedure tightened the cover to 150 kilograms per meter of tension, fully 36 percent more than on the *Hindenburg*, significantly dampening flutter.

They also changed the formula for the dope, better balancing water resistance with stability. The new dope, called #6252, contained a little less plasticizer than what was used on the *Hindenburg*, "a slight sacrifice being made in the resistance to moisture to gain a reduction in stretch," as maintenance records put it.

Finally, while workmen tied off the gas-cell wiring at its crossing places on the *Hindenburg* to protect the gasbags from dangerous chafing, they did so only at the very top of the ship. Evidently on the thought that too narrow an area of reinforcement may have been a factor in the *Hindenburg* fire, they fastened more of the gas-cell wiring on the LZ 130, nearly down to the middle line of the ship, the equator. That protected the gasbags on the entire top half of the Zeppelin. In notable German understatement, as maintenance records put it: "On the 130, the wiring was so tied off [to the equator] in order to avoid a recurrence of this difficulty."

Watching the LZ 130 on its test flights, Harold Dick, the Goodyear engineer, noted: "From the ground, the outer cover looks very good, and there is not much flutter, much less than with the LZ 129."

Shortly after the LZ 130's christening in mid-September, Eckener reportedly piloted the new *Graf Zeppelin* on an early spy flight over Czechoslovakia. Back in May, Hitler had instructed his generals to be ready to invade the country by October. As German troops concentrated on the Czech border, Czechoslovakia mobilized its armed forces there. France vowed to step in if Germany attacked, and Britain issued warnings. The Nazis promised to honor Czechoslovakia's sovereignty.

Closing in on invasion, Goebbels whipped up the German public in late September with falsified reports of atrocities and scare headlines in the Nazi press:

*WOMEN AND CHILDREN MOWED DOWN
BY CZECH ARMORED CARS*

*BLOODY REGIME—NEW CZECH
MURDERS OF GERMANS*

Under the ruse of a flight to Vienna on September 22, 1938, Eckener used his new Zeppelin to cruise along the southern border of Czechoslovakia. It was actually an advance scouting trip for an invasion. The dining room of the "passenger" ship was packed with twenty-four consoles to monitor radio transmissions. There were oscillographs to track electrical pulses, along with several dozen Luftwaffe signalmen, photographers, and language interpreters. Hitler's eyes and ears in the clouds.

Four Messerschmitt fighter planes accompanied the Zeppelin, masquerading in the green colors of the civilian police. Built for aerial dogfighting, they were there to defend the *Graf Zeppelin* in case the Czech air force tried to attack. The very same day, Neville Chamberlain landed in Germany. The British prime minister flew in to try to persuade Hitler not to invade. Hitler assured him he would not.

In October, Hitler's troops marched into Czechoslovakia's so-called Sudetenland area, ostensibly to protect Germans being victimized in the German border regions. It was only a first step. In less than a year, the Nazis would occupy the rest of the country. As 1938 closed, the LZ 130 would fly over Liberec, Czechoslovakia, where Hitler appeared for a large rally. From the Zeppelin, loudspeakers blasting music and Nazi propaganda, the crew dropped thirty large paper swastikas.

Czechoslovakia provided Hitler with a rich war chest, as he commandeered the bulk of the Czech arms factories, its rich metals industry, and a base to expand Germany into the "living space in the east," space the Führer insisted Germany's growing population needed. The Nazi war machine just got much stronger, with Hugo Eckener's help.

Harold Dick was supposed to report on airship construction to the president of Goodyear, Paul Litchfield, but he hit a stone wall called Knut. The Zeppelin company and Goodyear still had a partnership, and Hugo Eckener had agreed to cooperate with Dick. He even allowed his son, in charge of construction, to be Dick's main contact for information. But Knut Eckener withheld far more than Dick realized, his recent Nazi affiliation being just one thing. On the most important matters, the Goodyear man was left in the dark.

As the Czechoslovakia occupation was playing out, Dick could sense the nature of the Luftschiffbau Zeppelin was changing, from commercial to military. Berlin was mentioned far more in relation to the LZ 130. The Air Ministry requested special flights that had nothing to do with normal test-flying of the ship. He assumed that they were related to the unusual equipment installed in the airship, he wrote in his notes. It was all kept top secret, but he surmised it dealt with snooping on other countries' radar signals.

Until 1938, Dick would later recall, he could roam freely all around the factory, the shops, the wind tunnel, anywhere. Then, one by one, he was barred from certain areas. The wind tunnel was restricted because the factory had begun doing research work for Dornier Aircraft, which was constructing two-engine bombers for Germany's air force. If Dick had to go near the Dornier work, Knut usually had to escort him. As they walked through, Knut would caution Dick to keep looking at him and away from the work at hand. Dick recalled that he was advised to avoid the port-side passenger quarters of the LZ 130, where workmen had been installing signal-monitoring equipment.

It was pointless to stay in Friedrichshafen, given how much they were hiding. Dick returned to America at year's end.

Hugo Eckener began edging toward the Nazi military's inner circle.

At the shipyards at Kiel, the highest-ranking four officers of the armed forces and government and Nazi Party officials assembled on Thursday, December 8, 1938. They were there, along with thousands of spectators drawn by the bands and pomp, for the launching of Germany's first aircraft carrier. The battleship, christened the *Graf Zeppelin*, was a 19,000-ton monster, capable of carrying forty airplanes. She had sixteen six-inch guns. The shipyards had a sister ship under way.

After thunders of *Heil*s for Hitler, Göring took the podium to say the mammoth new ship was proof that Germany's armaments were now strong enough to enforce peace in a turbulent world. He reeled off the German naval achievements of the Great War and the Zeppelins that raided London. He praised Count Zeppelin, the namesake of the new battleship, as "a good German, a fearless soldier, who fought for an ideal."

Amid the pageantry, Hitler smiled and acknowledged cock-armed salutes. On hand, too, was Hugo Eckener, invited as Hitler's personal guest.

Distressed by the headlines out of Germany, British silent-film star Charlie Chaplin decided to use his celebrity to take a stand against Hitler. Some people couldn't help but notice that the Little Tramp and Hitler had virtually the same smudge of a mustache. Chaplin, upset by the oppression of Jews in Nazi Germany, began work on a sarcastic movie with the working title *The Dictator*, in which he would lampoon Hitler by playing the tyrant himself.

Even before film production began, Nazi officialdom was outraged. England, as part of an appeasement agreement aimed at not stirring tension with Germany, had agreed not to show *The Dictator* whenever it was released.

Hinting that the movie sounded splendid for American theaters, Harold Ickes quickly became one of the nation's first prominent anti-Nazi politicians. He had already blocked helium exports to Nazi Germany that summer, and by the end of 1938, his growing Nazi opposition flustered the U.S. Department and drew strong rebukes in Germany.

Ickes had to be somewhat diplomatic, as he was far more extreme at that point than his boss, President Roosevelt. On top of that, he was Secretary of the Interior, responsible for domestic affairs, not Secretary of State. In a Cleveland speech, Ickes denounced an unnamed dictator who had recently given awards to two prominent Americans, Henry Ford and Charles Lindbergh. "How can any American accept a decoration at the hand of a brutal dictator who, with that same hand, is robbing and torturing thousands of fellow human beings?"

The Roosevelt cabinet member said the mistreatment of Jews drove Germany back "to a period of history when man was . . . benighted and bestial." As Ickes was not Jewish himself, his outcry particularly affronted the Nazis.

Ickes was, in short, a real enemy of the Nazis. At that point, Göring knew hope was dead for helium from America. Helium would have provided at least two benefits: The Nazis were anxious to avoid repeating a *Hindenburg* flaming fiasco with the sister ship, and neighboring countries would not be nearly so nervous if the new *Graf Zeppelin*, filled with helium, occasionally drifted into their airspace, as it routinely did that first year. In Houston, the *Idarwald*, a German freight ship with a cargo of 200 empty steel bottles, intended for the first shipments of American helium, was recalled to Germany in mid-December.

Into 1939, the aerial surveillance Eckener allowed became a top priority for the Air Ministry. The spying of 1938 had revealed significant radio-signal activity among the air forces of Germany's neighboring countries.

Now the chief of the Luftwaffe's Air Signals Branch, Wolfgang Martini, anxiously wanted to pinpoint which airfields were generating the signals. Battle plans depended on it. The problem was the large metal frame of the *Graf Zeppelin* interfered with reception too much to analyze locations.

Then someone had the bright idea of reviving an old Zeppelin observation car, which was showcased at the recently opened Zeppelin museum in Friedrichshafen. During the first world war, searchlights on the ground allowed cities to spot Zeppelins overhead and easily fire upon them. To avoid that danger, a Zeppelin would hide in the clouds and lower a single-occupant car on a metal cable several hundred feet below, allowing the lookout man inside to search the ground for targets. He would then telephone his findings back up to the ship. It was frightening, hanging in the air like an unfurled yo-yo, but it worked.

And it solved problems a couple decades later. Lowered 500 feet or more, the little manned observation car escaped the troublesome interference of the ship, allowing the *Graf Zeppelin* to accurately identify the positions of transmitters of future enemies. The crew often vied for the chance to man the hanging car. It was the only spot one could smoke.

The Zeppelin spy flights were so important that the Nazis went to incredible lengths to orchestrate and camouflage them. In the summer of 1939, the Air Ministry amassed huge crowds for Sunday "Flying Days" in towns on Germany's border. With marching soldiers, swastikas waving, and military bands, they were a complete ruse. They were actually a cover for the *Graf Zeppelin*, flying beyond its borders between several of these events, to conduct its spy missions.

In what came to be called the Chain Home radar system, England had begun building a ring of towers on its shores. It was aircraft-warning equipment, and that worried Germany's Air Ministry. The *Graf Zeppelin* was ordered to snoop around England with a forty-eight-hour flight, beginning on Wednesday, August 2. At one point, Captain Sammt stopped his engines off of Scotland's coast, faking engine trouble, so they could drift over the suspect antenna masts. As the *Graf Zeppelin* approached, though, Britain's new Supermarine Spitfires suddenly appeared, darting menacingly around the large airship. Inside, Luftwaffe men quickly snapped photos of the Royal Air Force fighter aircraft, which they had never seen before. In a panic, the Zeppelin cranked up the little spy car, fired up the engines, and retreated.

Within weeks, Hitler's troops invaded Poland, and two days later, England and France declared war on Germany. With a couple dozen flights, the *Graf Zeppelin* had helped the Nazis gather intelligence to prepare and plan their attacks. But once the battles actually began, the Zeppelin was entirely too vulnerable to be useful. It would sit in its hangar until 1940, when Göring ordered it and the older *Graf Zeppelin* dismantled, the scrap metal to be used for airplanes.

That left Hugo Eckener with time on his hands. At seventy-two, he could have easily retired to his nice home in Friedrichshafen, gardened with Johanna, smoked his cigars, and written his memoirs. Instead, he soldiered on, soon to cross paths with a man named Georg, a rising SS commander from Auschwitz, who conducted business with a whip.

# "Enjoy the War"

*The clever and experienced minds among our people should put them-
selves at the Führer's disposal.*
—HUGO ECKENER, 1934 RADIO TALK ENDORSING HITLER

WERNHER VON BRAUN HAD THE BUTTERFLIES: TO MEET THE LEGEND-
ary Hugo Eckener face to face. Not yet thirty, von Braun was a genius, a
prodigy in the Third Reich's armaments world. He had recently written
a doctoral dissertation on rocket propulsion. From the time his mother
gave him a telescope as a child, von Braun was fascinated with space.

Hugo Eckener was another star von Braun had looked up to. But his
glory days seemed past. Once his Zeppelins were scrapped, their metal
reused for Luftwaffe aircraft, the Luftschiffbau Zeppelin had drifted. For
generations, it had expertly crafted light metals and aluminum. It had
little to offer in the war effort, though, little to lob at the enemy. In time,
work shifted to containers for dairy, brewing, and chemical industries,
along with bodies for passenger cars and buses. It did have an industrial
gear factory, which the army paid richly to crank up production for tanks.

Then Eckener began to make good on those contacts he made back
in 1936, when he began attending the beer evenings organized by the
Army Weapons Office. Another man lifting steins at the get-togethers
was Walter Dornberger, an army researcher, who headed a team of scientists working at a secret base near the old fishing village of Peenemünde
(pronounced *peen-uh-MOON-duh*) on the shores of the Baltic Sea.

What they were planning at Peenemünde was something the world
had never seen, a heavy bomb that would drop from the empty sky, with

no warning, no way to counteract it. A meteor. A terrorist weapon. Still in its infancy, the A4 rocket had many glitches to work out. Dornberger thought development should proceed with both researchers and factory experts simultaneously. Production could move quickly once the rocket was ready for deployment, with fewer manufacturing surprises. The whole project was veiled in secrecy.

Over beers years earlier, Dornberger began to consider the underused Zeppelin factory in Friedrichshafen for production of his rockets. On Wednesday, September 3, 1941, he sent von Braun and other rocket men to the town on Lake Constance, the birthplace of German aircraft, to discuss whether Eckener would offer his factory for production. Sturdy, lightweight metal, a Zeppelin specialty, perfectly fit the needs of a long-range rocket.

The entourage from the Peenemünde Army Command Center spoke with Hugo and Knut Eckener and with their longtime Zeppelin designer, Ludwig Dürr. They showed them a variety of drawings and documents. After speaking over two days, Hugo Eckener showed interest. The Peenemünde brain trust left encouraged.

Eckener had been busy that year. It was around this time that he began working with the Abwehr, the Third Reich's military intelligence operation, possibly as an officer, American intelligence would later discover. He would act as an Abwehr operative in Bucharest, Romania; Berlin; Istanbul, Turkey; and Sofia, Bulgaria.

He also began scouting for other sites to hide the important gear work for army tanks. Rockets were futuristic; tanks were rolling against the enemy every day. The war by 1941 was going poorly for Germany, and the Reich figured it best to split armaments production, to limit damages from possible Allied bombing. At the same time, the army raised its orders of gear and components for tanks.

Eckener scouted remote spots, away from the industrial cities that the Allies would surely target, in occupied territories including Balkan countries and Austria. He ended up locating a factory, which would make gear boxes for panzer tanks, in the German/Austrian border town of Passau. By 1941, the army had conscripted millions of able-bodied German men, gutting the manual labor force, so Eckener's new factory would soon consider something forbidden by civility and international law: prisoners of war as slave labor.

By the winter of 1941, the Japanese had attacked Pearl Harbor, and the United States joined the battle in the Pacific and Europe. Germany was clearly beginning to lose the war. Even with espionage from Eckener's *Graf Zeppelin*, Göring's formidable air force had failed to invade England, despite months of aerial bombing raids in 1939 and 1940. Germans began making jokes with gallows humor: "An airplane carrying Hitler, Göring, and Goebbels crashes. All three are killed. Who is saved?" Answer: "The German people."

Hitler was feverish to find a secret weapon to turn the tide. In February of 1942, he appointed a new armaments minister, the Third Reich's chief architect, a man he admired like a son, Albert Speer. Hitler's favorite architect had joined his inner circle nearly a decade earlier, partly because Hitler fancied himself an artist and an architect. On paper, Speer was his kindred.

One early project elevated Speer within the Reich. It was built in Nuremburg, a town renowned since the Middle Ages for its toys: carved and painted animals, dolls and doll houses, tin Prussian soldiers. Speer created an entirely new playground. He drew up vast stands and marching grounds around the Zeppelin Field, where Count Zeppelin famously landed an early airship in 1909.

Speer built a daunting stone grandstand at Nuremburg, based on an ancient Greek temple, and crowned it with an enormous swastika. Starting in 1933, thousands marched and cheered on the Nazi Party grounds, with propaganda-film cameras rolling. The outdoor arena was epic. Thunderous cheers from the stands. *Sieg Heil! Sieg Heil!* It was here that the *Hindenburg* tipped its nose to Hitler the year before it was destroyed.

If his fair-haired Speer could orchestrate armies of construction workers and tons of quarried stone into imposing buildings for the Reich, Hitler figured, he could work miracles with arms production. As Speer began reviewing plans for the latest in tanks, aircraft, and submarines, he was brought inside the top-secret rocket mission.

Four months later, Dornberger, von Braun, and their team were ready to demonstrate the A4. On June 13, 1942, a Monday, Speer flew from

Berlin with Germany's top arms chiefs to Peenemünde to witness the firing of the classified rocket. Peenemünde is on a slim island called Usedom, nearly evenly between Berlin to the south and Copenhagen to the north. The island is surrounded by tall pines, good cover for a secret base. The Peene River empties into the Baltic Sea.

At the test site, near the airfield to the north, stood the A4. At forty-six feet tall, it could fly distances of nearly 200 miles, four times the speed of sound. At its launch pad, the rocket was painted with a large black-and-white checkerboard across its body, making photographs of the missile in flight easier to study. "Before us in a clearing among the pines towered an unreal-looking missile four-stories high," Speer would recall.

Wisps of vapor surrounded the canister, which suddenly leapt from its pad, howled on a tongue of fire into the clouds, and disappeared. Von Braun watched his baby through binoculars. Moonfaced already at thirty, he was beaming. "I was thunderstruck at this technical miracle, at its precision," Speer recalled thinking that very moment. "It seemed to abolish the laws of gravity."

As the technicians began explaining the distance the rocket was covering—flying several times faster than the speed of sound—the army, air force, and navy officers on the field suddenly felt a shudder. They could tell from the nearing howl that the rocket was headed back to earth, back toward them.

"We all froze where we stood," Speer remembered. Within seconds, it landed, ground shaking, only half a mile away. The guidance system had failed.

Hitler was intrigued by the rocket, but thought it too fanciful. When Speer reported the test flop to him, the Führer had the "gravest doubts" they could ever perfect the guidance machinery. The A4 would not be the secret weapon hoped for.

Dornberger had staked his entire career on the rocket. He was crestfallen. Unless Hitler was a believer, they would never be allocated the raw materials or technical staff to move the A4 beyond testing. Hugo Eckener perhaps sensed a moment in the limelight. Dornberger needed to gain an ally for his A4, someone willing to gamble his own money on the dream weapon. Maybe then Hitler would take it seriously.

Ever since Germany's failure in 1940's air battle for Britain, Dornberger and his colleagues thought the only way to defend Germany in the west, if they even could, was to frighten its enemies into retreat with a series of guided missiles exploding on them. The sooner, the better. But Dornberger knew the strengths and weaknesses of his team at Peenemünde. Most everyone on the base was a research scientist, and no one really had a clue on how to mass-produce the missile.

Some of the production could begin at Peenemünde, but he needed manufacturing expertise from elsewhere. He decided to check back with Eckener. What could it hurt? He was desperate. His life's work was slipping through his hands. In the fall of 1942, they talked and talked. "I . . . managed at length to interest Dr. Eckener," recalled Dornberger, "and he agreed to put his Friedrichshafen establishment at our disposal as a second assembly center."

Hugo Eckener had just saved Germany's wonder weapon, in Dornberger's estimation. Years later, Dornberger would recall his remarkable relief at that very moment, at Eckener's eleventh-hour rescue, saying, "I breathed again."

The world would never be the same. At Peenemünde, on October 3, 1942, von Braun and his team shot the A4 to an altitude of sixty miles, the first time anything man-made had ever grazed space. It was a ballistic missile, meaning it used fuel to power its initial arching trajectory, and then fell with gravity onto its target. That day, a Saturday in October of 1942, would bequeath to the world a mad, unending arms race.

Speer reported the test to Hitler. A fourteen-ton rocket was launched on a 120-mile course, and it struck within two and half miles of its target. Suddenly, Hitler showed real interest, Speer recalled. By the end of the year, Hitler committed to mass production of the rocket, though there were known technical glitches, ones forecast to take at least six months to work out. Final technical data was supposed to be finished by the summer of 1943, and then production could proceed.

Fall of 1942. Puffing on his fat cigar, Hugo Eckener, along with son Knut and Dr. Dürr, were aboard an early train leaving Friedrichshafen. They were wearing dark, warm coats. It was Tuesday, November 3, and they were heading to northern Germany. They passed through Nuremburg, where Hugo Eckener had flown the old *Graf Zeppelin* over the first Nazi Party congress in 1933; through Leipzig, where he studied the human brain as a graduate student at the university; and through Berlin, where he had met and consulted with Göring and Goebbels.

The final train station was Szczecin in Poland, which had been occupied nearly three years earlier by Germany. There, a car was waiting. They were being chauffeured to the Nazis' most secret military installation: Peenemünde. The Nazis had bought the fishing and farming village a few years earlier, and cleared nearly all of the town for secret missile work.

Heavily guarded, the grounds had a series of security posts and fences the Zeppelin men had to clear. Their car was carefully checked, along with their papers. They were cleared again, at the main guardhouse, and finally arrived at the inner sanctum.

The base had an oxygen factory to create the liquid oxygen that fueled the A4. It had its own airfield and a dedicated water-treatment plant. There were several concrete bunkers for researchers to observe launches within protective enclosures, and several air-raid shelters. The living quarters, which had views of the sparkling waters of the Baltic Sea, accommodated more than 400.

The army considered the base so confidential, it installed artificial fog machinery to make it impossible for Allied reconnaissance planes to spot revealing structures, such as T-shaped launch pads, amid the wafting vapor. For extra security, the base was forbidden to employ any foreigners. Various areas of the property required special authorization. On their shirts and jackets, all employees had to wear identification and badges of different shapes and sizes. The army wanted no leaks, no security breaches. No one was allowed to set foot on the top-secret base unless the Nazis were completely confident of his or her loyalty.

At two the next morning, the Zeppelin men checked into "nice rooms" in the officers' quarters, Hugo Eckener wrote in a letter to his wife, Johanna, that evening. The lodgings were cozy, with manicured lawns and dormer windows peeking from steep, red roofs. The accommodations and meals on the island were sumptuous, far better than one could find elsewhere in wartime Germany. It was an oasis from the realities of the war.

He and Knut had lunch there that Wednesday with beef stew and generous portions, Hugo wrote to his wife, including fifty grams of boiled beef. It was so plentiful that neither Knut nor an accompanying officer could finish their meal, but he finished his, Hugo boasted. Knut was quite cheerful, he added, and in a good mood, as he always was.

The next morning, they further discussed production plans for Friedrichshafen. Before departing Peenemünde, they stood for a commemorative photo on four concrete steps outside an office building. Hugo Eckener wore a dark hat and stood with his hands in his black winter coat. He was next to Dornberger, in his army uniform, hat off his bald head. Next to Dornberger was von Braun, cigarette in hand. Knut Eckener was in back. They were surrounded by army officers in full uniform. Each wore his gray-and-green army-officer cap, its peak topped with a silvery eagle, wings spread, clutching a swastika. It was a photo Hugo Eckener could not avoid.

By the winter of 1943, Speer wanted an update. He summoned Dornberger and von Braun to Berlin.

The men showed up with a 1/100 scale wooden model of a launch site. They filled Speer in on the rocket's development and the problems that remained. After meeting with Eckener, Dornberger had requested that Hitler give the A4 a higher priority in the war effort, meaning more money and more technical staff, which would allow them to speed the work along. But Hitler was still not convinced the project was going to work, Speer told him. Dornberger was losing hope. That would change within days.

Russia, late January 1943. The Russian army encircled Germany's Sixth Army near Stalingrad. Nearly 150,000 Germans were killed or wounded, and more than 91,000 had been captured, including twenty-four generals. The toll was so staggering, the disaster so evident, that the Nazi press couldn't hide it, or even spin it. Hitler was growing increasingly desperate for a wonder weapon.

A week later, Hitler ordered Speer to form a special committee to create the rocket. Anxious, Speer gathered two dozen technical specialists from industry at Peenemünde. It was Tuesday, February 9, 1943. At this point, the Eckener name became part of the A4 Special Committee, whose memos were marked *Geheim!* (Secret!) with explicit instructions that they had to be hidden in a locked safe after reading.

Even while working on the rocket, Speer held on to an early, dark memory of Zeppelins. He had been in awe, and terror, of them since he was a child in Mannheim. It was 1915, and one of the Zeppelins used in the London bombing missions in the Great War was stationed there. The captain and his officers, after being guests in his house, invited little Albert and his two young brothers to tour the Zeppelin. As a ten-year-old, he stood before that monster of technology, climbed inside through the light-speckled hull innards, and got into the control gondola, Speer would recall. Later that night, the captain had the Zeppelin perform a loop over the Speer house, and the officers waved a sheet down at them.

The experience left the young boy shaken. "Night after night afterward, I was in terror that the airship would go up in flames, and all my friends would be killed," he recalled.

Speer carried that nightmare into adulthood, to Peenemünde. Hitler needed a terror weapon, quickly, and he was one of the Führer's most-trusted confidantes. Speer's newly assembled A4 Special Committee had to materialize it. Speer handpicked as chairman of the committee Gerhard Degenkolb, an industrialist and fervent Nazi whose acceleration of train manufacturing, to an astonishing 2,000 locomotives a month, connected Germany with its conquered areas throughout Europe. For filling that vital role, he was celebrated as the train "dictator."

There were thousands of parts in the fourteen-ton rocket. The committee would break the rocket into components and production steps, assigning each a dedicated group. Zeppelin and Daimler-Benz were responsible for Group 12, rocket fuselage and fuel tank production. Other groups worked on raw materials, factories, machinery, energy, vehicles, fuel, electrical equipment, delivery, assembly, and transport. Von Braun was in charge of "Final Approval."

Speer had proved himself adept at ratcheting up production. The prior year, he so dramatically increased manufacturing that it was called the "armaments miracle," a sinister pairing of quite different words.

With the A4, Eckener could really revive his career, and that of the Luftschiffbau Zeppelin. Having reached seventy-five, he could write a final chapter to his life. Rockets would catapult the Zeppelin works to the forefront of technology, and lucrative military contracting, from the technical obsolescence their trusty Zeppelins had sunk to. And, if Germany won the war, Eckener would become a hero again, having an important role in delivering victory to the Fatherland.

Large companies like Zeppelin and Daimler-Benz gained great clout. Because they controlled the factory floors, tooling, and equipment, they could call the shots, with or without army support. They also gained access to the latest in technology, without having to foot oppressive development costs, meaning fat profits. Eckener's own salary had risen to 91,396 Reichsmarks in 1942, making him one of the highest paid executives in Friedrichshafen.

The motto of the A4 Special Committee: "Enjoy the war—the peace will be terrible."

That they were even contemplating "the peace" in early 1943 is telling. Many company executives were heartened by Germany's rapid, early successes in invading neighboring countries in 1939 and 1940. They expected the soldiers drafted from their factory floors to vanquish the Russians quickly and return to work. In many cases, they didn't even look to fill the jobs, holding them open for the returning veterans.

But with the Soviet Union proving a far tougher foe than they imagined, Germany quickly became starved for laborers. By 1941, German agriculture and industry had nearly one million job vacancies. The country simply couldn't operate, much less wage war, without massive infusions of workers from somewhere.

The problem was solved at the top. Hitler and Göring in late 1941 developed a plan to allow forced workers into German industry. The so-called *Ostarbeiter*, or the Ukrainians, Poles, and Russians, would be deported from their homelands after German occupation and then dispatched by train to factories throughout the Reich. Some volunteered, hoping to earn money to send to impoverished relatives back home.

Luftschiffbau Zeppelin's German workforce had been gutted by the war. In 1942, 782 workers had been conscripted from its factory, handed rifles, and consigned mostly to the Russian Front. To keep the assembly lines running in Friedrichshafen, Zeppelin, under Eckener's leadership, ordered and received 1,219 of the forced laborers, nearly 1,000 of them men. They made up a little over a third of Zeppelin's total workforce, and had to wear special badges identifying them as foreigners, lesser people.

Their work conditions, and lives, were harsh. As at camps throughout Germany, the non-Germans were enclosed in residential barracks at the factory, fenced in and segregated by sex. They were supervised and guarded by security men, and, for any infractions, they typically faced punishments, including cleanup chores, labor gangs, and withdrawal of hot meals for a period of days.

Generally, they were prohibited from leaving, but some classes of foreign workers could take vacation time for visits home. This was a perk that was later discouraged at some companies, as workers, frazzled from strenuous conditions, simply deserted. In early 1943, for instance, more than 300 Dutch laborers, on the job only four months at Peenemünde, left for their Christmas vacations and never returned.

The forced laborers were paid a fraction of what their German coworkers were, and roughly a third to half of those meager wages were confiscated by mandatory Eastern-worker taxes and room-and-board fees automatically deducted by Zeppelin. They were also subject to harsh discriminatory laws. In Nazi Germany, racial purity was paramount, and the country created a strict system of apartheid. For violating race-separation rules, particularly having sex with a German, a foreign worker could be executed or dispatched to a concentration camp.

As the foreign workers marched into Zeppelin's factory gates, Werner von Braun visited Friedrichshafen in May of 1942 to tour the factory facilities there, to be sure it was fully equipped and staffed to be the sister plant to Peenemünde to build the rockets. He inspected the assembly halls, train tracks, and power equipment. He could see that Zeppelin had begun employing foreign workers to supplement its German workforce, but he thought the factory was still understaffed.

In a May 5, 1942, memo on the Zeppelin visit, von Braun recommended that "construction of fuel tanks can be done by foreign workers and prisoners of war." Using the prisoners in that way was a clear violation of international law, established by the Hague Convention, which forbade countries from forcing prisoners of war to make munitions and weapons.

Eckener appeared to have no problem with it. After checking the needs of the factory, a member of the A4 Special Committee in October ordered 200 prisoners of war for Zeppelin, including 100 mechanics, 10 toolmakers, and 10 lathe operators. The Armaments Ministry denied the request in November, however, replying that those work specialists were more desperately needed for the mining industry.

After that denial, the Zeppelin company apparently then worked behind the scenes to requisition prisoners outside the A4 Special Committee. In order to build the rocket, Eckener would need an engine-testing base, which would have to be built off-site, moving any accidental explosion dangers away from the population of Friedrichshafen. The plan was to locate it at Raderach, about four miles north of the main Zeppelin plant. At the same time, Zeppelin seemed confident that the A4 Special Committee would prevail in receiving priority for slave laborers, and plans were drawn up to convert part of the camp for the foreign workers into a full-fledged prisoner camp.

The move to seek prison workers put Zeppelin on an entirely different plane, legally and morally. It also put Eckener in the territory of the dreaded SS, which managed Nazi Germany's concentration camp network. Armaments companies were among the first to requisition prisoners from the SS, which in response created a rent-a-slave business.

The nearest big prison was in Dachau, to the north, near Munich. It was the founding SS concentration camp and had, at various points, 30,000 prisoners in its main location behind barbed wire. Starting in February 1943, Dachau prisoners arrived by train at Friedrichshafen and began building a Zeppelin concentration camp, which was informally called "Don." It would house still more prisoners.

Two months later, in April 1943, the A4 Special Committee set out to explore deeply the slave-labor idea. The committee sent a delegation to Heinkel, an aircraft factory in Oranienburg, north of Berlin, to study the feasibility of using a vast army of slaves for rocket production. By that point, the aircraft firm had 4,000 prisoners working on assembly lines, and they were kept in line by harsh SS guards, who crammed them into creaky bunks, behind barbed wire, guarded with machine guns from watchtowers. One of those touring the operation was Arthur Rudolph, chief engineer of the Peenemünde factory. Dr. Dürr, Eckener's longtime partner at Zeppelin, also visited.

Dismissing the brutal conditions, Rudolph drafted a memo to the committee, sounding every bit the engineer, assessing prison labor in cold terms of efficiency. "This system has worked well," he wrote, "and the employment of prisoners (*Häftlinge*) in general has considerable advantages over the earlier employment of (forced foreign workers), especially because all non-work-related tasks are taken over by the SS, and the prisoners offer greater protection for secrecy."

It was very clear that Rudolph and other members of the A4 Special Committee fully understood that they would be forcing enemy soldiers to create weapons that would be used against their home countries. That, naturally, would prompt some of the prison workers to try to sabotage the rockets. But Rudolph noted that the melting pot of nationalities—Russians, Poles, and French—helped undercut any attempts at resistance.

When the glowing testimonial came to the A4 committee, it enthusiastically agreed: Concentration camp prisoners were ideal. A representative for the committee would soon reach out to the SS, hoping the security agency would agree to allocate some of its precious living currency.

Eckener's standing was poised to grow in the Third Reich. The A4 rocket promised power, prestige, and access to raw materials and manpower, all things the has-been flying machine called the Zeppelin could no longer provide him.

According to press accounts, Eckener was emerging as a member of the Nazis' elite circle of arms merchants. On May 13, 1943, he appeared on the cover of *Berlin Illustrated* magazine, pictured in a tank, with Ferdinand Porsche, who wore driving goggles and gloves. In the Nazi-controlled newsmagazine, Porsche and Eckener, hailed as "armaments experts," were joyriding in a new Tiger tank with one of Germany's leading lights at the steering wheel, Albert Speer.

By the summer of 1943, just five months after the A4 committee first met, Hitler awarded Peenemünde top priority in German armaments. It happened on July 7, 1943, when Speer invited Dornberger and von Braun to headquarters in Berlin at Hitler's request. They showed the Führer a color film of an A4 launch. The camera motor hummed. Spooling film clicked. Images flicked on the screen. Hitler for the first time saw the majesty of a great rocket thundering into the stratosphere.

Hitler was mesmerized. He turned to Dornberger and told him he wished Germany had had these rockets earlier. Now, Hitler added, there was no end to what Germany could do with them.

Dornberger replied, "No defense against the rocket exists." After years of hesitation, Hitler suddenly believed that the rocket could turn the war. He ordered anti-aircraft guns out to Peenemünde for protection.

The rocket would not exist without the genius of von Braun. Speer immediately recommended to Hitler that he pronounce von Braun a "Professor," the title Hitler had previously awarded to Eckener. Hitler agreed. The room was buzzing. All smiles, they started talking about the "wonder weapons" they would unleash on the unsuspecting world.

When the Peenemünders left, Speer and Hitler were alone. Hitler rhapsodized that the A4 could decide the war. It would electrify Germany if they attacked the British with it, he said. Hitler ordered Speer to accelerate development of the A4, and promised to provide whatever labor and materials he needed. Hitler added one other thing: "God help us if the enemy finds out."

The enemy was already onto it. Two Polish janitors, part of the growing underclass of exploited foreign workers throughout Germany, heard something frightening in the northern sky one night in early 1943. They were on the southern part of Usedom Island, and they had the unenviable job of cleaning latrines and drains around the Peenemünde technical complex.

As they rolled along with their pots and horse cart, they saw off in the distance a small winged projectile making a loud, vibrating noise they had never heard before. They mentioned it to another Pole whom they regularly ran into on their rounds. He had an intelligence contact in Warsaw, and their rocket sighting made its way to London in an encoded message.

Since late 1939, a young British scientist named Reginald Jones had been on the lookout for secret weapons in Germany. Trained at Oxford, he was only twenty-eight when the British government enlisted him. His assignment began after Hitler made a cryptic speech in Danzig, warning that the Nazis had "a weapon which is not yet known and with which we ourselves cannot be attacked." That was September 19, 1939. Jones's job, as a scientific advisor to the government, was to work with British intelligence to identify Hitler's secret weapon—or determine if the whole thing were a hoax.

The report by the Polish janitors corroborated other intelligence, including aerial surveillance around Peenemünde. But within the tight group of British security experts, few really believed the Germans had anything close to a missile that could be aimed at a target one hundred miles away or more. It seemed more like rank rumor. The British certainly had no such capability. And the whole thing seemed too advanced, too futuristic, something straight out of a *Buck Rogers* comic strip.

Jones and his intelligence team in London kept gathering string. Within a few months, they got a big break. Two German generals had been captured in northern Africa at El Alamein in late 1942. They were being held at Britain's Interrogation Centre, and on Monday, March 22, 1943, the two were recorded in a bugged room. Their conversation turned to "this rocket business."

In hushed tones, Wilhelm von Thoma spoke to the other officer as the hidden microphones picked up revealing fragments: "I saw it once with Field Marshal Brauchtisch. There is a special ground near Kummersdorf . . . They've always said they would go 15 kilometers [9 miles] into the stratosphere and then . . . You only aim at an area . . . Every few days . . . Frightful . . . The Major there was full of hope. He said, 'Wait until next year, and the fun will start!'"

Though their prison location was supposed to be secret, von Thoma told his comrade that he knew they must be near London. And since he hadn't heard any booming explosions, he said, there must've been a glitch in the rocket development.

Jones and his team were jolted. It was a vital espionage breakthrough, from a highly ranked, knowledgeable officer of the Third Reich. Unless the generals were cleverly misleading them, it was the first credible confirmation that the frightening, long-range rocket they suspected really did exist. A far more specific intelligence report on the Nazi rocket would soon reach Jones via a Frenchwoman who could flirt in impeccable German.

By May 1943, the Allies began planning for an invasion of Germany across the English Channel. Ever since 1941, when Germany invaded the Soviet Union, Joseph Stalin, its dictator, had hoped America and the Allies would open a second front on Germany, compelling it to divide its forces in the east and west. But Dwight D. Eisenhower, supreme commander of the Allied expeditionary forces in Europe, was anxious about the intelligence on Germany's secret weapons: winged bombs and long-range rockets.

On Europe's north coast, the two sides were preparing for an epic showdown. Hitler and his generals anticipated that an Allied invasion was likely through the north of France, and he appointed General Erwin Rommel, known as the Desert Fox, to protect the Atlantic coast with thick walls, heavy artillery, and fortresses. Hitler would later order launch sites for the secret rockets to be positioned at cities along the shoreline, including Normandy. To counter any landing invasion, Germany could fire missiles at the ports across the channel in southern England, cutting off the advancing soldiers from their supply lines.

This was all something entirely new for Eisenhower to contend with. Missiles that could appear without warning, raining down on his troops, and no known way to counteract them. Unless the Allies could find the German missile factories quickly and destroy them, Eisenhower worried it would be difficult, if not impossible, to proceed with plans to invade the Continent, something that would become known as D-Day. Then Hitler could roll through Europe. At that moment in the spring of 1943, Eisenhower was sizing up the unthinkable: Unless he could somehow stop the dreaded missiles, Germany could win the war.

Hugo Eckener, hailed as a heroic Zeppelin captain and builder, had a troubling Nazi past that rendered him an unreliable narrator. © ARCHIV DER LUFTSCHIFFBAU ZEPPELIN GMBH, FRIEDRICHSHAFEN

Ernst Lehmann, the "Little Captain," revealed a hazard on the *Hindenburg* weeks before the tragedy. © ARCHIV DER LUFTSCHIFFBAU ZEPPELIN GMBH, FRIEDRICHSHAFEN

The *Hindenburg* under construction; its pillowy gasbags are visible here. Their protective wiring would later prove menacing. © ARCHIV DER LUFTSCHIFFBAU ZEPPE-LIN GMBH, FRIEDRICHSHAFEN

The ship's outer cover had to be installed, tensioned, and brushed with various coatings by workers on rolling ladders at dizzying heights.

© ARCHIV DER LUFTSCHIFFBAU ZEPPELIN GMBH, FRIEDRICHSHAFEN

The *Hindenburg* name is painted in script on a panel prior to being installed on the airship. © ARCHIV DER LUFTSCHIFFBAU ZEPPELIN GMBH, FRIEDRICHSHAFEN

The *Hindenburg* first arrived in America in 1936 at Lakehurst, New Jersey. WIKIMEDIA COMMONS

The ship's elegant dining room featured sumptuous meals. © ARCHIV DER LUFTSCH-IFFBAU ZEPPELIN GMBH, FRIEDRICHSHAFEN

Passengers were fascinated by the aerial views out the angled windows. © ARCHIV DER LUFTSCHIFFBAU ZEPPELIN GMBH, FRIEDRICHSHAFEN

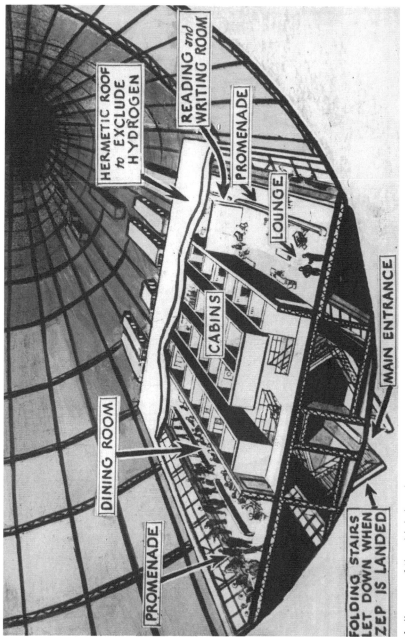

A diagram of the ship's interior. WIKIMEDIA COMMONS

The labels in the diagram read:

HERMETIC ROOF to EXCLUDE HYDROGEN

READING and WRITING ROOM

PROMENADE

LOUNGE

CABINS

MAIN ENTRANCE

DINING ROOM

PROMENADE

FOLDING STAIRS LET DOWN WHEN ZEP IS LANDED

Men look like ants next to the massive *Hindenburg* at Lakehurst, New Jersey, in 1936. WIKIMEDIA COMMONS

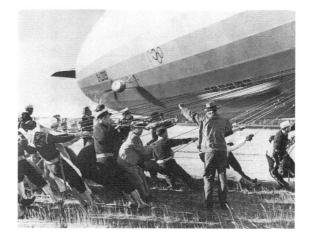

Lilliputians struggle to
tame the monster.
WIKIMEDIA COMMONS

It took careful team-
work to tug the big
ship around the land-
ing field. WIKIMEDIA
COMMONS

Charles Rosendahl, who was commander
at the Lakehurst naval station when the
*Hindenburg* caught fire, buried a whistleblower's tip about prior damage to a
hydrogen gasbag. WIKIMEDIA COMMONS

As the *Hindenburg* approached its mooring mast on May 6, 1937, the top of the ship burst into flame. WIKIMEDIA COMMONS

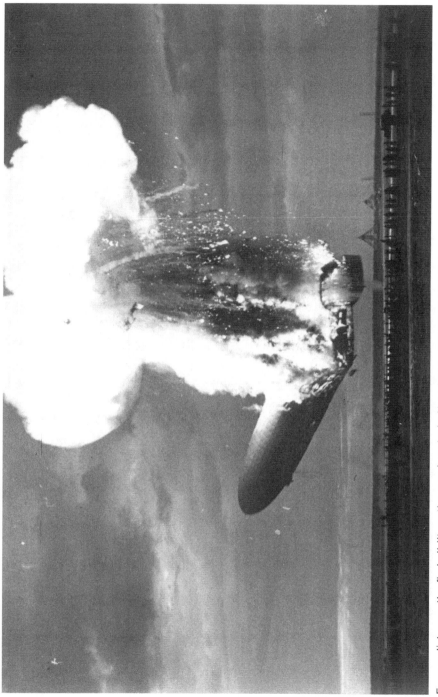

From a distance, the fireball lit up the evening sky in New Jersey. WIKIMEDIA COMMONS

In less than a minute, the mighty *Hindenburg* became a charred skeleton.
WIKIMEDIA COMMONS

Hugo Eckener (third from left, on bottom step) and his son, Knut (in dark hat, tallest man in back row), attended a 1942 meeting at the super-secret V2 rocket installation at Peenemünde, Germany. At far right in the front row is Wernher von Braun, later an architect of America's space program. Only trusted people could set foot on the Nazi base. © ARCHIV DER LUFTSCHIFFBAU ZEPPELIN GMBH, FRIEDRICHSHAFEN

The V2 rocket, which Hitler hoped would turn the war in Germany's favor, terrified the Allies. WIKIMEDIA COMMONS

Nummer 19 13. Mai 1943
Copyright 1943 by Deutscher Verlag, Berlin

**Berliner**

52. Jahrgang Preis 20 Pfennig

# Illustrierte Zeitung

Speer am Steuer . . .

Zusammen mit deutschen Rüstung-Fachleuten wie Porsche (rechts), Maybach (Mitte) und Eckener (im Hintergrund links) erprobt Reichsminister Speer Leistungsfähigkeit von Motor und Fahrgestell eines neuen deutschen Panzers.

Aufnahme: Willi Ruge

The Nazi-controlled *Berlin Illustrated Magazine* of May 13, 1943, shows Hugo Eckener, seated on the far left, in a tank being driven by Albert Speer, the Nazi arms minister. The caption calls the occupants of the new German tank "armaments experts." AUTHOR COPY

Hugo Eckener, far left, listens in as Hitler's arms minister, Albert Speer, speaks to a German air force officer in August 1943.
ULLSTEIN BILD/GETTY IMAGES

Moisej Temkin, a Russian soldier, survived several concentration camps, including one at the Zeppelin factory, by keeping a secret about his identity.
COURTESY OF ALEKSANDR AND BENJAMIN TEMKIN

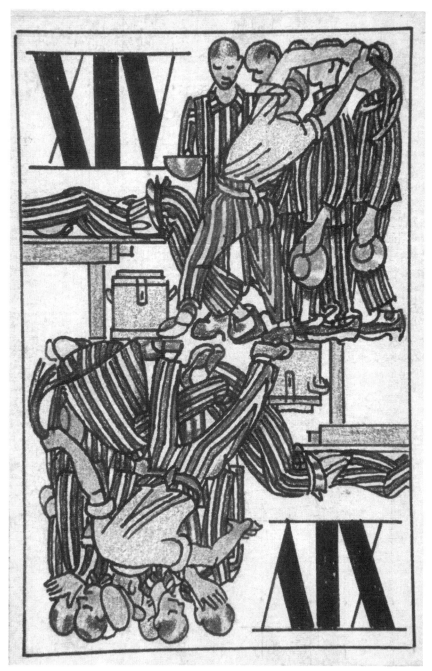

Forced to construct rocket parts at the old Zeppelin factory, slave laborers were sometimes brutally flogged. This tarot card was drawn by a prisoner of several Nazi camps, Boris Kobe, a Slovenian artist and architect. COURTESY OF JURIJ KOBE AND THE NATIONAL MUSEUM OF CONTEMPORARY HISTORY, SLOVENIA

# EARTH

*In a century of Zeppelins and stupid deaths . . . why fight against the flesh when the terrifying problem of the spirit exists?*

—Frederico García Lorca

# 13

# Illicit Fruit

*In the midst of a chaotic world and with human raw material partly*
*sunk to deep moral depths . . . stern, indeed drastic interventions and*
*methods are unavoidable.*
　　　　—Hugo Eckener, 1934 radio talk endorsing Hitler

It had been almost three years that he carried a gun. Then
Moisej Temkin was captured by the Germans in June of 1941. Imprisoned, head shaven, the young Russian soldier, not yet twenty-six, hadn't
seen his thick, dark hair in over two years.

When the trainload of Red Army men arrived inside the barbed-
wire fence that summer of 1943, Temkin looked around, his eyebrows still
thick, stunned at how large the prison was. Barracks after barracks after
barracks—it was a town unto itself. At the north end of the camp, dark
smoke wafted from a tall brick stack.

As Temkin was taking the place in, SS guards suddenly beat him and
the other Soviet soldiers with rifle butts and fists, shepherding them into
a tarp-covered truck. They were crowded inside and motoring away, somewhere. Temkin couldn't tell why they were taken away so quickly from the
large camp, or where they were now, a short drive away. He did not know
he was at an SS shooting range called Herbertshausen, where firing squads
shot more than 4,000 Soviet soldiers to death in 1941 and 1942.

He came to a wide courtyard with a large iron gate. Across from
it, there was a long, high wall spattered with blood. He was white with
fear. As he began taking in the ghastly surroundings, guards milled about.
Gestapo men ordered the Russians to undress and line up in rows of five.

It was clear they would face a firing squad. Suddenly, one of the Gestapo men shouted "*Genug!*" or "Enough!" The men were then ordered to dress again and jump onto a truck.

The truck returned to the big camp. Temkin did not know why the Gestapo men called off the execution. He stood bewildered in the large camp again.

"Do you all know where you are?" said one man in prison stripes, speaking in his mother Russian tongue. "This is one of the most famous camps in Germany—Dachau." It was August 1943.

At the turn of the century, the remote land of Dachau was an artists' town. It had unrelenting winters, with heavy snow falling into April. The bleak terrain of peat bogs and moors drew landscape painters, who could afford to live there more simply and cheaply than in nearby Munich. They were inspired by the beauty of the Alps in the distance. An artist colony formed. They painted the marshy uplands and especially loved to paint one particular old cottage nestled by timeworn poplars.

In 1933, the Third Reich converted the painters' colony into a penal colony. With fanfare, Heinrich Himmler, chief of police in Munich, announced in the newspapers the formation of *ein Konzentrationslager*, "a concentration camp," to remove as many as 5,000 political prisoners from good German society. The inmates were deemed a national security threat. The bad elements were concentrated together, away from society.

Built from the ruins of a World War I explosives factory, the Dachau grounds were earmarked by the Nazi Party for a complex of "protective custody" barracks and offices. From the beginning, the camp planned to extract free labor from its prisoners.

Sometime after Dachau opened, the SS, the Reich's political police and administrators of the camp, created a museum where visitors could come and view wax and plaster models of Dachau prisoners, all types of regime enemies. Criminals had hideous scars on their faces. Jews were portrayed haggling with others, and robbing them. Sometimes, SS tours concluded by displaying a live prisoner handicapped somehow or disfigured physically. The point was to portray how repulsive the prisoners were, to justify their removal from society.

Dachau became the model camp for a vast network of prisons across Germany and its occupied territories. It was a Nazi laboratory for terror. Three months before its gates opened, the SS drew up a disciplinary and penal code, a canon of brutality. In its introduction, it states: "Tolerance is a sign of weakness."

Temkin was lucky to arrive alive. He was young—that helped. After captivity out east for nearly two years, he had been cooped up in a freight train for nearly 1,200 miles, traveling from a concentration camp in southern Latvia, packed into a padlocked boxcar with dozens of other men, sweating and vomiting. There were no toilets on board, and food was very sparse. Their trip lasted more than a week. Temkin and his new arrivals were regarded, for registration purposes, as a "shipment."

For two years or so, Germany had been methodically ridding the lands it had conquered of hostile combatants and resisters, executing many and locking away tens of thousands in camps. As the war worsened for Germany by the winter of 1942, the Nazis began raiding their eastern camps and transporting trainloads of those prisoners to the Fatherland, forcing them under the most brutal conditions to dig trenches, tunnel out bomb shelters, and work at Peenemünde, Zeppelin, and other armaments factories.

Temkin and his fellow soldiers were more fortunate than their comrades who arrived in Dachau the previous November. Their journey through wintry Poland and Czechoslovakia and into Bavaria took ten days. The prisoners were given enough food for only two days. When the train pulled into Dachau, there were 300 bodies dead on arrival. Some of the famished men grew desperate. Six of the corpses had been gnawed into.

On reentering the grounds at Dachau, Temkin and his Russian compatriots were escorted inside the wrought-iron entrance gate. Woven into the ironwork were the words *Arbeit Macht Frei*: Work Sets You Free. Squared watchtowers looked down upon the grounds, with machine guns pointed outward.

The Russians stood face to face with jackbooted SS guards, with steel helmets, skull and crossbones pins, and whips and pistols at the ready. They shouted insults and obscenities at the new prisoners: "Communists, bastards, Russian pigs!" Some pointed guns at the prisoners and joked they would happily shoot them down, except that it would waste a bullet, which cost chicken feed, three *Pfennig*. Temkin would face much worse if they discovered what he was hiding.

After registering and being photographed front and side view, Temkin and the others were led to the barbers. Some of the haircutters were untrained prisoners, who sometimes cut the prisoners' scalps. Haste, inexperience, worn blades. Mandatory disinfectants sprayed would then burn their head wounds.

Stripped naked, they stepped into showers with SS men leering. Once finished, the prisoners relinquished any personal belongings, which were supposed to be catalogued, and were handed a striped uniform, galoshes or clogs, a mug, fork, and spoon. Doctors hastily looked them over, and dentists looked for gold fillings, noting them on a detainee's file for extraction in case he died.

Uniforms usually didn't fit, and being handed two shoes of different sizes was not unusual. Some men struggled to button their shirts; others had to roll trouser cuffs up. They had to sew on their uniforms the badges that listed their prisoner number. For Temkin, 38681. Temkin's triangular badge had a large *R* on it, denoting Russian nationality. This marked him, along with the Italians and Jews, for extra-severe punishment under the SS prison mentality.

Temkin and the others were kept in quarantine for several weeks. The precaution was to quell the spread of any disease. On arrival, nearly every prisoner was weak, thin, and malnourished. They were kept isolated in their own barbed-wire pen. They were humiliated and initiated, taught that they had no rights, that they were at the whims and mercy of their guards.

Addressing the "filth" and "pigs" with great disgust, SS men shouted that the smallest defiance meant execution and the crematorium, Temkin would recall. Before he arrived, the original crematorium hut was replaced by a larger building to accommodate more and more corpses. Polish priests, who were trained as bricklayers, were compelled to build it. With the prevailing west winds and the camp chimney wafting smoke day and night, there was no escaping the dismal stench of burnt flesh.

Over a few weeks, the prisoners were drilled in how to march in a column to roll call, which occurred every morning and evening, where they stood for forty-five minutes or more while guards accounted for every single prisoner in the entire camp. Temkin, who didn't speak German, had to learn to sing German marching songs, including one popular number among Nazi youth groups and soldiers, "*Die blauen Dragoner sie reiten*," or "The Blue Dragons, They Are Riding."

He learned to distinguish SS ranks, from the lowest private to the Reichsführer Himmler. He learned just how to react to the two-word command "*Mützen . . . ab!*" ("Caps . . . off!"). He had to move his right hand to his head at first command, then on the second, remove his cap and quickly clench it against his right thigh. He had to respectfully beg to visit the latrine.

Temkin settled into his new routine. Twice a day, in the morning and at night, he and the others had to take a cold shower, with guards inspecting. Anyone who cheated, trying not to stand under the cold water or taking a quick shower, was severely beaten, he would recall. In the morning, breakfast was a cup of black tea; dinner, a serving of spinach or turnip soup and a bit of bread. At bedtime, one of the prisoners who acted as a superintendent took out an illicit harmonica and quietly played the dozing men Soviet songs.

About the time Temkin was to be released from the quarantine-barracks block, he got word he was on a list for a transfer—always a frightening prospect. It was to a new camp called Friedrichshafen.

On June 20, 1943, a squadron of four-engine British Lancasters roared into Friedrichshafen and bombed the main buildings of the Zeppelin complex, the historic cradle of most of the world's airships. Britain's Royal Air Force carried out the attack after intelligence showed the old Zeppelin factory was producing Würzburg radar equipment, critical for Germany's air force. The Air Ministry in Berlin announced that the surprise attack, which penetrated deeply into Germany, rendered heavy damage throughout the industrial city of 30,000 people.

It was misinformation, to throw the Allies off the scent. The bombers did not touch the Reich's classified new project, Hall 3, which was about to start A4 rocket production, and its secret Zeppelin slave camp, just completed and ready for a thousand prisoners. Temkin would be arriving soon.

Construction of the Friedrichshafen camp, Don, began in early 1943. Plans called for seven barracks for slave workers and one for SS administrators. An electrically charged wire, about seven feet high, would surround the slave barracks. Apple orchards bordered the concentration camp.

After the meetings with the Peenemünde planners, Zeppelin agreed to accept a loan of nearly five million Reichsmarks to fund construction of Hall 3, the A4 factory to be hidden in Friedrichshafen, about as far from the shores of Peenemünde in Germany as possible. It was massive, 750 feet long, nearly as long as the *Graf Zeppelin* that Eckener had once flown around a very different world.

Eckener was excited about Hall 3's prospects. "This facility," he raved in one corporate report, "is our greatest and most modern manufacturing plant. . . . Steam, water, electricity, gas, compressed air, etc., can be fed to every part of the facility, without much effort, through concrete traversable channels that run lengthwise and crosswise and that conform to manufacturing requirements."

He dreamt of a new future with his modern factory, subsidized by the Third Reich. Hall 3, he promised, would "continue to be the main business of the LZ when production resumes after the war." Important raw materials had to be ordered to make the rocket a success: aluminum, magnesium, people.

A little over one hundred miles northeast of Friedrichshafen, Dachau was emerging as a central warehouse for slave laborers in southern Germany. Eckener needed more than 800 units, and Don was built solely to accommodate workers for the A4 rocket. Under an ambitious production schedule, Zeppelin was to fabricate 300 of the A4s a month, while Peenemünde was responsible for another 300.

Using slave labor to construct the camp, Don was rushed into existence in a matter of months, starting in late 1942. It cost 597,635 Reichsmarks. The project ate up a nearby farm, and the owner had to take a loss on his property, as the purchase was needed for the war effort. The Zeppelin factory grounds were near a Friedrichshafen main street, the *Hochstraße*. Hall 3 and the prisoners' barracks were arranged closely for quick marches to and from work.

Moisej Temkin was part of the "shipments" sent from Dachau to replenish the workforce at Zeppelin. Of the nearly 800 German Zeppelin workers drafted into service in 1942, 56 had already died in battle. According to contract terms with the SS, the Luftschiffbau Zeppelin would pay at a typical rate of four Reichsmarks a day for unskilled workers and six Reichsmarks for skilled ones. Zeppelin managers told the workers what to do. The SS did the rest, supplying security, food, clothing, and slave quarters. The spare, inhuman conditions the SS provided barely kept the prisoners alive.

With the army's secret blessing for the rocket, the Luftschiffbau Zeppelin actually leapfrogged other firms vying for prison labor. Given the urgency of the A4, Dachau pulled skilled laborers from granite quarries and prisoners were moved from other concentration camps, including Mauthausen and Buchenwald, to supply manpower to Friedrichshafen. They also press-ganged Temkin.

At Dachau, Temkin and another hundred inmates quarantined by the SS were disinfected. They had their clothes laundered and boarded the national railroad, the Reichsbahn, under stern surveillance, for Don.

It was a mercifully short train ride, in steamy August of 1943, and beautiful when Temkin arrived in Friedrichshafen. He could see the Alps in the distance, and could hear the bells ringing in the Palace Church, which had onion-bulb towers, like the ones at home in Russia.

Between thirty and forty SS members ran the Friedrichshafen camp. There was a dog kennel, with German shepherds, Rottweilers, boxers, and Great Danes. The camp commandant was Georg Grünberg, still baby-faced at thirty-seven. The tall SS lieutenant walked the grounds with jackboots and a whip. He would have discipline, as the prisoners would learn, answering even tenderness with cruelty. He needed to be able to answer his superiors, at any given moment, supported by the correct regulation, that all was in order: *Alles in Ordnung.*

Grünberg came to Friedrichshafen from Auschwitz, where he began his SS training in 1932. He beat some prisoners himself, but usually left the job to subordinates like the thug who liked to bludgeon prisoners with his fists and feet.

Temkin found conditions similar to Dachau. Wooden bunk beds had to be made quickly each morning, with military precision. His cot had to be wrinkle-free and neatly creased. Failing an inspection invited all kinds of abuse, being kicked repeatedly in the shins with heavy boots being one. Some prisoners so feared this that they cowered all night on the floor, afraid to mess up the bed for the morning inspection. But sleeping on the floor was forbidden as well.

After showering, and trying to use the latrine with dozens of other men and no privacy, workers were assembled on a square in front of the camp for roll call. Guards took inventory, counting them. They were in assigned groups of twenty to one hundred and marched with barking guards and dogs to Hall 3. They had to show a special ID to enter.

They were not allowed to discuss their work with other laborers, who only knew Hall 3 as "the secret department." Knut Eckener was boss of plant operations, and he and his father oversaw the important military project work at the factory. They couldn't have helped but notice how much the ribbed inner structure of the rockets taking shape resembled the Zeppelins they once built there.

In the hall, Temkin and his coworkers stood at row after row of tubular metal frames, the outer cover for the rocket. Over the eleven-hour workday, with an hour break, they would lift, weld, rivet, saw, pack, and assemble curved panels into missile bodies. Temkin was a manual laborer, sturdy. He carried boards and iron to the cramped work stations and sawed pipes with a hacksaw.

As at other armaments factories, prisoners looked for opportunities, putting their lives at risk, to yank out wires, solder welds too weakly, or tighten nuts too much or too little. There were thousands of parts to the A4 rocket. The cost alone was about 100,000 Reichsmarks each. Tampering with rockets in progress meant they might malfunction when fired. Anything to save Allied lives.

According to SS camp regulations, what constituted sabotage was widely interpreted. Tampering in any way with barbed wire, electrical boxes, water pipes, even telephone lines, could mean immediate execution. If the damage was caused by innocent negligence, the guilty party would be impounded in dreadful solitary confinement. "Doubtful cases," the rules conclude, "will be treated as sabotage."

For breakfast, Temkin and the other inmates usually had only a bitter cup of substitute coffee. Made from cheap roasted grains instead of coffee beans, it was warm at least, staving off hunger a bit. Ribs protruding, he and his fellow prisoners in Friedrichshafen found themselves preoccupied with food, talking about it all day, hoping for some extra potato peels at dinner. Usually they had only watery soup, a scrap of bread. If they were lucky, there was sometimes some jam or margarine. Some of the civilians in the factory took pity on the prisoners, Temkin would later recall, secretly giving them a plum, a pear, a piece of bread, or a cigarette.

The SS dog kennel was near the kitchen in the compound for the SS administrators and soldiers. The dogs were there to menace the workers, to hunt for any escapees. The SS hounds were generally well-fed, with meat, bread, potatoes, and milk. Prisoners who worked at the kennel were envied; they had a chance to filch some of the dogs' rations. The hounds would be employed in a most hideous way when a Russian prisoner tried to escape.

The dogs barked constantly, and the guards never took their eyes off the prisoners. Most guards were failures at their civilian jobs or ex-convicts, who were schooled in the ways of brutality, told they would never advance in the SS unless they had a record of being cruel, merciless.

Under SS regulations, three or more prisoners congregating, speaking together, constituted a possible rebellion and invited severe punishment. The guards courted secret informants from the prisoners' ranks, with gifts of cigarettes or extra food, making everyone wary of everyone else.

Under Rule 11 of the camp penal code, death by hanging awaited anyone suspected of instigating "subversion." That could include loitering with others or trying to communicate with the world outside the barbed wire, by tossing notes attached to stones or other projectiles outside the camp.

It crushed Temkin, to work ten hours a day, dizzy from hunger, menaced by guards and growling dogs, with no end in sight, to build weapons to help the Third Reich kill Russian comrades. Weapons that would prolong his very imprisonment.

By fall, when Temkin slipped back into bed for lights out, it began to get chilly, and there was typically only one worn blanket to make it through the night. The barracks were unheated. To keep warm, shivering men huddled together overnight, exhausted. "Then we slept like the dead," he recalled.

As 1943 wore into winter, Sundays and mail offered some hope. Sunday was the only free day. Allowing the prisoners a day of rest was not altruism. The idea was to raise morale so they would work harder the rest of the week. Some read the few old newspapers that were passed around. Some slept. Some wrote letters.

Letters were allowed, and prisoners craved keeping in touch with their loved ones in the outside world. Content was restricted to family matters; regulations strictly forbade putting in writing anything about camp conditions. Mail was censored at Dachau before being sent on to Friedrichshafen. A suspicious sentence, even a clause, would end the mail privilege. One of the harshest penalties the SS could impose, they learned, was to revoke it. The threat alone won utter submission.

At the Don camp, the slaves were housed right next to the thundering anti-aircraft artillery, on the western edge of the camp. The slave quarters were only 300 yards from the factories, which the German air force and army must have known would become a target of Allied bombing attempts at some point. With no bomb shelter to protect them, the prisoners in Friedrichshafen were sitting ducks.

Trying to escape was futile. Temkin and other prisoners would whisper to one another when someone had tried to, or was accused of trying to, the outcome often being the same. One day, a Polish prisoner, a man of thirty-five, was suspected of planning an escape to Switzerland. After appearing before Grünberg, the accused was sentenced to torture, which was never carried out in the factory for fear of later incriminating SS guards. Their code called for secrecy about their doings.

An instrument of torment common to Nazi concentration camps was called the Bock. It was a wooden table with its center scooped out. The Friedrichshafen guards laid the alleged escapee face down into the depression and fastened his hands and feet to the Bock. The SS men then loudly flogged his back with an *Ochsenziemer*, a whip usually used to corral stubborn cattle. It was made out of dried ox penis.

Each time they struck the prisoner, he had to call out the number. *Eins. Zwei. Drei* ... Most of the victims slurred the numbers, or lost count or consciousness, around eighteen. Typical sentences were twenty-five to thirty lashes. The Polish prisoner's flogging ran to forty-eight. When they unstrapped him, he had to be carried to the sick barracks, where his wounds were treated with iodine tinctures. He was ordered back to the factory the next day. He was an essential welder of aluminum containers.

*Alles in Ordnung.* All is in order.

Even German prisoners were dealt with severely in Friedrichshafen. Two men, Otto Jung and Karl Schuler, were caught flirting with a French woman and a Ukrainian one at a neighboring detention camp in November of 1943. Jung was only twenty-three and ended up in Dachau, swept up by the Gestapo after fighting on the wrong side in the Spanish Civil War. He was a political prisoner, number 43585. He arrived in Friedrichshafen earlier that year with Schuler, a thirty-two-year-old German carpenter. Accused of being a Communist, he was prisoner number 932.

For two weeks, the German prisoners would signal the women and then throw little love notes tied to twigs or stones over the fence. Romance over barbed wire. One day, the men carved out apples and stuffed notes to their sweethearts inside. Schuler signed his letters "H," apparently for cover in case he was discovered. When Schuler tossed his apple over the fence into the other camp, another prisoner picked it up and turned it over to an SS guard.

Jung and Schuler were summoned before Grünberg, the commandant of Don. It was Wednesday, November 3, 1943. In his jackboots, Grünberg interrogated them both. When he sized up the situation, the commandant ordered both men to suffer twenty lashes on the Bock.

The punishment order cited a "love affair," smuggling letters over the fence, and using impermissible words such as "swine-dogs" to refer to SS guards. A little over a week later, on November 12, Grünberg had them both sent 300 miles away from their women friends, to the Buchenwald concentration camp.

Deposited in the Zeppelin camp disciplinary records is the note Schuler stuffed in the apple. It reads in part:

*My dear child!*

*Remain my little star, my golden child, remain true to me. Don't be so sad, everything will turn out well. . . .*

*Child, there's also something urgent I have to tell you, the watchman you gave the apple to yesterday, be on your guard with him. That swine-dog just wants to possess your body. He said something in my presence that I'd rather not repeat to you. . . .*

*Child, my dear child, don't leave me, I'll never forget you, never, never ever,*

*Your H*

# 14

# The German Missile Crisis

In the waning months of 1943, Zeppelin and the A4 Special Committee would begin hiding the rocket's factories, in a game of cat-and-mouse between the Nazis and the Allies that would stretch across Germany. And underneath it.

It was idyllic the previous summer of 1943, the little Baltic island paradise that was Peenemünde. Isolated from the war in Germany, it was removed from the ration cards, the air-raid alerts, the bombings. There was the one air attack near the base three summers earlier, when a British plane got lost and released a bomb on a local farm, leaving casualties of a haystack and a noncombatant cow.

Otherwise, rocket work progressed quietly. In the year or so since Hugo and Knut Eckener had been there, the base had become home to 12,000 people, with its own restaurants, shops, and other nightlife. German engineers with slide rules in their pockets calculated trajectories, thrust, and throw weights in their offices by day, and strolled with their families along the Baltic shoreline in the evening. Nightfall was over sparkling water.

Hugo Eckener returned at least twice more over several years, recalled Eberhard Rees, a head of technical development at Peenemünde. "He was very much interested in our work there," Rees would later recount. Because Eckener was such a celebrity from his Zeppelin days, Rees added, "It was always quite an event when he came to Peenemünde."

British reconnaissance planes kept a steady eye on the little island, even as England's top military strategists still squabbled over the credibility of the missile threat. One dismissed the whole rocket business as a "mare's nest," a hoax. German army officials, worried about leaks from its growing base of forced foreign workers, developed a cover name for Peenemünde, a word that was banned from all correspondence starting in June. The new authorized name was Home Artillery Park 11.

On a Wednesday evening, August 17, 1943, 600 British bombers flew under a full moon toward Peenemünde, loaded with over 1,600 tons of explosives. The attack was ordered after Winston Churchill reviewed the intelligence indicating Peenemünde was a true threat, an important arms laboratory that was finishing up a novel rocket invention. The bombing raid destroyed some key buildings, but failed to halt development. It also missed its objective of assassinating the scientists who developed the A4 by striking their living quarters. Bombs struck a camp nearby, though, killing more than 500 foreign laborers.

The Peenemünde air raid was part of a concerted Allied campaign, to be code-named "Crossbow," to seek and destroy the German secret armaments network. That mission would soon target Friedrichshafen. The word was out. It wasn't only making radar equipment, it was part of the terrorist-rocket industry.

The raid rattled Hitler. Three days after it, August 20, the Führer ordered Speer, Himmler, and others from his inner circle to meet to plan a move of the Peenemünde operation to some secret new location underground. Allied airpower was just too overwhelming. The A4 Special Committee chose a spot smack in the center of Germany, in the Harz mountain range, near a town called Nordhausen. The industrialists on the committee took advantage of the ruins of Peenemünde to seize greater control of the rocket project from the army.

The A4 Special Committee, led by the train dictator Degenkolb, requisitioned some 30,000 prison laborers from the SS that August to begin a near-impossible plan: gore out the inside of a mountain and hide a modern industrial factory inside it. It would require an elaborate network of tunnels, some big enough for locomotives to chuff in and out. The rapid tunneling and fabricating of a new underground factory put the businessmen behind the rocket in an irreversible alliance with the SS, Germany's powerful terrorist police.

The committee set recklessly fast deadlines to transfer machine tools from Friedrichshafen and Peenemünde. There were already some tunnels bored out for a fuel depot there, but slave labor would soon be dispatched to blast and dig more. Top to bottom, the whole operation was a rush job, to be completed in months, one that would prove deadly for thousands of slave laborers.

As the tunneling got under way, Berlin also decided that Zeppelin would make only the propellant tanks and the twenty-foot middle fuselage of the rocket, important parts, but a downgrade from full production. Friedrichshafen was too vulnerable to aerial attack, it was felt, on the southern edge of the Nazi empire. Eckener could not hide his bitter disappointment, reporting in the Zeppelin annual report for 1943: "It was decided by those higher up that we were no longer to build the whole machine." The A4 he camouflaged with the word "machine."

Even at that, to hold on to the contracts he had, Eckener had to spread his production to other locations, for secrecy. One place chosen was the little, rural village of Saulgau. Spy planes would never look there. A farm-equipment company, Josef Bautz AG, had just built a large factory, 95 feet wide by 500 feet long, to make a harvesting machine called a grain binder. It also had a railway line, crucial to get the rocket components north to the mountain factory for final assembly.

Knut Eckener, as operations director of the Zeppelin company, approached Bautz in October 1943, explaining that he needed their factory for the war effort, but the managers resisted. They were not interested in making armaments, and some objected to the slave labor they knew it would entail. Knowing he had the clout of Arms Minister Speer on their side, Knut pressed ahead. As a first step, he had prisoners drag out the mowing machines stored at Bautz and dump them in a gravel pit.

Six army trucks later arrived with the first production machines from Friedrichshafen. This time, the managers kept the factory gate locked and resisted. Over several hours, phone calls were made. The Bautz factory director was told he had to surrender the factory for military needs. The district administrator and the Gestapo arrived outside the gate to back up Knut Eckener's demands to be allowed in. At 5:45 in the evening, the Bautz director relented, barely avoiding Gestapo arrest for resistance.

The gates swung open, and the army trucks rolled in. The empty grain-binder factory was filled with rocket-production machines. Within weeks, the Luftschiffbau Zeppelin transferred 335 of its prisoners to Saulgau to begin producing A4 shells and propellant tanks, the same work they had done in Friedrichshafen. Moisej Temkin would also work stints there.

In reality, the new camp was a mini-Don, surrounded by barbed wire, built for sixty prisoners. Armed guards manned four watchtowers in the corners of the camp. A road through the site was named Zeppelin Street. Georg Grünberg became commandant for Saulgau as well, commuting the thirty miles between there and Friedrichshafen to make periodic inspections of the prisoners and guards.

From now on, the farm-machine factory would pound plowshares into swords.

Once Peenemünde was bombed, the Allies fully expected the Germans to move production to new locations—that is, if they guessed correctly that the rocket was beyond test stage and ready to manufacture in numbers. That fall, Reginald Jones, the British expert in charge of assessing the missile threat, had been sorting through vague and conflicting reports. Then one particular memo stunned him. It came from France.

"It appears that the final stage has been reached in developing a stratospheric bomb of an entirely new type," the memo said. "Trials are said to have been made, without explosive charge, from Usedom towards the Baltic. . . . The trials are understood to have given immediate excellent results as regards accuracy, and it was the success of these trials that Hitler was referring to when he spoke of 'new weapons that will change the face of the war' when the Germans use them."

The memo for the first time named a key German officer in the rocket program. It included details on the color-coded IDs needed to enter the Peenemünde technical complex, and described plans for reinforced concrete platforms to launch the weapon. It was precise, detailed, convincing. The Nazi rocket was ready to roll along assembly lines.

The surprising intelligence came from an attractive twenty-three-year-old woman in Paris, Jeannie Rousseau, who spoke perfect German and worked as an interpreter for a group of French businessmen, helping them negotiate contracts with their German occupiers. Over weeks, she cozied up to some German army officers, who did not know the woman they knew as Madeleine Chauffour actually worked for the French Resistance.

Over drinks each night at the Hotel Majestic, where the German military commander's staff was based, she teased and taunted the soldiers who bragged to her about working on a secret project. Looking at them wide-eyed, she would recall, she kept insisting they must be mad, with all this talk of an astounding new weapon that flew over vast distances, faster than any airplane. "I kept saying, 'What you are telling me cannot be true!'"

It was all so technical that she couldn't understand much of what they told her. To impress her, one officer began to show her diagrams. Without ever writing anything in the officers' presence, she memorized every detail she heard and saw, passing it along to her intelligence contact. It was an amazing act of bravery, given that she faced horrible torture by the Gestapo along with execution had they figured out she was a spy. Relying on this information, the British organized another bombing raid against Peenemünde, and hunted in earnest for where the Germans moved the operation.

The German missile threat gave Eisenhower, the Allied supreme commander, fits. As early as the fall of 1943, Churchill began sharing his alarm with Roosevelt. "During the last six months, evidence has continued to accumulate . . . that the Germans are preparing an attack on England, particularly London, by means of very long-range rockets which may conceivably weigh 60 tons and carry an explosive charge of 10 to 20 tons." A British home security official recommended emergency plans be drawn up to evacuate one million Londoners.

Eisenhower, in turn, had to pacify Churchill as well as concern himself with what a German rocket offensive might mean as he helped plan what would be a historic massing of troops and ships in southern England. He needed to analyze—with a smuggled sketch, resistance reports, and the best intelligence available—how seriously a missile onslaught on London could disrupt a continental invasion. No one among the Allies had even seen an A4 yet.

In the final months of preparing for the Normandy invasion, Eisenhower was forced to turn much of America's firepower to neutralize the rocket threat. After December 5, 1943, in fact, bombing German secret-weapons sites took priority over the offensive bombing against major German cities and the country's aircraft industry. Targeting suspected rocket sites, the Allies attacked with B-17s, B-24s, B-26s, A-20s, Mitchells, Bostons, and Mosquitos.

"We bombed the suspected launching sites along the coast of northwestern Europe," Eisenhower would recall, "where our reconnaissance photography showed numerous facilities and installations that could not be interpreted in terms of any known weapon." British and American planes would fly thousands of individual sorties solely to target secret-weapons sites.

Germany might easily have been defeated by the end of 1943 but for one thing. The exploitation of millions of foreign workers and concentration camp prisoners allowed Nazi Germany to wage war months after the German workforce had been depleted. In agriculture and arms alone, a third of the workforce was forced labor of one stripe or another.

Eckener exploited an even heavier load of unfortunates. In his final reckoning for the Luftschiffbau Zeppelin for 1943, only about 42 percent of the 4,563 workers were German. More than half were forced laborers and concentration camp prisoners, 1,202 of them from Dachau, including Temkin.

Eckener noted in the Zeppelin corporate report for the year that 120 German workers were recruited into military service. "We recall with gratitude and reverence our 82 other fellow workers who lost their lives in the field and at home in the struggle for our people's continued existence," he wrote in the report.

And the Luftschiffbau Zeppelin, under Eckener, began managing a forced labor camp on its property. "The civilian laborers' camp operated by the German Labor Front was taken over by us and continued as the factory's own camp," Eckener wrote in his review of 1943. He seemed to take pride in managing the camp better than the Reich's main labor organization had. "Through intensive protective measures in the camp and in the plant, it was possible to limit a typhus epidemic originating in the camp to a small circle."

The Zeppelin company was raking in money from the war. It booked revenue of 12.8 million Reichsmarks for radar equipment and, for the new A4 project, another 5.4 million RM, which equaled about $2 million then, or $29 million in 2019 dollars. By comparison, the *Graf Zeppelin* and *Hindenburg* brought in only 1.7 million RM in the company's last full year flying Zeppelins, 1936.

The Zeppelin company was enjoying the war. "We were fully occupied with armament production; the manufacture of peacetime goods ceased completely," Eckener wrote in his review of 1943. "Hand in hand with the intensification of war production, there were increasing difficulties . . . obtaining laborers and raw materials. The assignment of foreign laborers and of prisoners from the Dachau concentration camp would not have been able to remedy the lack of personnel if our German staff had not been compensated by increased performance and by taking on greater responsibility. We are happy to be able to state this, with thanks and acknowledgment."

With a black pen, he signed the report, "Eckener."

## 15

# "An Inside Job"

MOISEJ TEMKIN COULD HEAR THEM COMING. BOMBERS HOWLED FOR several minutes through dark skies toward the Zeppelin complex, Thursday evening, April 27, 1944. They were British planes. The anti-aircraft artillery right next to Temkin's barracks began to thunder. He and the other inmates instantly dove anywhere they could for cover, sick skeletons in chaos. For hours, fire, shrapnel, shrieks, explosions. It rained bombs.

"Prisoners ran around the camp as if possessed," Temkin would recall, "and SS men with German Shepherds ran around the fence." All the barracks and the kitchen would burn down, but the barbed wire held up.

"Many prisoners died that night, but the SS men did not care," Temkin remembered. "The main thing was that no one had escaped."

On their mission, the Royal Air Force (RAF) planes would drop 3,500 tons of bombs in that one massive assault. For two weeks straight, the Allies bombed railroads, factories, military bases, the entire Nazi war machine. Gearing up for an Allied invasion of the Continent, more than 6,000 British and American aircraft unleashed 65,000 tons of bombs in Europe in the last two weeks of April.

In the attack on Friedrichshafen, thirty-six RAF planes were shot down in heavy anti-aircraft fire from the ground, as the Germans tried to protect their tank-motor factory and their coveted rocket works.

Months earlier, Zeppelin management had approved tunneling at Friedrichshafen for a deep bombproof shelter, up to seventy feet belowground, with seven entrances, capable of protecting 5,000 people. But it was still under construction. It was not yet large enough for anyone other than the German employees of the Luftschiffbau Zeppelin. Entrance required an ID. Two dozen of the 1,200 prisoners died in the bombing, along with five SS guards.

After the attack, many people evacuated the town of Friedrichshafen, convinced the Allied planes would return. Hall 3 was not very damaged in the bombing. Temkin and the other prisoners were ordered to clean up the debris around it. Some also had to defuse the duds, the bombs that had failed to explode.

By this point, Germany had more than 1.6 million prisoners of war working as slaves in its war industries. Many were housed near the factories that would only continue to draw heavy bombing. There were few bomb shelters, and with armed guards around, no way to flee the grounds in an aerial attack. It was a miserable predicament.

The Reich was not holding together. Supplies of everything were thinning. Allied planes were meeting less and less resistance, and Russian forces were advancing from the east. It was just a matter of time, everyone knew, before Allied forces would invade continental Europe.

Fears of security leaks and sabotage rose. Knut Eckener, who supervised production at the main Zeppelin factory, gained a new role. He was appointed an *Abwehrbeauftragter* at the plant, meaning he had to report any suspicious activity to military intelligence. It was an important security job. Knut was expected to help unearth any suspected sabotage efforts by the prisoners and pass reports up the chain. Without many questions, those so reported could be hanged.

As digging continued on the air-raid tunnel at the Zeppelin factory that summer, the Allies finally landed. D-Day. June 6, 1944. More than 150,000 Allied troops arrived on the northern coast of France, as history's largest seaborne invasion. Withstanding heavy fighting at Normandy, the Allies had finally cracked the continental fortress of the Nazis.

Though the A4 rockets weren't ready in time to stop the invasion, Hitler and some of his generals continued to believe that they were strategically important, to repel the Allied forces and to terrorize England. Never before had a single weapon, in such a dark hour in Germany, given the Nazis such hope.

"What an inspiring murder weapon!" Goebbels reflected in his diaries. "When the first of these missiles screams down in London, something akin to panic will break out among the British public!"

After all the airstrikes and the Normandy landing, Hitler seethed for revenge. Yet to be fired, the A4 gained a new name in beleaguered Germany: *Vergeltungswaffen*, or Vengeance Weapon. A winged flying bomb, also being readied, was named the V-1. And henceforth the A4 rocket became known as the V-2, Vengeance Weapon 2.

On July 20, a little more than a month after D-Day, Hitler and some top generals were strategizing in a conference room at his Wolf's Lair compound in East Prussia. The army's chief of operations was spelling out just how dismal the war was on the Eastern Front. Suddenly, a blast. Shrapnel, chaos. A bomb in a briefcase under the conference table had exploded. Hitler survived the assassination attempt, but he had a lacerated back, a punctured eardrum, and burns on his legs and face.

Thinking Hitler had been killed that afternoon, a conspirator in Berlin moved quickly to order the arrest of key figures in the Nazi leadership, ordering Otto Ernst Remer, a young leader of an elite guard battalion in the capital, to arrest Goebbels. When Remer and his soldiers arrived at the Propaganda Ministry office, a terrified Goebbels assured them that Hitler was, in fact, alive. To prove it, Goebbels connected Remer by phone to Hitler.

Hitler told Remer that he was now in command of all Berlin's troops and to crush the coup attempt. A tall, thirty-two-year-old officer with a skeletal face and pointed ears, Remer quickly encircled several key army buildings, trapping some of the ringleaders. Within hours, order was restored in Berlin, and the attempted revolt fell apart. The Gestapo would begin a campaign of widespread disappearances, killings, and trials in retaliation. Some 2,000 army officers and resistance suspects would lose, or take, their lives in what would become a sequel to the Night of the Long Knives.

On the Thursday afternoon of the bombing, Germany was rocked by radio reports of the inside job. "A bomb attempt was made on the Führer's life today," DNB, the official news agency, reported in Germany. "The Führer, himself, besides light burns and bruises, sustained no injuries. He immediately took up his routine work afterwards, and, as it had been planned, received Mussolini for a lengthy discussion."

The very same day, the skies over Friedrichshafen blackened with planes. American B-17s, stationed in Italy, flew north and dropped bombs for hours, and this time they destroyed Eckener's pride and joy, Hall 3, the future of the Zeppelin firm, as he once called it. British bombers that day also attacked suspected launch pads for Vengeance Weapons in northern France.

In Friedrichshafen, seventy-two people died in the attack, and the damage was so extensive that the Zeppelin works was finally silenced there. Hall 3 was smoldering ruins, and most of the critical buildings were on fire. Railroad tracks curled in mayhem, and the grounds were pockmarked with craters.

On the evening of September 8, 1944, the first V-2 rocket exploded in London, five minutes after liftoff from Holland. That landmark in weaponry, the first ballistic missile, followed the June firing of the first V-1, the pilotless, winged bomb. It reached London a week after the Normandy landing. A strange hybrid of a plane and a rocket, the V-1 was loud and terrifying. It had a variety of nicknames, including buzz bomb, doodlebug, and flying bomb. The barrage of both V-weapons would pick up, landing by the hundreds.

The terror of the Vengeance Weapons was immediate. After the Allied landings at D-Day, the British were greatly relieved, thinking the worst of the Nazi danger was past. But, Eisenhower would recall, with the new weapons exploding all around London, hope collapsed. "The depressing effect of the bombs was not confined to the civilian population," he would recall. "Soldiers at the front began again to worry about friends and loved ones at home, and many American soldiers asked me in worried tones whether I could give them any news about particular towns where they had previously been stationed in southern England."

To restore its operations bombed in Friedrichshafen, Zeppelin planned to move them to a new underground site, nineteen miles northwest. One detachment of prisoners followed Georg Grünberg to the new subterranean camp, Überlingen, along the shore of Lake Constance. In many cases, working in squalid conditions, the prisoners arrived simply to dig their own graves. About 700 prisoners were forced to tunnel underground at Überlingen, in a plan to reopen assembly operations for Zeppelin and its associated military contractors, Dornier Aircraft and Maybach Motors. On hand were twenty-five SS guards, headed by Grünberg, who marched around his tunneled-out new fiefdom with his whip.

Work constructing Überlingen's tunnels was treacherous, dangerous. The prisoners worked twelve-hour shifts. Within the first six months, at least 170 died, some from accidents in the suffocating tunnels, many because of sparse food and poor hygiene. The bodies became hard to dispose of. At one point, ninety-seven corpses were stuffed into bags. A farmer was hired to haul them into a grove. When they were later found, one man still had a noose around his neck, and one in ten of the corpses had dog bites.

A Russian prisoner who tried to escape became an example under Grünberg's iron-fist rule at the new Zeppelin operation. Wassilij Sklarenko, prisoner number 33639, was twenty-one when he and the other prisoners were forced to witness the fate of their Russian comrade at Überlingen. The SS guards captured the escapee outside the camp. They brought him back and threw him into the dog kennel, where he was viciously torn to death by the hounds.

To terrorize them, the prisoners were forced to watch, Sklarenko recalled. "Everyone was deeply affected."

While some of his fellow prisoners were dispatched to Überlingen, Moisej Temkin was rolling north in a boxcar toward the Nazis' last hope for the war, the underground mountain factory that would restore the V-2 program. He was among 762 prisoners vacated from Friedrichshafen on September 30, 1944, after the deadly airstrike. The A4 Special Committee formed a new quasi-public corporation called Mittelwerk as owner of the new factory.

When Temkin arrived, there were nearly 14,000 prisoners already there, a nightmare camp given a woman's name, Dora, which is based on a Greek word meaning "gift." People in nearby Nordhausen referred to the parade of men in prison stripes as "zebras." Armaments Minister Speer took great interest in the project and visited the secret weapons installation the prior year, as its conversion was under way. In only four months, the army, the Armaments Ministry, and the SS had evacuated all the A4 production from its planned factories, including Friedrichshafen, and reassembled and plunged it all into a modern arms plant belowground.

For six months, many Mittelwerk prisoners hadn't seen the sun. Paul Bouteau spent an entire fall and winter living in the bowels of the earth, like a mole, dust in his eyes, mouth, and nostrils and no way to wash. He was one of thousands of men enduring life in the mountain that the Germans forced them to tunnel out, with picks, hammers, hand tools, and, at times, their bare hands. The blaring sun would give Bouteau so much joy when he arrived aboveground at last. It also brought tears to the eyes of an old Russian prisoner in his work group, who died a few days after he finally saw the sun again.

There was no water in the tunnels for washing and little for drinking, and their concentration "camp" was an underground pit. It was dark as night, barely lit by single dim lightbulbs every 300 feet. At the end of their exhausting days, prisoners had to sleep on straw in the cold, dark tunnels. One prisoner, Otakar Litomisky, would share a blanket nightly with a fellow Czech. The men would spread the straw on the hard stone and lay as close together as they could. They would finally fall asleep in a huddle, he would recall, "like two cats."

Desperate, forced to live in filth like beasts, some of his fellow prisoners used their own urine, or some of their rotten coffee, to wash the dust from their faces. One water pipeline ran through the tunnel, but the men who tried to wash themselves with its leaking drips were beaten by SS guards. There were no toilets in the tunnels, and men by the hundreds relieved themselves into old gasoline drums cut in half, with boards laid across. The stench was miserable.

The A4 Special Committee was responsible for this, though the prisoners did not know it. The panel had decided that the priority was to dig out a main tunnel—twenty-three feet high, thirty feet wide, big enough for a train to pass inside—as quickly as possible to relocate the rocket's assembly lines and restart production. The men also had to excavate smaller side tunnels throughout the mile-long Kohnstein mountain.

It was a mammoth, inhuman task, all to hide the Reich's all-important rocket project from the Allies. Before the war, the Harz mountain region was a resort area, with numerous hotels and villas for people to escape the bustle of nearby cities, including Berlin, Hamburg, and Leipzig. Once the Nazis took over an old storage depot already built in one tunnel there, they began expanding a second tunnel to create a complex for the rocket's production.

There were plans to build rudimentary barracks with bunk beds for the concentration camp prisoners outside, at the base of the mountain. But the prisoner camp wouldn't be built, according to strict orders from the Special Committee, until the tunneling for the new factory was complete. Storage tanks and V-2 assembly line equipment from Peenemünde, Zeppelin, and other factories had to be installed first as well.

That mandate sentenced several thousand prisoners to a catacomb of agonizing death. The men, mostly Poles and Russians, subsisted on a starvation diet of soup and bread. In a matter of weeks, they looked like fleshy skeletons, whites of eyes and teeth on filthy faces. There was no adequate medical care, and SS guards tormented the weakened workers with rifle butts and boots. The air was hazy with dust, and the tunnels constantly rocked with excavation blasts.

"The noise bores into the brain and shears the nerves," recalled Jean Michel, a French prisoner held at Dora. "Some are too weak and collapse. They have dysentery. They foul their trousers. They no longer have the strength to sit over the barrels—even to get to them. The SS beat them."

Within six months, a staggering 3,000 prisoners died at Dora. At first, the corpses were hauled off to a crematorium, but Dora later had to build its own incinerator. A prisoner named Jacky, his head constantly covered with a Russian chapka, rolled a small, squeaking cart throughout the tunnels. As chief of the undertaker's gang, he was on the prowl eleven hours a day, looking for corpses to haul away. One day, he found a dozen gray bodies near a door, probably placed there by prisoners trying to distance themselves from the smell of the departed.

By the time Temkin arrived in late September 1944, the barracks aboveground were completed, and the prisoners no longer had to sleep in the tunnels. He had been a captive in the Nazi prison state for over three years. At Dora, he became prisoner number 91408. Among the Russians, Yugoslavs, Czechs, Poles, and Frenchmen he met there, Temkin, his twenty-seventh birthday days away, encountered the first man he had ever seen with black skin. He was a Haitian who had been arrested by the Gestapo in France.

In the dead of the winter of 1944, Temkin faced a new peril: He was freezing. The SS men warmed themselves by the fire, in warm clothes, while he and his compatriots unloaded cement from freight cars or loaded open cars with metal scraps. They worked without gloves.

There was a field of sugar beets within reach, but the SS guards and prisoners called *Kapos*, who supervised their prison peers for extra rations and other privileges, refused to let Temkin or the others pick them from the ground. He was weak, tired, and famished. The gossip around the camp was that the Allies were making good progress toward Germany, and his Russian compatriots, too. One prisoner could see a map in a manager's office with pins showing the position of Allied forces closing in around Germany. His updates got passed prisoner to prisoner. Temkin worried he would not live to see what was on everyone's lips, a single word: liberation.

About one-third of the prisoners at Dora were highly coveted electricians, welders, machine operators, and other skilled technicians. They got to work in the shops and on the assembly lines, with jobs that required light, nimble work, not the heavy, exhausting labor of the other two-thirds of the prisoners.

Temkin had no particular skill useful in rocket-making, but he decided to take a chance when he heard there was an opening underground for a locksmith. He thought the only way he could survive was by taking an "inside job," he recalled. He took a risk, pretending to have lock-making and repair skills. He knew how dangerous it was. If it came out later that he had lied, he would undoubtedly be killed.

For a few days, the locksmith impostor wandered from tunnel hall to hall, carrying a toolbox, looking for an assignment. In some of the tunnels, welders fastened large middle sections of the rocket together. Elsewhere, men were stringing wiring or connecting the tail fins. The walls were bare, scalloped rock, scarred from blasting. The only light was artificial, bright lamps occasionally breaking the dark. Men with clipboards walked around, inspecting.

Soon, Temkin was assigned to a transport group, the so-called *Transportkolonnen*. It was one of the heaviest jobs in the entire factory. In one of the tunnels, workers painted the sections of the rocket, and Temkin was a slight man on a brawny team who carried hulking parts on their shoulders. The middle section they began carrying, Temkin knew well. He had seen the half shells, the curved sectional fuselages, as a Zeppelin prisoner in Friedrichshafen and later in Saulgau. The rocket *Halbschale*, or half shell, was still being made in Saulgau.

And now Temkin was shouldering Hugo Eckener's contribution to the Reich's wonder weapon. The outer shell of the rocket was important. Made of rolled sheet steel, with supporting ribs, the fuselage had to absorb the vibration and punishment of thrust forces on the missile, much as the outer cover of the *Hindenburg* was supposed to. Eight men on each side carried the curved section, teams of sixteen laborers lugging the single largest part of the rocket, at twenty feet long. The tunnels were humid, forty-six degrees on average, and miserable, but the fumes of the painting room were suffocating.

By now, the factory was producing twenty of the enormous rockets every day, and Temkin and his team lugged loads for twelve hours, with only a thirty-minute break. When they left the tunnel exhausted, they could hardly stand, Temkin recalled. But they dared not sit down, rest. There was a dreaded SS guard, and all the prisoners, in whatever their language, called him the same name: Horsehead. He had an elongated face and a short temper. When he saw someone sleeping, Temkin would recall, he would shoot the dozing man with his pistol. Horsehead was so brutal, prosecutors would seek him years later, threatening to expose any link between Zeppelin company employees and Mittelwerk and Dora, whose operation top to bottom was nothing short of criminal.

Dora's camp doctor at one point complained to the management that prisoners had been hospitalized for being "beaten or even stabbed with sharp instruments by civilian employees for any petty offense." In the summer of 1944, Georg Rickhey, a top Mittelwerk supervisor, followed up with a written warning to the engineers: Punishing prisoners was the SS's exclusive domain. A wind-tunnel engineer, Peter Wegener, visited the factory one day and was mortified by the conditions he saw. Unable to forget the way the prisoners eyed him, he would later write, "I have never before experienced such glances of hate."

By the end of the year, with Temkin still new to Dora, the SS began viciously suppressing a group of Soviet resisters, factory slaves suspected of planning to sabotage the V-2 rockets. It took extraordinary willpower even to contemplate sabotage, as most of the prisoners were consumed with survival, daily struggles against cold and hunger, anxiety about sickness.

Breaking from normal protocol of executing prisoners outside the factory, the guards conducted one mass hanging inside the factory to terrorize the workers. Twelve accused saboteurs were lashed with nooses to the boom of a factory crane, which slowly rose. Hands tied behind their backs, wooden gags wired in their mouths to muffle screams, they dangled there suffering, kicking, then twitching, then still.

Work shifts were stopped. The prisoners all had to parade past the hanged men. The lifeless bodies were left up for twelve hours, to ensure that both work shifts would witness the barbarism. Suspended there, they looked ghastly, like bent, gray puppets.

"Most of their bodies have lost both trousers and shoes, and puddles of urine cover the floor," recalled a French prisoner, Yves Béon, forced to witness the horror. "Since the ropes are long, the bodies swing gently about five feet above the floor, and you have to push them aside as you advance. . . . The corpses, pushed against each other, begin to spin around."

As 1945 opened, more madness was in the offing. Temkin was right. Everyone felt it. Liberation was floating in the air. They heard the civilian engineers at Mittelwerk whispering that Hitler was finished.

By the spring, the German arms makers could sense the end was coming. Germany couldn't defend itself. German society and its vaunted order were rapidly breaking down. Throughout the Fatherland, army officers, local mayors, mothers, factory workers, and farmers—all were scrambling to hide everything they could from vanquishing forces.

The industrialists didn't want to be caught red-handed with factories full of slave laborers when the occupying powers took over. They demanded the SS evacuate the prisoners, immediately. To avoid detection for their war crimes, they collectively shoved tens of thousands of prisoners back onto the SS, knowing full well its violent ways. The security agency, suddenly overwhelmed, had a logistical nightmare on its hands. Its solution did not involve the care and safe passage of the prisoners, their unwanted cargo.

Throughout Germany, the SS stampeded groups of sixty to one hundred prisoners into rail freight cars and locked them in. In cases where they transported the inmates using open flatbed cars, armed guards stood watch, on six-hour shifts, at each of the four corners. The German national railroad made passenger cars available for SS men accompanying the transport. Prisoners would soon begin rolling away from Dora and other concentration camps throughout the Reich.

About ten days before Easter of 1945, orders were relayed from the Buchenwald concentration camp, the official feeder camp for Dora and the rocket work, on how to dispose of the prisoners. Apparently, the original plan involved sealing them in the tunnels and gassing them to death. The SS even constructed a wall at one end of one of the tunnels to conduct the mass extermination. But, in some confusion, trains were ordered to evacuate the prisoners instead.

Temkin vividly remembered being stuffed with his fellow prisoners into a freight car. Guards barred the doors, and the train set off for God-knows-where. The train went forward, then backed up. Wherever they were, he could hear shots fired. For four days, they got nothing to eat. Finally, the train stopped, and the doors creaked opened. Loaves of bread and canned meat flew into the car. The doors slammed shut, and it was pitch black again. Men began shouting and fighting one another in the dark over the bread and cans, trying to rip food from one another's hands. The weaker men ended up empty-handed. The train took off again.

Another four days passed without food or water. In the cars, men began dying from hunger and thirst. The train again stopped someplace, and the skylight in Temkin's car opened. German farmers brought them raw potatoes, raw turnips, rutabagas—whatever they could—in wheel-barrows. The SS guards allowed them to throw everything through the skylight, and the prisoners divided the food among themselves. They didn't have enough strength to squabble, as they did days earlier. Everyone ate. Guards gave them glasses of water through the window.

On all these evacuation trains, the prisoners, locked up and packed in, had to relieve themselves where they could. Weak prisoners knelt down or laid down on the railcar floor and never got up. Many of them. "We awaken to find that there are dead bodies everywhere," recalled Yves Béon. "They take up room, and we'd like to throw them over the side, but the guards refuse to allow it. They have no orders about this, so we living prisoners must sit on top of the dead." The lifeless bodies even provided some comfort to the survivors. Sitting on a corpse, Béon noted, offered "a softer cushion than the railcar's flooring."

After more than a week of rolling somewhere, Temkin's train finally stopped. The SS guards unlocked the doors. Without being told where they were, Temkin and his trainload of prisoners were told to step off and to march in columns, with guards to either side and behind. They were a pitiful procession, so skeletal, so weak, the guards didn't bother to hurry them along with rifle butts and stabbing bayonets, or even order them to march in straight lines.

Why the change of rules, never broken before? There was no village, no other people around. All Temkin knew was that it was early April. All he could see was a thick forest. They marched into the darkening woods.

Another train, headed north as well, stopped in Mieste about one hundred miles from Nordhausen. The route of the train, with more than 1,000 prisoners from Dora and another concentration camp, had just fallen into Allied hands. Some eight miles away, American troops were closing in on the prisoners and their SS guards. The SS called on a local Nazi district leader, Gerhard Thiele, for help managing the large band of prisoners. Thiele gathered reinforcements from the Hitler Youth and the *Volkssturm*, the national militia of the Nazi Party recently formed to help protect German towns from enemy forces. Some of the SS guards on the evacuation train had just deserted.

It was Friday, April 13, 1945. Pointing rifles, the guards herded the men in their striped uniforms by the hundreds into a massive brick barn in the nearby town of Gardelegen. It was seven in the evening. After dousing tangled straw on the floor with gasoline, they slammed the doors and set the building afire.

Amid shouts of agony, some tried to escape, crawling under wooden planks, but the guards stationed like snipers around the barn shot them to death. When a group of Russian prisoners tried to ram a barn door, they were struck with the rat-a-tat of machine gun and rifle fire. Soldiers threw grenades into the barn, fueling the blaze.

When the flames subsided, 1,016 of the evacuated prisoners had been burned to death. The toll was as if the *Hindenburg* disaster had repeated itself every single day for a month.

# 16

# Swastikas in the Closet

*We must establish incredible facts by credible evidence.*

—Robert Jackson,
chief U.S. prosecutor of Nazi war crimes at Nuremburg

In the final days of World War II, it was Nordhausen that began to expose the Nazi concentration camp horror. On April 11, 1945, Colonel James L. Collins was leading American infantrymen toward Nordhausen. He knew it was an industrial city in central Germany, and he had intelligence that there was a German military installation there. Those two things, the colonel was prepared for. Then his liaison officer, who was already there, radioed.

"Colonel, you'd better get up here and see what we've got," the officer said. "It's terrible."

Collins and his infantry unit came upon the base of the mountain, just outside the tunnel entrance. Arriving, they couldn't take the smell. They saw thousands of cadavers, stiff, waxy, twisted, in row after row on the ground. It looked like an entire cemetery had somehow surfaced aboveground. The soldiers were horrified and "terribly angry at what the Germans had done," Collins recalled.

Army photographers walked between the rows, with boxy cameras, cigarettes in their lips, and started snapping. Their photos shocked the world. They were some of the first images of Nazi atrocities to scar human consciousness. A little later, two army squads showed up on the camp grounds: The first was a set of army war-crimes investigators; the second was a shadowy group, an ordnance technical intelligence team.

As the American Third Armored Division began to liberate the Dora camp in the second week of April 1945, maps showing Allied positions in U.S. newspapers back home made it clear: The Third Reich was on the verge of collapse. The Russians were already in Berlin, and American forces were closing in on the capital from the west. For days, those hopeful maps with arrows converging on Berlin ran side by side in the papers with photos of all the piled-up corpses at Nordhausen.

Long rows of trenches six feet deep were filled with ravaged, bony corpses. The American military authorities, who began transporting survivors to hospitals, ordered the local administrator of Nordhausen to call up 600 townsmen to bury each of the victims. They arrived in suits and hats, with shovels on their shoulders. Over a few days, details surfaced that there were 2,700 rotting, unburied corpses there, along with another 3,000 men barely alive. About 600 had died of starvation in the previous two weeks. They were Russians, Poles, Belgians, Frenchmen, and Czechs.

The world shared outrage. "Things came to a head here at Nordhausen when thousands of American soldiers viewed the shriveled bodies of great hundreds of people who had been done to death by the Nazis in local concentration camps," one editorialist wrote. "Unless a more convincing and explicit official Allied policy toward war criminals is quickly announced, there is going to be an unofficial one . . . frontier law."

The war was nearly over, and already sentiment was building for revenge. Two weeks after the liberation of Nordhausen, Hitler was holed up in his underground bunker in Berlin. On the last day of April 1945, he put a bullet in his head.

Days later, a fiery U.S. congresswoman from Connecticut completed a two-month tour of European battlefronts and shared her findings back in Washington in a speech to the House. Clare Boothe Luce singled out the freshly discovered secret factory for the V-1 and V-2 weapons, saying that its prison slaves lived in "the bowels of hell."

"It seems clear to me from what I have seen myself of these camps, and heard about them from our military authorities," Luce said, "that the beatings, burnings, hangings, clubbings, foul mutilations, and massacres practiced in these charnel houses were merely hellish interruptions of a clearly held Nazi policy of death by slow starvation. . . . The dead and the dying were difficult to tell apart in the hideous barracks of Nordhausen."

The use of prisoner slaves, who were unable to escape or communicate to the outside world, only enhanced the weapons secrecy of the Nazis, she said, and prolonged the war. "The Nordhausen camp provided this factory with a great pool of slave labor who could be counted upon to take the secrets of the diabolic weapons, upon which they worked, into the burning kilns with them," the congresswoman added. Three days after her address, Germany surrendered. The war in Europe ended.

The technical intelligence group that arrived with the GIs at Nordhausen was on a secret mission. It was one that, in an unintended twist, would eventually help Hugo Eckener escape Germany, to the safety of American soil.

With Germany vanquished, things shifted quickly from victory to justice. For the United States, apprehending war criminals now fell to President Harry S. Truman. He had just assumed the Oval Office four weeks earlier, after Roosevelt had died of a cerebral hemorrhage. Truman couldn't let those responsible for Nordhausen, or whatever other atrocities the Allies might discover, escape justice. He quickly appointed Robert Jackson, a former U.S. Attorney General, as lead American prosecutor of Nazi criminals. The main trials, it was thought, would be held in Nuremburg, notorious by that point as the cradle of Nazism.

Some officials among the Allies had advocated for straight-ahead vigilante justice. Winston Churchill and other British authorities, in fact, tried to establish, through old "outlaw" principles, how they could legally subject captured senior Nazis to summary execution. Other Allied leaders, however, insisted they could only win world regard in the long run not by shooting suspects but by trying them in legitimate court proceedings. The high road beckoned.

The first week of June 1945, Judge Jackson submitted to Truman an outline of procedures that essentially became the operating manual for Nuremberg. "Fair hearings for the accused are, of course, required to make sure that we punish only the right men for the right reasons," Jackson wrote.

Given the vastness of criminal actions by German politicians, military officers, doctors, and industrialists, the major Allied powers formed a special court called the International Military Tribunal, which hung the flags of the United States, Soviet Union, France, and Britain. Germany itself was carved into four zones, with each of those countries responsible for one part. The Zeppelin company was in geography to the south, under French control. Nordhausen and the V-2 factory in central Germany fell in the American zone, though the Allies occasionally squabbled over the boundaries themselves.

The commanders in the four zones were instructed to arrest and deliver for trial anyone suspected of crimes against peace, war crimes, or crimes against humanity. Military-government courts in each zone were supposed to try the accused. From the spring of 1945 on, thousands of suspects were detained in Germany's four zones while prosecutors gathered evidence. Punishments ranged from forfeiting property and deprivation of some civil rights, all the way up to fines, imprisonment, and execution.

Jackson saw more than immediate justice at work in these proceedings. Posterity concerned him. He thought the accurate portrayal of history was at stake. The record of the Nazi movement must be written clearly and precisely, he wrote. The trials must show that justice awaits anyone whose actions similarly offend civilization. Army prosecutors would soon begin amassing evidence against those responsible for the V-2 factory near Nordhausen, and for its nightmarish Dora concentration camp.

Within a few weeks, Hugo Eckener resurfaced in the news. Whatever he was up to during the war was anyone's guess. The last the world had heard of him, he was trying to get helium for his new airship after the *Hindenburg* disaster. That was back in 1938. That seemed, to him, like a good place to pick up.

In July of 1945, Eckener gave an interview with an American reporter. Hitler by then had been dead for several months. The article described Eckener as "the Zeppelin builder." He had a gloomy view of the future of airships, the story said, which was ruined by "that fool with criminal instincts, Adolf Hitler."

It was perhaps the first public rebuke of Hitler ever by Eckener. And it signaled the tenor of his plan to revise his wartime record completely.

The interview took place "at his villa near the bomb-scarred Friedrichshafen Zeppelin plant, where French occupation forces have allowed him to live unmolested since the surrender," the news story said. The world-girdling aviator "still clings firmly to his personal dream of international air transport by dirigible," it noted.

But Eckener told the reporter that the Nazi Air Ministry ordered him to destroy a big Zeppelin he had under construction in 1939. He said he was also ordered to convert the Friedrichshafen plant, where he was managing director for many years, to making aluminum castings for the German Ford Motor Plant at Cologne and light metal parts for other factories. No mention of rockets or slave camps.

"The air ministry people," Eckener said, "did not like us."

But Hugo Eckener was soon cornered.

The eyes of the world were on Nuremburg in November of 1945, when the historic war-crimes trial opened for two-dozen officials of Hitler's Nazi apparatus and German army leaders. Two of the defendants, Hermann Göring and Albert Speer, Eckener had previously worked with, either on Zeppelins or the war. One day after Hitler committed suicide in his underground bunker, Goebbels killed himself.

The Nuremburg trial was front-page news around the world. Photographs of the defendants, sitting side by side in the dock, would become staples of World War II history books. For now, each was fighting to avoid death by hanging.

Eckener's association with two of the top Nuremburg defendants must have unnerved him as the four Allied powers spread a vast dragnet to capture and punish other Germans who ardently sympathized with, supported, or otherwise collaborated with the Nazis. That broad investigation had a clunky name, denazification. Across occupied Germany, the plan was to purge any remnants of Nazi ideology from German government, universities, culture, and industry. It was not enough simply to defeat the Nazis militarily—Nazism had to be rooted out entirely from all corners of German life.

"If anybody believes we're going to leave anything for Germany" to start another war, Eisenhower told reporters, "he's crazy."

This posed an immediate problem for Eckener, who joined his fellow Germans in facing a mandatory Nazi-background check. It started with a questionnaire, ordered by the Allied powers. In it, Germany's citizens and her returning soldiers were required to disclose memberships with any Nazi group, along with other related political or military activities, during the years of the Third Reich. The dreaded form, known in German as the *Fragebogen*, was the first step toward penalties that could mean losing one's job or property, imprisonment for ten or more years, and even, in the severe cases, execution.

Friedrichshafen, as a major armaments center of the Third Reich, seemed like a Nazi hothouse. The local denazification board, called the Krua, operated in the French zone of conquered Germany. It was charged with determining if business executives in the arms business voluntarily sought the work from the Nazis or were forced into weapons production. Were they war profiteers?

In a remarkable stroke of luck for the industrial executives, denazification authorities apparently decided early on to absolve many of them from responsibility for exploiting foreign civilian workers and concentration camp prisoners, on the mistaken notion that they had been compelled to by the Nazi labor organization or the SS. It was a blunder no one in industry apparently tried to correct.

The denazification officials did not expect Nazi supporters to come completely clean, however, so they conducted their own background checks. Given the magnitude of their task, with some half-million *Fragebogen* submitted for processing in the French zone alone by the end of 1946, they were quickly overwhelmed.

The local tribunals were run not by professional jurists, but by political party members, trade union officials, and clerks. To investigate suspects, they mostly spent hours flipping through magazines and yellowed newspaper pages, looking for any incriminating statements or published letters from individuals under investigation. If it wasn't in the public record, the tribunals had almost no way of learning it. It became trial by paper trail.

There was typically no court appearance. The accused was presented with evidence, he or she was allowed to respond, and if the tribunal still recommended punishment, the judgment with recommended penalty went to a regional commissioner for final judgment.

In the summer of 1946, the panel looking into Eckener and the Zeppelin executives worked on a shoestring. At one point, a clerk wrote to the district office, requesting a new typewriter. The tribunal's one typewriter couldn't, exactly, type. Office space was sometimes difficult to find in bombed-out Friedrichshafen, and some of the proceedings took place in the town of Riedlingen, to the north, in a gym.

Eckener seemed to think he could fool the tribunal, stop the investigation cold at the initial step. When he filled out his *Fragebogen* on April 14, 1946, he was seventy-eight years old, an advanced age to face prison time. By the end of that year, Germany would see 90,000 Nazis locked up in concentration camps through denazification and other judicial actions, and nearly two million Germans stripped of their chosen professions, forbidden to do anything but manual labor.

Eckener tap-danced around some questions, and omitted his entire war record. Asked if he ever belonged to the Nazi Party, or the SS, or any of fifty other specifically named Nazi-affiliated groups, he replied "*Nein.*" Those dozens of cultural, financial, and military associations were intertwined throughout Nazi German society and helped keep the Hitler machine running. And, asked whether he had received any award from any of those groups, he also reported, "*Nein.*" Eckener did not mention that Adolf Hitler himself had bestowed on him the honorary title of "Professor."

Knut Eckener was also under investigation, along with pretty much every other executive at Zeppelin and related arms companies. In his *Fragebogen*, Knut confessed to joining the Nazi Party in the winter of 1937. He admitted to being an *Abwehrbeauftragter*, a security officer for the German military, at the Zeppelin company, a position he said was assigned to him in 1944.

The Eckeners were lucky to be facing a French denazification proceeding. The French, for all their animosity toward Germany, were less harsh in charging Germans with being Nazi supporters than the other occupying powers. French proceedings more often ended in demotions and fines than imprisonment. At one point, Eisenhower, acting as U.S.

military governor, even complained about French "laxity" in the drive to rid the world of onetime Nazi supporters.

France, in fact, seemed intent on moving forward, with an eye toward long-term reconciliation with a country on its border. French denazification sought to determine the real character of the suspects, the real Nazis. They wanted to sift out those who were "spiritually and practically devoted to the Nazis," as one official put it. Being a Nazi Party member, as roughly one in ten Germans had been, did not constitute automatic guilt. The term for the French proceedings was not denazification, but *épuration*, purification. It was all less about revenge than rehabilitation.

But Hugo Eckener would still have to get past Gerhard Hermann Müller, a leading commissioner for political cleansing, who recalled from his law-school days in Tübingen an Eckener radio address he could not forget. Müller rose to the role of Nazi hunter honestly. In 1937, the year the *Hindenburg* was destroyed, he was twenty-five years old, a fresh law-school graduate. He had just taken a civil service job when he was suddenly pressured to join the Nazi Party. Instead, he resigned. "I was unwilling to be a member of the National Socialist organization," he would later write, "which made it impossible for young lawyers to remain in civil service."

For the next three years, Müller cobbled together income writing freelance articles for newspapers and magazines. In 1940, he was conscripted into the infantry. When the war ended, French military authorities were impressed that he had sacrificed his legal career rather than serve the Nazis. Müller stood out as a true Nazi opponent. So, they selected him, as one of the honorable German citizens, to help them purge former Nazis from society.

That effort was in full swing in the fall of 1946. The first trial at Nuremburg had just ended, in early October. Twelve of the defendants were sentenced to death, and seven were given prison terms of ten years to life. Albert Speer, who broke from the others by voicing guilt, and even contrition, for helping the Nazi war machine, was spared death. Though he was deeply implicated for his role in the use of slave labor in the war, including at the underground V-2 factory, Speer was only sentenced to a twenty-year prison term.

The threat of prosecution was relentless. Hjalmar Schacht, who was Hitler's Minister of Economics, was one of the few men acquitted at the world-famous trial at Nuremburg. But one week later, he was arrested near Stuttgart by German police and locked up all over again, to be tried by a denazification panel. Having escaped Nuremburg, he now faced a new tribunal that could punish him with a ten-year prison term, confiscation of his property, and a ban from politics or leadership in industry. Meanwhile, the denazification workers looking into Eckener kept flipping through newspapers and magazines through the fall of 1946, and Müller was waiting for Eckener's case to reach him.

Around the same time, a watch list of German generals in the British and U.S. zones of occupation was drawn up. The roster listed the most notorious German officers, suspects Allied military intelligence should keep under surveillance for a possible Nazi revival. One of those on the list was Major General Otto Ernst Remer. Hitler rewarded Remer's loyalty for his role in decisively stopping the July 20, 1944, attempted coup, which came to be called Operation Valkyrie, by appointing him his chief bodyguard. Remer's watch list file categorized him as "a fanatical Nazi."

That designation would make all the more troubling the looming association of Remer and Hugo Eckener.

The American military pondered a Faustian pact, just before the Germans surrendered. Spellbound by German missiles and buzz bombs, cutting-edge weaponry never seen before, the U.S. military decided to raid the crumbling nation's technical brain trust. As the Allies moved from the beaches of Normandy deeper south into Europe and eventually into Germany itself, scientific investigators trailed just behind the front lines. They were hunting through the newly captured territory for Nazi research labs, technical institutes, and scientists. The hope was to export enemy men and machines to the United States.

Weeks before he died, President Roosevelt was asked for his opinion of a secret plan to bring the most brilliant of the German scientists to America. He was not lukewarm in his response, and seemed to have anticipated someone just like Eckener. Roosevelt wrote a memo in December of 1944, trashing the whole concept. "We may expect that the number of Germans who are anxious to save their skins and property will rapidly increase," he wrote. "Among them may be some who should be properly tried for war crimes or at least arrested for active participation in Nazi activities."

After Roosevelt's death, Truman approved the covert military project in September of 1946. It had the code name Paperclip. In time, hundreds of German scientists would be put to work in America, to help the United States gain a technical edge in arms.

Within a few months, a large military transport plane from Frankfurt landed at Westover Field, a huge U.S. base near Springfield, Massachusetts. The four propellers of the C-54 Skymaster stopped whirling, and a stooped old man from Germany stepped down the staircase. It was Saturday evening, April 26, 1947.

Hugo Eckener was back in the United States. Having crossed the Atlantic on a Zeppelin sixty-nine times, this was his first transoceanic trip by plane. And there was another difference. This time he intended to stay in America, seeking asylum. His application cited as character references the chairman of the Goodyear company, Paul Litchfield, and Eckener's old friend from the *Hindenburg* days, Charles Rosendahl.

Eckener was hoping to emigrate to the United States secretly, to flee from justice in Germany. His application, however, omitted the most salient of details. Two years after the war's end, he was facing fines and censure for being a Nazi supporter and war profiteer. Even more foreboding, a U.S. military court was gathering evidence for a war-crimes trial around the murder and systemic persecution of prison laborers at the V-2 rocket factory outside Nordhausen. Within a few weeks, one defendant in that case would hang himself before the trial began.

In Massachusetts, someone seemed to have tipped off reporters. This was a big story. The Associated Press and other news outlets sent reporters over to the air base. The grand old man of Zeppelin fame—who knew he was still alive?—was back in the United States again. After the *Hindenburg* tragedy, Eckener's name had virtually disappeared from the news.

His first plane trip across the Atlantic lasted twenty-nine hours, less than half the duration of a Zeppelin trip. Spotting reporters waiting for him, Eckener stepped briefly to the porch of the airfield's lounge and spoke to the newsmen. Photographers were barred from snapping pictures.

"I am very sorry to say I cannot give you any interviews," Eckener said. "I am under instructions not to say anything about the purpose of my visit."

Eckener spent the night at Westover Field. In the morning, Army Captain Frederick Smith of the European Command escorted him to an unannounced destination. They were on their way to Lakehurst, and the Pentagon.

Truman had finally signed off on the project to bring Germany's scientists to America after he was assured that no one who substantially supported the Nazi war regime would be included. The top brass of the military had told him privately that the War Department would exclude anyone with Nazi or clearly belligerent records. And they offered a backup: Any of the scientists who might later face allegations of war crimes would be immediately deported to face trial. Truman took them at their word.

In truth, the War Department was lax in screening candidates for Operation Paperclip. The military, coveting the best and brightest of Germany, conducted virtually no background checks. If something was uncovered, it wasn't pursued or was often omitted from the files.

The American mission had changed. Two years after the war, the country was transfixed with a new enemy, the Red Peril. Paperclip grew out of three intelligence agencies of the U.S. military, and they eagerly wanted to know just what the Germans knew about technology in the Soviet Union. Each German expert was debriefed before he started working in the States, and, after they all began, their mail was secretly read for scraps of intelligence. Paperclip participants were technically considered enemy aliens under military custody.

The Joint Intelligence Objectives Agency, an arm of the military's Joint Chiefs of Staff, was largely responsible for Paperclip. It took a lot of heat from the State Department and even from FBI director J. Edgar Hoover, who repeatedly warned intelligence officials about the security threat of bringing German scientists, their Nazi pasts lightly investigated, into America's secret weapons installations.

Early on, a main overseer of Operation Paperclip, Bosquet Wev, wrote a memo to Stephen Chamberlin, the army's director of intelligence, arguing that allowing the German experts to slip into Russia was a graver security threat to America than any Nazi work they did in the past or any sympathies they may still harbor. Thus, he complained about wasting time investigating the wartime pasts of the German scientists, which he called "beating a dead Nazi horse."

All of this was playing out behind closed doors. The American public was in the dark about the fact that some of the scientists here on America's dime had been architects and operators of the V-2 rocket operation that killed some 20,000 slave workers. Among the technical specialists recruited to the United States were Walter Dornberger, Wernher von Braun, Arthur Rudolph, and Georg Rickhey.

By late 1947, critics in Germany argued that they couldn't properly run denazification trials because most of the 300 or so scientists in America had simply fled Germany for Paperclip. Eventually, pressure built on both sides of the Atlantic for the program to go public in some fashion. Several hundred men with German accents suddenly showed up in the grocery stores and movie theaters of small towns in Ohio, New Mexico, and elsewhere. Some returning soldiers were angry to see men they considered the enemy months before, now in canteen lines for meals with them at army bases back home.

So, several military bases employing the Germans, including Wright Field in Ohio, got clearance to hold open houses for the press to interview the scientists. The idea of the tightly controlled press briefings was to downplay Nazi pasts and spin the coverage as a positive for America's future.

In December of 1946, *Newsweek* headlined its story "Secrets From Hitler." The report said that roughly 300 handpicked German and Austrian scientists, engineers, and technicians were spread throughout the United States, busily melding Germany's wartime projects with America's postwar technology. Hundreds more were expected to join them from Europe.

"The transplantation of the enemy's technical brainpower has been going on since September 1945 at an increasing rate and in comparative secrecy," the article continued. "The censorship has now been lifted." At

Wright Field, Ohio, and Fort Bliss, Texas, *Newsweek* said, news reporters recently had been allowed to interview a couple dozen of the scientists, to discuss their lives and work.

"All of them are officially still under the jurisdiction of the United States occupation forces in Germany and can be disciplined under the denazification program. Many were former Nazi party members, although none was in the political leadership," *Newsweek* told readers. The article noted that many of the experts were employed at White Sands, New Mexico, testing V-2 rockets the Allies captured. Among them was Wernher von Braun, chief inventor of the V-2.

The same week, *Life* magazine also contributed to the news presentation of Paperclip, as staged by the military. Its article was headlined "Nazi Brains Help U.S." *Life* had large photos of German scientists being taught in a classroom at Wright Field, as an instructor in a suit and tie wrote German and English phrases on a chalkboard. "Though the other nations bid high and sometimes successfully for the cream of German science, the U.S. got pretty much what it wanted," the *Life* article said. "The reason was that the German scientists liked America best—or feared it least."

Behind the facade, some Nazi supporters were enjoying jobs and homes in America immediately after the conquest of Germany. Through the duplicity of the American military intelligence establishment, some 1,600 researchers, scientists, and technical experts would eventually be employed on U.S. soil. After American soldiers gave their lives to fight Nazism, some of the men associated with the crimes of the Third Reich were simply imported to help the United States develop postwar space and weapons programs.

Hugo Eckener's six-page Paperclip contract was dated March 10, 1947. It was on a form called "Special Contract for the Employment of German Nationals with the War Department in the United States." He was to be paid 30,000 German marks for a minimum of six months' work. He listed one dependent, his wife, Johanna, who was seventy-seven. The United States would pay the cost of transporting Eckener to and from Europe. Baggage allowance was 175 pounds, not including the weight of scientific books or equipment. Medical care was paid for. The requesting agency for Eckener's Paperclip work: the U.S. Navy.

That was the first document in the U.S. military's classified dossier being assembled on Hugo Eckener. On the form called "Civil Fingerprint Card," Eckener pressed his inky fingers into ten boxes. He scowled at the camera for a mugshot, with a black-and-white photo straight on and side view.

Even his basic physical characteristics were marked "Restricted." They read: 78 years old, 5'9", 168 pounds, blue eyes, grey hair. Complexion: Ruddy. Distinguishing Marks: None. Physical Condition: Good. Birth date: 10 August 1868, Flensburg, Germany. Principal Occupation: physicist, airship constructor. Employment History: Luftschiffbau Zeppelin 1924–1947, RM 35,000.

On the form, under "Honorary Awards, Membership in Professional Societies," he told interrogators, "Too numerous to mention." He did not report his honorary Professorship from Adolf Hitler.

Military Service: None. Contacts in the USA: "Admiral Rosendahl, Paul Litchfield, President, Goodyear Tire and Rubber Co. Met all Presidents since Coolidge . . . and all other Secretaries of State."

On the "Personal Data" form, filled out by Eckener, he reported that he had been living in Konstanz, Germany, for the past thirty-six months, but was forced to leave his previous home in Friedrichshafen. "My home was burned by bombs," was his typed response.

The last line of the first page said: "I desire to emigrate to _____." He typed, "The United States." His reason: "To continue research work."

Asked about any military activity in Germany, Eckener wrote, "I have stayed away from any action taken by a state-sponsored organization or group, and have limited myself entirely to the work for my group."

For Paperclip clearance, Eckener was required to fill out another *Fragebogen* shortly after he arrived in the United States. Apparently, no one in America had ever heard about his pro-Hitler radio endorsement from 1934. And he omitted it. Eckener's answers on the new form contained huge holes. His replies were written entirely in German.

On separate pages, he was supposed to disclose all the public addresses he'd made since 1932. He reported giving many lectures, "several hundred having to do with airships and airship traffic, and I have done so in many countries, such as Germany, the USA, England, Holland, Denmark,

Sweden, Switzerland, Austria, etc." He added, "I can naturally give no further details about all these lectures from here and can only say that they were neither purely scientific nor political, but almost entirely propaganda in favor of airships."

He added: "I have also often spoken on the radio, including once on a political topic at the request of Chancellor Brüning in 1932, on the reparations question. This radio address earned me the anger of Hitler and Goebbels and without Hindenburg's intervention would have led to my imprisonment in a concentration camp at the time of the so-called takeover of power in 1933." Briefly chancellor of Germany before Hitler, Heinrich Brüning was an actual enemy of the Third Reich, who fled Germany in 1934.

Asked about denazification proceedings, Eckener confirmed he was being investigated, in the town of Reutlingen, by the French military government, but noted that he was not forbidden from working, as the proceeding was still under way. He denied being a Nazi Party member. Asked about family members, he fudged on Knut's party status. "My son, Knut Eckener, came under pressure in Friedrichshafen from the NSDAP [Nazi Party] in 1938 because of the Zeppelin works in Friedrichshafen and was threatened with resettlement."

To question 103, about any support of the party, Eckener replied, "I have not directly or indirectly supported the party."

Eckener faced prison for any misleading responses. On the last page was a declaration: "The statements on this form are true, and I understand that any omissions or false or incomplete statements are offenses against the Military Government and will subject me to prosecution and punishment."

Under that pledge, he filled in the date, April 14, 1947, and signed it, "Hugo Eckener."

The Office of the Military Government of the United States, abbreviated OMGUS, was responsible for providing a security report for all Paperclip candidates. OMGUS was to analyze army intelligence, interviews, inquiries, tips, character references, and so forth to determine whether a candidate was a security threat to the United States or an "ardent Nazi." The army defined as "ardent" any Nazi Party member prior to 1933, when Hitler came to power, along with all party leaders. The definition also included anyone convicted by denazification panels and those convicted, or even accused, of war crimes.

OMGUS issued its security clearance for Eckener two weeks before he even filled out his *Fragebogen*. Dated March 26, 1947, the two-page security report gave this analysis: "Subject has no governmental (German) connections, employment or otherwise, in projects or enterprises of industrial or scientific nature or military planning."

It is remarkable that the U.S. military government occupying Germany didn't know, or didn't acknowledge, that Eckener had been involved in production of the V-2 rocket from its initial stages or that, while he ran the Zeppelin company, it used slave labor for arms manufacturing.

The report concluded: "Based on available records, subject has no criminal record or charges of suspicion of being a war criminal. Based on available records, subject is not a war criminal, was not an ardent Nazi, and, in the opinion of the Military Governor, OMGUS, is not likely to become a security threat to the United States."

It was signed by Colonel C. F. Fritzsche, Assistant Deputy Director of Intelligence, European Command, authorized representative of the U.S. Military Governor for Germany.

Eckener was good to go.

He was not brought to the United States to continue working on rockets, as many others from the V-2 project were. Instead, his mission was to help with airship research—hardly the cutting-edge technology of missiles. Eckener was able to flee Germany, with his denazification case still under way, based on the slimmest possibility of a revival of airships, a campaign driven by Charles Rosendahl, then fifty-five, and Paul Litchfield, who, at seventy-one, was the longtime chairman of Goodyear.

Fully ten years after the *Hindenburg* disaster, the two men remained fanatically convinced that airships could still be used for commercial or military reasons, an alternative means for transporting cargo over long distances. In the intervening years, materials had gotten lighter and stronger. Helium, as it always had been, was safe. Rosendahl, in fact, was urging President Truman's special merchant marine committee to subsidize airships. He was trying to raise $70 million to build seven super airships, each a third larger than the *Hindenburg*, the largest flying object ever. Eckener was to work as a consultant to Goodyear on airship design.

It's not clear what, if anything, Rosendahl or Litchfield knew about Eckener's wartime activities or his brewing denazification case. But the navy maintained that Eckener, "The Pope" from his former Zeppelin glory days, and his plan to immigrate to the United States stood to benefit Goodyear as well.

A graduate of the Massachusetts Institute of Technology, Paul Litchfield began leading Goodyear in 1926 and had built the company into a global powerhouse. He founded a research and development department that created state-of-the-art airplane tires, truck tires, and conveyor belts.

Litchfield was fascinated with flying, and during the war, Goodyear had 37,000 workers making aircraft and plane components. He had also sunk millions of dollars into airship development throughout his entire career and had little to show for it but the Goodyear blimp, an oversize balloon for publicity flyovers. When Eckener arrived in Akron, Ohio, on Saturday, May 3, 1947, Litchfield put him up in his own house.

In Akron, Hugo Eckener would soon make the society pages, photographed attending concerts and other events, just as Ernst Lehmann had regularly been in the newspapers years before when he worked for Goodyear. Back in Germany, denazification kept sending people to prison, and the trials at Nuremburg had turned to Nazi doctors and judges. From Ohio, it all must have seemed so far away.

But then prosecutors started charging business executives with Nazi ties. The day Eckener arrived in Akron, the United States filed indictments in Nuremburg against top officials of IG Farben, a large chemical company. The charges, which closely mirrored some of the work of the Zeppelin company, could have made the blood drain from Eckener's face.

"Ostensibly acting only as business men, Farben officials carried on propaganda, intelligence and espionage activities indispensable to German preparation for, and waging of, aggressive war," the indictment read. Eckener, of course, recorded a propaganda speech in favor of Hitler in 1934, then charged the Reich for propaganda flyovers with his Zeppelins, and then authorized spy flights with the sister ship to the *Hindenburg* that allowed Hitler to begin his invasions of Europe.

For exploiting forced laborers and concentration camp prisoners, the Farben executives were charged with committing war crimes and crimes against humanity. The indictment charged them with "the use of prisoners of war in war operations . . . including the manufacture and transportation of war material and equipment; and the mistreatment, terrorization, torture and murder of enslaved persons. In the course of these activities, millions of persons were uprooted from their homes, deported, enslaved, ill-treated, terrorized, tortured and murdered."

These acts were, the indictment continued, "part of the slave labor program of the Third Reich, in the course of which millions of persons, including women and children, were subjected to forced labor under cruel and inhuman conditions which resulted in widespread suffering and millions of deaths.

"At least five million workers were deported to Germany. Conscription of labor was implemented in most cases by brutal and violent methods, among which were included systematic manhunts in the streets, motion picture theatres, houses of worship and other public places, and frequent invasions of homes during the night. Workers deported for the Reich were sent under armed guard to Germany, often packed in trains without heating, food, clothing, or sanitary facilities, as a result of which many of them were dead upon arrival, and most of the survivors were seriously ill."

The charges against one top Farben executive specifically cited organizing his company for war mobilization, including the use of slave labor, just as Eckener had done. The indictment further stated that exploitation of enslaved workers and of prisoners of war directly connected with war operations was standard policy of Farben. Another Farben officer was cited for detailing the use of slave workers in a company business report, just as Eckener had done in discussing the 1,202 prisoners Zeppelin acquired from Dachau.

Prosecutors charged Farben for having slave camps "enclosed with barbed wire . . . guarded by SS men. Deportees from Eastern-occupied countries were guarded by armed plant guards accompanied by watch dogs." The Zeppelin company had done the very same thing. Thirteen Farben officials were sentenced to prison, in terms up to eight years.

In many cases throughout Germany, the use of prison labor was initiated by a company, not the SS. In fact, not every business caved to using slave labor. Erich Bachem, the inventor of an experimental rocket plane that excited the SS weapons office in late 1944, rejected an offer by Himmler to set up a concentration camp in the town of Waldsee to ensure that there was a sufficient labor force. Bachem declined, without suffering any reprisals from the SS, explaining that what he needed was workers, not slaves.

The arrest sent a shock wave through the Paperclip men.

Georg Johannes Rickhey, who was general manager of the V-2 Mittelwerk factory, had been comfortably cocooned at a special barracks with 140 other Germans in the Paperclip project at Wright Field in Ohio. He played cards with them at night, drank too much. Then on May 19, 1947, he was suddenly arrested by MPs and flown back to Germany to face the death penalty, as prosecutors had finally brought criminal charges related to the underground installation.

What was perhaps most troubling for Eckener, and other executives who could perhaps be connected with V-2 production at Mittelwerk, was that Rickhey was a civilian manager, just a businessman like him. Just as with Farben, criminal prosecution was now arriving at the doorstep of supervisors and executives. When Rickhey arrived days later at Dachau, where he would be held awaiting trial, another defendant in the same case, Kurty Mathesus, who had been compound commandant at the Dora camp, had just hanged himself in the prison hospital.

Opening arguments would begin in a barracks in the Dachau complex in August 1947. The parallels between Mittelwerk and its Dora prison and Zeppelin and its concentration camps were unmistakable. In his opening statement, Lieutenant Colonel William Berman, the chief prosecutor, described Dora as particularly sinister. In the vast prison state that was Nazi Germany, Dora was a camp founded solely to supply the war machine. And Dora and its subsidiary camps, Berman said, provided a workforce in the thousands to help foster secrecy at the V-2 factory. Collectively, he referred to the whole operation as Nordhausen.

Called to the witness stand, Rickhey could provide damaging testimony about other civilians who worked in the plant or regularly visited
it, and who couldn't have missed how horrible conditions were. He could
name names. Zeppelin's Knut Eckener, keeping an eye on production of
the rocket's center sections, attended at least one meeting there.

Rickhey knew about forty-two boxes of Mittelwerk management
documents. He could direct prosecutors to evidence that could incrimi-
nate others. He knew where the skeletons were. Would the Americans
seize and extradite other Paperclip experts back to Germany?

The figures prosecutors cited were chilling. Between the summer of
1943 and April 1945, there were about 15,000 recorded deaths at the
Nordhausen concentration camp. The actual number was closer to 18,000 to
20,000, they argued, not including deaths during evacuations. That worked
out to about one in three of the 60,000 prisoners forced to work there.

Aside from Rickhey, defendants included eighteen men who worked
for the SS or who were Kapos, prisoners deputized by the SS to supervise other inmates. They were charged with killings, beatings, torture,
starvation, and abuses of "many thousands." The Nordhausen concentration camp was under the supervision of SS Major General Hans Kammler, who had made a name for himself at Auschwitz with more efficient
machinery for mass extermination.

Conditions tunneling out the factory in 1943 were hellish, prosecutors said. Beds were built of boards, four tiers high, stacked so tightly one
on top of another that it was impossible for prisoners to sit up in bed.
The mattresses were paper stuffed with straw, and they soon became filled
with lice and vermin. The prosecutors detailed pitifully filthy and unsani-
tary conditions in the tunnels and the lack of facilities for delousing.

The number of prisoners mushroomed, from around 4,000 in October 1943 to 10,000 in December 1943. Overcrowding meant two or
three inmates had to share a bed. The beds never got cold; as soon as
one got up to go to work, another crawled into the same bunk. There
was not even one blanket for each bed, and some inmates had to cover
themselves with their coats. At one point, the camp had a shortage of
8,000 blankets, as well as a considerable deficiency of jackets, trousers,
caps, shirts, stockings, and shoes. When the beds were moved from the

tunnels to the barracks aboveground in the spring and summer of 1944, dead bodies of inmates, some decomposing, were found in water underneath wooden floorboards.

The prosecutors kept the outrage building. The principal means of killing was shooting, hanging, strangulation, beating, starvation, exposure, deprivation of medical attention, and overwork. The inmates were beaten with iron bars, rubber hoses, rubber cables, wooden clubs, and heavy boards.

Prisoners were forced to work twelve-hour shifts, seven days a week. Roll call took from one to four hours. They typically could muster only five or six hours of sleep a day. Blasting operations in the tunnels day and night created dust and gases, which coated the inside of their noses and mouths. Many prisoners became so thirsty and dirty from the dust, they attempted to drink urine or use it for washing. Doing so prompted beatings, sometimes to death, by SS men. Many others acquired pneumonia from the dust and dampness, which developed into tuberculosis.

The early miserable conditions were directly the work of the A4 Special Committee, which devised an inhuman schedule to bore out the tunnel, move machinery, and begin production—even before any quarters had been built for the prisoners. This part of the trial could prove a problem for the Zeppelin executives, as the surname Eckener appeared on at least one Peenemünde Army Institute document naming members of the A4 Special Committee. Whether it referred to Hugo or perhaps Knut, it was trouble.

Back when it was all playing out, the A4 Committee members were heroes to Hitler. In December 1943, Albert Speer wrote a letter of praise to Hans Kammler, the overseer of that abomination. "The leader of the Special Committee A4, Degenkolb, reports to me that you have brought the underground installations . . . to completion out of their raw condition in the almost impossibly short period of time of two months," Speer raved. "You have transformed them into a factory which has no European comparison and remains unsurpassed even in American conceptions."

Zeppelin officials may have had a hand in other misdeeds. Mittelwerk management and the SS were constantly on the lookout for sabotage. After all, the prisoners were Germany's enemies. The slave workers knew the weapons they were forced to make would blow up their own countrymen, would prolong the war.

Equipment tests became a critical way of spotting sabotage efforts. Civilian engineers and technicians tested parts and assemblies frequently as they made their way along the assembly line. The Army Acceptance Office used inspectors from contractors to help hunt for sabotage, and some of those inspectors were apparently officials from Luftschiffbau Zeppelin. Any knowledge of how sabotage suspects at Mittelwerk were brutally executed could have incriminated those Zeppelin employees.

Specific sections of the tunnels in the underground complex created each part, subassembly, and general assembly. Should any given part appear to have been tampered with, the civilian engineers could then pinpoint precisely when it was made and, unfortunately for the prisoners, who worked on it at a given time.

Whenever a prisoner was accused of sabotage, a noose awaited. At the bunker, the prosecutors established, prisoners to be publicly hanged were gagged with a piece of wood, wired from their mouth behind their head to prevent screaming. Hangings were carried out at least two different times in the tunnels, where all work was stopped and the prisoners were forced to witness them.

The prosecutors painted a gory portrait of the men who had been hanged on the electric crane, as it rose slowly. The victims writhed and strangled for about ten minutes, they said, after which the bodies were let down. SS personnel then fired "mercy shots" into any victim still alive in some degree of agony. This horror played out once in February 1945, when nine were hanged, and another time when sixteen were hanged.

About 310 inmates were hanged at the main camp, about 120 suspected of sabotage. As many as fifty-seven inmates were hanged on one occasion in the roll-call square in March 1945. Once, when the victims were still alive after being cut down from the gallows, the prosecutors accused the chief hangman of unthinkable cruelty. Citing witness testimony, they said the hangman approached the men who were still alive and smashed their heads with a footstool.

## 17

# "I Don't Believe in War"

WHILE HUGO ECKENER KEPT HIS HEAD DOWN IN AKRON, PAUL LITCH-field and Charles Rosendahl appeared together at a hearing in Washington that fall. They were testifying in late October before President Truman's recently appointed Air Policy Commission. Now that the war had ended, Truman wanted to chart the future of aviation for America, and the panel was hearing from dozens of aircraft makers and military officers. The 1950s were soon coming. The United States needed to be pushing ahead with jet planes, supersonic aircraft, and guided missiles. Space travel seemed surely in the offing.

None of that is what Rosendahl and his friend from Goodyear wanted to talk about. They wanted to revive a relic, the old airship. Litchfield said he had even brought a statement from Hugo Eckener, the world-renowned expert, who just so happened to be working with Goodyear to develop balloon ships that would be twice the size of the *Hindenburg*. The Eckener name was storied. He was an aviation pioneer. He flew the *Graf Zeppelin* around the world, as everyone knew. But that was all some time ago. What had he been up to lately?

Litchfield explained that Eckener was a visiting German scientist, much the same as the V-2 developers who were now in New Mexico and elsewhere working for the U.S. military. He stressed that Eckener was never a Nazi and had barely escaped being locked up in a concentration camp during the war.

The Eckener statement in Litchfield's hands expressed complete confidence in dirigibles, despite the *Hindenburg* tragedy and the loss of the *Shenandoah*, *Akron*, and *Macon*, much of the U.S. Navy's airship fleet. Litchfield and Rosendahl called the floating aircraft "neglected" and asked that a national airship policy be formed.

Rosendahl, promoted to rear admiral during the war, said there were many military capabilities for airships, including carrying modern electronics equipment such as radar. He did not mention, if he knew, how Eckener had already helped pioneer such espionage, in advance of Hitler's invasions. Rosendahl told the panel that airships could patrol America's long coastlines and might be equipped to "deflect" guided missiles.

For months, Rosendahl had been issuing a warning. It was about Russia. His information, he said, was that Russia had begun some sort of airship program and had managed to secure some helium, though the United States was generally understood to be the only country with enough helium to be practical. He would keep the embers of the Red Scare glowing.

As the hearing proceeded, President Truman appeared at a somber gathering nearby, the first mass burial of American soldiers who had died overseas. In a dark coat and gray striped pants, the president stood with chiefs of the army, air force, and navy as twenty soldiers were laid to rest in Arlington Cemetery. Eventually, another 6,000 bodies of slain Americans would be brought home from foreign graves. A bugler played taps. Rifles cracked three volleys. Families standing in the autumn cold wept. An eighty-six-piece army band played "Nearer My God to Thee."

Two days later, a significant deadline passed. In the two years since World War II ended, the Allies had grown weary of trying war crimes. U.S. Army military courts and commissions in Germany tried more than 1,600 defendants in nearly 500 cases. The United States and Great Britain had decided to close their military proceedings down. Their statute of limitations for accepting evidence or extradition orders against suspects would expire November 1, 1947.

Two weeks after that date, Eckener would be on a plane back to Germany. He had been in America during the entire Nordhausen trial at the Dachau prison, and it was clear he would neither be called as a witness nor charged. The trial was about to move to sentencing. Having celebrated his seventy-ninth birthday in the United States, Eckener told his American military supervisors his wife was sick and requested his return to Germany.

That set off classified Paperclip paperwork.

*To HQ EUCOM, Frankfurt Germany*
*Subject PAPERCLIP*
*Dr. Hugo Eckener departing US by air Westover Field on Novem-*
*ber 13 . . . Terminate contract on arrival. Eckener paid in full by*
*Goodyear Aircraft Corp . . . Subject returning due to illness of wife.*
*Request return to residence be expedited. Not considered security*
*threat. Dossier follows by airmail.*

After Eckener flew back, Bosquet Wev, the director of the Joint
Intelligence Objectives Agency, wrote a memo to J. Edgar Hoover, the
FBI director. The FBI wanted to keep a close eye on German characters,
recently enemies, whom Hoover thought were suspicious. "Dr. Eckener
was repatriated to Germany by air transportation on 14 November 1947,"
Wev wrote. "The dependents of Dr. Eckener were not brought to the
United States. Dr. Eckener has been in the United States under limited
military custody since 29 April 1947. He was returned to Germany due
to the illness of his wife."

Just after he left, the Associated Press carried a story about Eckener's
stay in the United States. He was happy to talk about his days flying the
*Graf Zeppelin* and the *Hindenburg*. He delighted in talking about how
new materials could lighten the weight of a Zeppelin by four to five tons.
Other advances would allow typical airship speeds to increase by five to
ten miles an hour. But when the reporter asked why Eckener kept running the Zeppelin company during the war and about military possibilities for a Zeppelin, Eckener snapped, "I don't believe in war."

The war-crimes trial over the Nazi underground factory at Nordhausen
closed on Tuesday, December 30, 1947. The commandant, Hans Moeser,
was sentenced to death by hanging. Fourteen others faced prison terms
from five years to life. Based on the testimony on the viciousness of the SS
guard nicknamed Horsehead, it became evident to the prosecution that
they had missed something by not charging him.

Georg Rickhey, the single civilian in the case, was acquitted. Rickhey had argued he was only responsible for budgeting, and he blamed any abuse and exploitation on the technical director, who happened to be missing.

Rickhey's defense attorney requested that Wernher von Braun, Arthur Rudolph, and other Mittelwerk managers, who were cocooned in the Paperclip project in the United States during the trial, appear to testify at the Dachau proceeding because Rickhey faced a possible death penalty. Their knowledge of the management structure could help defend him, the attorney argued. The U.S. military, however, refused to release them, citing the national security risk if the rocket experts fell into the hands of the Russians. For his part, Rickhey asked the court to credit him for his good work helping the Americans under Paperclip.

There was still one more chance to bring Eckener to justice. Months before he returned to Germany, the first phase of his denazification case established a troubling wartime record through clippings from newspapers and magazines. Hugo Eckener worked for the armaments industry since 1939, investigators believed. In *Berlin Illustrated* magazine, he appeared on the cover in a new Tiger tank with Minister of Armaments Speer. On Eckener's seventieth birthday, Hitler awarded him the honorary Professor title. And Eckener steered the Zeppelin company into making V-weapons.

The district denazification committee was unconvinced of Eckener's assurances that he opposed the Nazis. It ruled that he was essentially a Nazi supporter and proposed that Eckener be stripped of the chairmanship of the Zeppelin company and face heavy fines.

The regional committee, reviewing the case, reiterated the earlier charges and suggested that 50 percent of Eckener's total assets be confiscated and that he be barred for a decade from managerial employment, along with all political rights revoked. That panel charged that Eckener had contributed to Hitler's takeover of power, especially after his speech supporting Hitler in August of 1934.

Eckener must have known his "noble wine" radio endorsement of Hitler—in the immediate aftermath of the Night of the Long Knives massacre—was surely incriminating. So, he argued that he did write a

Hitler speech, under duress, but it ultimately was not acceptable to Goebbels's Propaganda Ministry and was never broadcast.

In fact, he further claimed, the Gestapo was looking to eliminate *him* during the Long Knives purge. Luckily, he said, he was in Buenos Aires, and when he returned days later, the executions had ended. He also played up the brief Propaganda Ministry censorship of him in the press, back in 1936, saying he was branded an opponent of the movement.

Eckener still needed some explanation, however, for why a professed enemy of Hitler wasn't simply snuffed out by an unrelenting terrorist government. He provided an extraordinary reason. Eckener contended that Hitler had wanted to send him to a concentration camp at some point, but did not do so because President Hindenburg, shortly before he died, made Hitler promise not to harm him in any way. Eckener really seemed to think he could convince them that Hitler and his henchmen would have spared a known enemy of the Nazis.

Then he reached back a decade, to the aftermath of the *Hindenburg* disaster. As hated as Nazi Germany was in 1937, he argued, there's no way the United States would have agreed to sell helium to a German executive had he been an ally of Hitler's. The House and Senate had agreed that "contrary to the existing helium export bans, helium would have to be made available to me, so I was not regarded as a helper of Hitler."

In late 1946, the Political Cleansing Committee at Ravensburg ruled that Eckener should be fined 100,000 Reichsmarks and banned for five years from political rights and administrative jobs. Without even considering the Zeppelin slave workers and all the suffering of the prisoners, it found that Eckener was a Nazi and a war profiteer.

The committee was eager to fine him and other armaments executives in Friedrichshafen because it found them partly responsible for the mass destruction of the city. They put their technical genius and their organizing skills at the service of the Nazi war, the committee alleged. Their actions to turn Friedrichshafen into an arms center merely put it on the map for Allied bombing raids. The fines would help rebuild the ravaged city.

Early on, Eckener not only failed to condemn the Nazis, the committee argued, but he recommended Hitler in a public speech, decisively influencing millions and enabling the Nazis to hold themselves in power. And Eckener, it added, knew professionally the great influence of public opinion.

Knut Eckener was also found to be a Nazi and war profiteer. Knut played a decisive role and made a considerable investment in the manufacture of V-weapons in Friedrichshafen, the committee said, and had a great hand in the subsequent destruction of the city. There was "great anger" among the people of Friedrichshafen toward those responsible, the ruling said. Ultimately, Knut was fined 5,000 RM and prohibited from taking any executive positions for five years.

In his defense, Knut Eckener noted that he only joined the Nazi Party to soften the government's campaign against his father and to avoid having a different party member forced upon the company's upper management. He said he was "personally against the Party."

In 1942, Knut acknowledged, the Luftschiffbau Zeppelin had begun making parts for long-range artillery weapons, specifically fuel containers and outer casings. He claimed not to have known that the parts were for V-2 rockets, though they did speculate as much. He also said he treated the forced foreign workers and the prisoners mercifully, being particularly humane, benevolent, and understanding, and in doing so raised the suspicion of the Gestapo.

Hugo Eckener's claim that the pro-Hitler speech was never broadcast infuriated Gerhard Müller, the commissioner for political cleansing. He recalled hearing the three-minute radio address in the summer of 1934, when he was a law student. After the war, he managed to secure a transcript of the speech, and reviewed its poisonous phrasing.

*One firm will has to command in a dictatorial fashion. . . . Weakness of thought here would be weakness of will. . . . Stern, indeed drastic interventions and methods are unavoidable in this. Mistakes and excesses may have occurred—how could they be avoided in such times?—pressed grapes are sour and cloudy as they ferment, but a clear and noble wine will one day result. . . .*

*The clever and experienced minds among our people should put themselves at the Führer's disposal and help to solve the dreadful*

*problems, instead of just making negative criticisms. . . . What is at*
*issue now is the conviction that the Führer's will is pure and sincere*
*and that his goals are good and great. . . .*

How could he? And how dare he, so shortly after Hitler's murderous Long Knives purge? Müller released a proclamation lambasting Eckener. He said Dr. Eckener's resistance claims were so vague, it was hard to tell whether he had remotely offset the considerable support that he had provided to the National Socialist regime, particularly by making his radio address in 1934. "There must be thousands who distinctly remember what a great impression this address made on the public, precisely because Dr. Eckener was not considered to be a National Socialist, and furthermore, how clearly the address praised the Regime as good and Hitler as the leader of the German people beyond any doubt."

The next winter, the French tribunal declared Eckener a Nazi and a war profiteer. The news hit the American newspapers in late January 1948. Hugo Eckener, Knut Eckener, and two other wartime airplane manufacturers and an engineer had been fined a total of 712,000 Reichsmarks (about $71,000 then) by a French zone denazification court. The Eckeners; warplane manufacturer Claude Dornier; Karl Maybach, who made motors for Dornier's planes; and a chief engineer were charged with having been Nazi supporters and with profiteering during the war. All five were forbidden to be managers for five years and lost their voting privileges. Not everyone under investigation in Friedrichshafen was found guilty. The longtime Zeppelin designer Ludwig Dürr, for one, was found innocent of all charges.

There was no appeal. But Hugo Eckener managed to have the last word on it.

# 18

# "Hunger Cages"

HUGO ECKENER MAY PERHAPS HAVE BEEN EMBOLDENED BY THE RULING. No one brought up the Zeppelin concentration camps. The one at the main factory in Friedrichshafen had been bombed and dismantled. Gone from the face of the earth, there was nothing left to liberate. Zeppelin's other detention camps in the south were minor outposts in the vast Nazi prison state. Eckener had no obvious connection to the V-2 rocket factories in the north. As with the *Hindenburg*, there seemed to be no evidence with which to charge him, if anyone even knew enough at that point to look.

For a decade, Eckener had lived a double life. He worked behind the scenes to help Hitler's cause in Germany, and before and after the war when he stepped to podiums and witness stands elsewhere in the world, he clammed up about anything that might hint of Nazi connections. He privately tossed off occasional jokes about Goebbels, whom he personally disliked, which further threw reporters off the scent.

Eckener knew well how to manipulate people, and the press. His doctoral training years earlier at Leipzig had given him insight into the brain and the way humans process information. He knew the wrinkles of rhetoric and celebrity, of truth and lie, of credibility and gullibility. Deep down, he knew how to tell a damn colorful story, one with legs. Repeat it enough, it's true.

To clear his name, he had spent months conjuring up a memoir, the Hugo Eckener autobiography. In it, he painted a self-portrait of a hero. It was a story of epic courage, of one man's open resistance to unspeakable evil. In a bad war, the Good German.

This brazen revisionism wouldn't matter except the fictional account helped Eckener to escape justice, and it became the narrative spine of every subsequent book on the airship age. The biography was so intricate, so replete with rich anecdotes, it would fool generations of historians trying to pin down the history of the Zeppelin company and the infamous *Hindenburg* disaster.

In Eckener's telling, the *Hindenburg* became the main wedge between him and the Nazi regime. His deception would sweep up Goebbels, and Göring, and the U.S. government. Along the way, he would smear his loyal companion who lost his life on the *Hindenburg*, the Little Captain, Ernst Lehmann.

When the Nazi penalty against Eckener was announced in the winter of 1948, he was eighty years old. He was living at his daughter Lotte's home in Konstanz, his hearing worsening, working on the book. The city was the childhood home of Count Zeppelin. Konstanz was on the Bodensee, across from Friedrichshafen. It was so close to the Swiss border that Konstanz residents left their lights on at night during the war to fool Allied planes into thinking the city was in Switzerland. The ruse worked.

The 565-page hardcover book would eventually be published in Eckener's birthplace of Flensburg. He titled it *Im Zeppelin über Länder und Meere*, or *In the Zeppelin over Countries and Seas*. Published in 1949, it would end up in the tiny-type citations of nearly every major book subsequently written on Eckener, Zeppelins, and the *Hindenburg*.

Before it was even completed, he used alibis and arguments he had formulated for it to defend himself in denazification proceedings. The work in progress would become particularly important in 1948, when Eckener faced new legal scrutiny in the American zone after he applied for a job in the town of Schwäbisch Gmünd, near Stuttgart. The tales in his book remained the backbone of his defense, a fabricated anti-Nazi record.

Opening chapters covered the *Los Angeles*, the Zeppelin that kept the Friedrichshafen factory alive after World War I, and the *Graf Zeppelin* and its round-the-world flight. The book ended with the rise and fall of the *Hindenburg* and a chapter titled "Helium Troubles and a Gloomy Ending."

Just before his sections on the *Hindenburg* and helium is a chapter that didn't really fit in the arc of the narrative. Everything else moved apace chronologically. The misfit chapter, an amalgamation of arguments Eckener had belatedly concocted to beat Nazi charges, he titled "My Encounters with Hitler and the Nazi Party 1929 to 1939."

The grand pretense, as laid out by Eckener, began with a 1932 newspaper poll. The large, well-known Milan newspaper *Corriere della Sera* asked its readers to name the most popular public figure on earth at the present time. By an overwhelming majority, he wrote, readers selected the name of Dr. Eckener.

But, the famous man wrote, celebrity did nothing for him. Throughout those years, he had been fully occupied with his own work and plans (the *Graf Zeppelin*'s world voyage, the South America trips, and on and on). He hadn't a care in the world for a rising politician named Hitler.

In 1932, Eckener wrote, a National Socialist Party member, a district leader in Friedrichshafen, approached him, requesting that he loan the party his large airship hangar, with voluminous floor space, for Hitler to speak to a gathering. Eckener explained that he refused, forcing Hitler to speak at a smaller venue elsewhere. At that moment, he wrote, he became branded as a Nazi enemy.

In April of 1933 came the creation of the secret police, the Gestapo, charged with neutralizing all "dangerous" adversaries by locking them away in concentration camps. The author did not mention that the first such camp was founded that year at Dachau. He worried, or so he said, that barbed wire would be his fate.

Eckener said he only discovered years later why he had been spared. He learned this from Ferdinand Sauerbruch, a doctor attending to the dying President Hindenburg in the summer of 1934. Eckener claimed that Dr. Sauerbruch confided to him that Hindenburg had learned that Hitler wanted to imprison Eckener in a concentration camp after January 1933. Then, according to Eckener's account, Hindenburg ordered Hitler to leave Eckener alone. "So," Eckener wrote, "I had Hindenburg to thank that I was spared. . . . Hitler, such the singular mixture of lies and truth that he was, kept the promise he made to the president."

The unlikely story line continued, gaining steam. In June 1933, Eckener learned through a naval officer friend that the head of the Gestapo, Rudolf Diels, had been gathering evidence of his criticism of the Nazis and wanted to speak to him. Or so Eckener wrote. The next night, the Gestapo chief arrived at Eckener's room at the Hotel Esplanade in Berlin. Diels told the Zeppelin captain that he had a fat dossier on him, filled with dissenting and hostile statements he had made about the ruling party. He suggested Eckener make a pro-Nazi public address, to clear his name of any trouble.

Face to face with the agitated Gestapo chief, Eckener recounted how he then outfoxed him. Eckener explained to Diels that he had a Zeppelin flight to Rio in a matter of days and needed to get back to Friedrichshafen in the morning by train. He would consider the proposal and get back to him, but then he just never did. Why didn't Diels follow up? It had to have been the secret order from the dying President Hindenburg not to harass Eckener in any way, he wrote, that's all he could figure.

Then, in late 1933, Eckener relayed how the *Graf Zeppelin* had been invited to the World's Fair in Chicago, and he gladly agreed to fly there. Given its South American schedule, the *Graf Zeppelin* would have to fly north from Brazil. His memoir then worked in his supposed aversion to political prisons, a passion that welled up in him as they passed over the infamous Devil's Island, a penal colony in French Guyana, off the South American coast. For certain undesirable political actors and major criminals, he wrote, France had its tropical-oven prison, Russia had its Siberian ice cellar, and Hitler had his "hunger cages in the concentration camps."

When the *Graf Zeppelin* finally arrived in Chicago, Captain Eckener was stunned to discover that anti-Nazi sentiment was powerful in America. After reaching Chicago around eight in the morning, the *Graf Zeppelin* did a few loops around the city and then was informed that it couldn't land near the fairgrounds because the local sheriff's office had received letters threatening sabotage to the airship. So, Eckener wrote, the sheriff arranged for a landing spot in a safe location well north of the city.

The next plot point in the deception: the end of June 1934. Eckener and his crew were leaving Buenos Aires when the radio man came breaking into the control room, warning him about British reports he had heard about the arrest of Ernst Röhm, a loyal lieutenant of Hitler, and the executions of Kurt von Schleicher, the former chancellor, and many others in authority. The radio man whispered, "Everything in Germany has turned upside down." On the entire trip back to Germany, Eckener and his crew followed developments on the radio.

And then Eckener relayed that he had learned something disturbing: He himself was supposed to be snuffed out during the Long Knives massacre, and had only escaped because he was somewhere over the Atlantic Ocean at the time. Or so he said, with no evidence to back it up. Eckener contended that two men who looked like police officers showed up at his home, asking for him on the morning of June 30. The housekeeper explained that Dr. Eckener was away on a flight, and the men disappeared. By the time he got back to Friedrichshafen, the notorious purge was over.

Eckener began to relax a bit, he wrote, but in view of the Gestapo's increasingly brutal attacks, he had to be very cautious. Within weeks, Hindenburg died, and Hitler made the bold stroke of fusing all the leadership powers into the title *Führer*. To legitimize it, he would hold a popular vote in Germany, to show that the move was the will of the people. Eckener snidely called the whole election a farce, drummed up by Hitler.

Things turned serious on August 10, Eckener's birthday, when the Ministry of Propaganda requested he record a radio speech in favor of Hitler's move. This speech would then be broadcast by radio on all stations nationwide. Worried about a civil war in Germany if he didn't add a calming voice to the situation, Eckener said, he relented. He wrote and recorded a speech. He could reach out to his fellow citizens and ask the important questions at this momentous point in time.

Eckener flashed forward, to immediately after the war, acting as the narrator addressing the reader directly. Today, he said, it is easy to see Hitler as a "consummate criminal," but back in 1934, the overwhelming majority of Germany was behind him, as he had won over even the intelligent and cautious.

Eckener claimed that he recorded the Hitler-Führer speech, but it never made the airwaves because it was too weak an endorsement. He again flashed forward in time. In 1946, he wrote, people found the manuscript of his radio address and then tried to brand him a supporter of Hitler. He argued that the prosecutors mischaracterized the speech simply by excerpting parts, out of context, that only made him seem to favor Hitler.

Next came the climax of Eckener's self-proclaimed anti-Nazi record and the slander of Captain Lehmann. It was 1936, and Hitler had remilitarized the Rhineland. Through his retelling, Eckener took advantage of his dustup that year with Goebbels. The newspapers back in 1936 had a heyday with the story of how the foolhardy propaganda minister blacklisted the famed Zeppelin pilot; how grand, old Eckener was to be erased from the daily record of events.

Again, seeking legitimacy, Hitler called for a popular vote, to show that the German nation, not some rogue leader in Berlin, backed the show of force in the Rhineland. In advance of the vote, the Propaganda Ministry asked for two things. First, the *Graf Zeppelin* and brand-new *Hindenburg* were supposed to participate in flights over all the major towns of Germany, to drop propaganda leaflets in favor of Hitler's muscle-flexing. Second, Eckener himself was called on again to make a radio speech, this time endorsing the Rhine move. The Nazi Party, in Eckener's telling, simply couldn't resist exploiting the most popular man in the world.

But Eckener refused to make the speech, telling the sinister propagandists that the territorial move was a political event, one outside his professional expertise. He did, however, grudgingly agree to the request for his airships. "I considered it a tasteless abuse, a kind of desecration of the airships, and I declined to travel along myself," he wrote.

The divide between him and the Nazi regime then came to a head with the propaganda flights and an early accident with the *Hindenburg*. To make the election aerial tour, Captain Lehmann brought the *Hindenburg* out of its hangar amid a very gusty wind. The injudicious attempt to take off in such heavy winds ended up in an accident, in which the tail fin was damaged on the airfield at Frankfurt.

Eckener asserted that he berated Lehmann, who had endangered the *Hindenburg* simply to support the Nazis. He wrote: "I . . . said something like this: 'How could you, Mr. Lehmann, order the ship to be brought out in such windy conditions? You had the best excuse in the world to cancel this ridiculous trip; instead you put our new ship directly at risk, just so as not to annoy Mr. Goebbels.'" Lehmann replied that he could make emergency repairs in two or three hours and would then catch up with the *Graf Zeppelin*. Eckener then became completely enraged, he wrote, and furiously upbraided Lehmann for conducting nonsense flights just to appease Goebbels.

Eckener's chief concern, he wrote, was that the engines weren't properly tested—untrue—before their looming first trans-Atlantic flight, scheduled for two days later. Eckener cared about the safety of the ship; Lehmann merely wanted to impress Nazi officials. The equation: Eckener safe, anti-Nazi; Lehmann reckless, Nazi puppet.

The upbraiding of Lehmann was so loud, or so Eckener claimed, that one of the Nazi propaganda aides on board the *Hindenburg* heard and dutifully reported Eckener's poisonous remarks back to Goebbels. The propaganda minister then promptly blacklisted Eckener, ordering that the Zeppelin man's name and image be stricken from the press.

Eckener only learned of the blacklisting himself when a reporter asked him about the rebuff while on a Zeppelin flight over the Atlantic days later. Back in Germany, he learned that Göring had summoned him to Berlin to discuss the matter. And then it dawned on Eckener: His charisma and popularity was probably a political threat in the upper circles of the Nazis, including perhaps Hitler himself.

It is true, the *Hindenburg* did smash its tail on takeoff on March 26, 1936. However, the cloak-and-dagger remainder of the story appears to have come solely from Eckener's imagination.

Lehmann showed no particular leaning toward the Nazi Party, and a surprise gust of wind over the hangar caused the damage on what was otherwise a day of light breezes, according to others present in the ship and on the field that day. A newspaper account the next day praised Lehmann's skill in getting the *Hindenburg* off the ground after the accident, and his caution in making an emergency landing to repair the damage before returning to the air. No eyewitness account seems to corroborate Eckener's ever screaming at Lehmann that day.

Equally telling, the daily diary of Goebbels makes it clear he became annoyed with Eckener for one thing only: agreeing to endorse Hitler and the Rhineland move in a speech on March 29, 1936, and then backing out at the last minute. "A true patriot!" Goebbels wrote, sarcastically. The tiff had nothing to do with anything that Eckener did say; rather, it was what he didn't say.

After the war, other Germans seeking to paint themselves as Nazi resisters similarly played up incidental brushes with party officials, and Eckener seized upon his with vigor. In December 1948, Eckener wrote an article in the large German magazine *Der Spiegel*, rebutting his denazification judgment, saying his derogatory remarks about Goebbels sparked a press ban of him that lasted two full years. It actually lasted two weeks, at most.

Eckener apparently counted on people to have moved on and forgotten that history: the short duration of the ban, his attempts to reconcile with the Nazi government in 1936, and what he told foreign reporters during his brief censorship. "I never protested against the use of the airship in the election propaganda," they quoted Eckener saying. He also told them back in 1936, "I always say 'Heil, Hitler!' when the occasion demands it, contrary to certain reports."

No matter, the Eckener line in his deceptive memoir was building: The Nazis nearly destroyed the *Hindenburg* on its maiden ocean voyage, with supposedly sympathetic Lehmann's complicity. Eckener next recounted the engine troubles on the *Hindenburg* in April 1936, more than 300 miles off the coast of Africa. Because Lehmann and the Propaganda Ministry had conspired to use the *Hindenburg* for propaganda, the ship hadn't undergone thorough engine tests, he erroneously charged, and could have plunged into the ocean when the motors subsequently malfunctioned.

Eckener didn't explain why he himself rode off over the Atlantic Ocean on a ship he supposedly thought wasn't properly tested, but he did portray himself as the heroic captain who saved the *Hindenburg* once peril surfaced on that flight. During the flight, two of the four engines broke down. The open ocean was below, he wrote of the drama, and the Sahara Desert lay off the starboard side. There were seventy-five people on board. The situation was perilous. He quickly considered trying to rush back to Brazil. Then he considered diverting the *Hindenburg* to a quick landing in the African desert, in case, say, another engine failed. He imagined a scene in his mind:

a crash in the desert; seventy-five people, shouldering water and provisions from the *Hindenburg*'s wreckage, making their way to a remote village for help. "I admit that I have hardly ever felt myself in such great spiritual need as in these hours of vacillation and perplexity," he wrote.

Eckener, who was solely on the flight as a passenger, did a crafty rewrite of events. Lehmann was captain the whole flight. Eckener, who had been removed from flight operations, was not in command of the *Hindenburg* on that flight. It seems Eckener had enmity toward Lehmann after turns of events left Lehmann commander of the *Hindenburg*. After Lehmann died, and could not, of course, contest the account, Eckener simply wrote how he wished events had transpired.

It was none other than Hitler himself who put the final nail in the coffin of the grand Zeppelin experiment—this was the conclusion Eckener's memoir was building to. The reader couldn't help but follow the unfolding logic. Eckener loved Zeppelins and devoted his life to them. Hitler's warmongering kept the United States from providing helium to the Germans after the *Hindenburg* disaster. Eckener's life work came to a jarring end, sealing forever his hatred of Hitler and the Nazis.

To make that story line work, Eckener had to lie about a few other things. After the English airship R 101 burned in France in October 1930, he wrote that he attempted to get helium from America, but was turned down. The *Hindenburg*, built for helium, therefore had to be filled with hydrogen, he wrote.

Actually, before the tragedy, Eckener had never tried to get helium, the gas that can't catch fire. He seemed to think the Germans' long record of safety with flammable hydrogen would hold indefinitely. After the *Hindenburg*'s first season, the Nazi Air Ministry even urged Eckener to use helium in airships for safety; he stalled, complaining to the air-service authorities about the increased cost, telling them he would study it further. He admitted as much, in a letter to his wife, days after the disaster, written while aboard the *Europa* steamer bound for the *Hindenburg* investigation at Lakehurst. He told her days after the tragedy that he regretted not ordering helium for the *Hindenburg*. He steadfastly had refused it.

His memoir offered nothing about the structural defect in the *Hindenburg* that wore a gas cell down its first season, and the hasty repairs made just weeks before to keep the ship on schedule for its second season. Captain Lehmann was so anxious about whether the repairs would hold, he rode the *Hindenburg* on its fateful flight, as an observer, just in case.

Eckener then steered the Commerce Department investigation to a faulty finding, posing a speculative theory that pilot error, an overly sharp turn at landing, possibly caused a tear in a gas cell that led to the *Hindenburg* disaster. The leaking gas, he speculated, was probably ignited by atmospheric electricity.

His memoir would recount that a flight engineer testified at the hearing in Lakehurst that the third gas cell from the stern was nearly completely empty just before the fire broke out. That observation certainly helped give credence to Eckener's idea that a shear wire tore into a gasbag, making hydrogen gush out and emptying the gas cell quickly.

It's just that no such testimony was ever given at the investigation. Eckener invented that.

Eckener's theory that a sharp turn and torn wire caused the catastrophe was convenient for him. It shifted blame first from the design of the ship to its pilots. More important, it suggested that had the crew executed the exact same overly tight turn and had fireproof helium aboard, the *Hindenburg* disaster would never have happened. A single deflated gasbag was a manageable problem.

Eckener was personally absolved by his speculative version of events. He neither steered the ship into disaster nor could he operate it with safe helium since America supposedly withheld the fireproof gas from him.

The *Hindenburg*'s design flaw was so dangerous, actually, it wouldn't have mattered what gas it was carrying, helium or hydrogen. With any loss of two or more cells as they became frayed, buoyancy would fail for the entire ship, sending it plunging from the sky. It would have weighed too much for the remaining full gas cells.

By keeping the investigators in the dark about any structural defect, Eckener managed to avoid responsibility for any wrongdoing in the deaths of thirty-six people. Had investigators have known, had they had the benefit of what Leonhard Adelt disclosed about gasbag damage, they could have at least requested maintenance records to further explore the possible role of known mechanical problems with the *Hindenburg* disaster.

At the time Eckener appealed to Congress to amend an export-control law so Germany could buy helium after the *Hindenburg* caught fire, no one knew that he had endorsed Hitler to his Germany countrymen in 1934, recording the radio speech that helped cement Hitler's ascent to Führer. Eckener's assurances that Zeppelins were obsolete for any military use would have had quite a different ring for U.S. lawmakers had they known that.

Eckener had been building his case to this final point: "Since we could not fly without American helium, however, I therefore had to conclude that Hitler had sent Zeppelin transportation to its grave."

Such a stark conclusion. No one would reasonably suspect Eckener as a Nazi supporter. His anti-Nazi credentials, his hatred of Hitler, sounded so solid. The war years, he dismissed in a few sentences. The Luftschiffbau Zeppelin was gradually drawn more and more into armaments production under military law, he wrote. There was no way to fight it. "Every director of any industrial plant," he wrote, "if he had a German sensibility, had to help win this war, in order to avoid the catastrophe into which we have now fallen. Acting in any other way would have been treason pure and simple."

Eckener professed that both he and Count Zeppelin were goodwill ambassadors to the world and that the Zeppelin was a tool of diplomacy. The Zeppelin was conceived by the Count from the beginning as "an instrument of peace and peaceful exchange" and only later, while planes were in their infancy, did the Zeppelin become an attack vehicle, Eckener wrote.

Wrong. The Zeppelin was conceived as a weapon. Of the 119 Zeppelins the Luftschiffbau Zeppelin built, 103 were for the military. And the V-1 and V-2 weapons were the fulfillment of Count Zeppelin's long dream of a German attack weapon for aerial warfare. Eckener trained more than a thousand crew members for Zeppelin bombing missions. The air raids were shocking in that they were the first use of strategic aerial bombing. By late 1915, Count Zeppelin was crying for all-out war with his flying ships. "All England must burn!" he shouted back then to an army officer.

The V-2 rocket was the final curtain of the Luftschiffbau Zeppelin as a war-industry company. Those rockets rained on England and the

European continent for months. Before Winston Churchill addressed the House of Commons on April 26, 1945, telling them the attacks had finally ceased, a thousand V-2s had killed over 2,700 people in England and seriously wounded another 6,500.

November of 1944 saw the British capital's most deadly attack, in London's suburban New Cross. A V-2 hurtled into a five-and-dime store there at the busy noon rush. In all, 167 died and another 100 pulled from the rubble were injured, mostly women and children. The rocket attacks finally stopped after Allied troops overran the launching sites in Holland.

In the final reckoning for the V-2, an estimated 10,000 slave laborers died in producing the rocket, from illness, execution, or exhaustion. That is double the estimated number of victims who died from V-2 strikes. In all, 3,000 of the rockets were fired at England and the Continent from September 1944 to March 1945.

None of that made the account of the good and high-minded author, who likewise steered clear of any mention of concentration camp prisoners. Eckener would close his chapter detailing his long resistance to the Nazis with a coda. Referring to his denazification sentence and fine, he denied being a party member or a profiteer.

If he were guilty for work that helped the war effort, he wrote, then one would have to similarly punish every potato farmer who fed a German soldier. "I laughed about my punishment," Eckener wrote, and everyone who knew him laughed about it, or were infuriated by it.

There was one bizarre aside. Some reports suggested that Eckener had fallen into disfavor with the Nazi regime because he christened his new ship the *Hindenburg*, rather than the *Hitler*, as some Nazis had advocated. Eckener wrote that he wished to correct that: It was Hitler himself who rejected the notion of a Zeppelin *Hitler*, fearing any disaster would tarnish his name.

The second proceeding on Eckener's Nazi past took place in Schwäbisch Gmünd, a town near Stuttgart, in the American zone. The tribunal's ruling came in July of 1948. It ended up exonerating him, citing these reasons: He was not a Nazi Party member. There were no known facts suggesting he supported, or even agreed with, the Nazis. On the contrary, the ruling added, Eckener himself had prevented the *Hindenburg* from being named the *Adolf Hitler*, as some had advocated.

"The defendant did not want to have anything to do with National Socialist politics," the ruling said the evidence showed, "but lived only for his company and the airship plant's longstanding tradition."

# Epilogue

He survived.

In early April 1945, SS guards marched Moisej Temkin and his companions into a woods after they left the train evacuating them from the Dora rocket-factory camp. When they came to a clearing, they were standing outside the barbed wire of Bergen-Belsen concentration camp, in northern Germany. In the past few weeks, the Allies closing in on all sides, the SS rushed evacuees from all over the country to Bergen-Belsen. It had become a dumping ground for some 60,000 prisoners.

Temkin, then twenty-seven, was astonished at how ghastly conditions were. He had seen calamities over nearly four years in five camps, he would recall, but he had never seen anything so terrible as Bergen-Belsen. Hundreds of people were dying daily from starvation and typhus. The crematorium couldn't keep up with so many bodies, and guards began piling them in the woods.

Row after row of wooden barracks, each infested with lice, and virtually no food or water. Prisoners were simply left there to die by the thousands. Men laid on mattresses next to corpses, too weak to remove them. Prisoners began digging ditches. They would tie strings or straps around the stiff-stick bodies and drag them off to the makeshift graves.

For days, Temkin licked at drops dripping from a pipe in a barracks, the only water he could find. Guards were around, but all was in disarray. He was able to scrounge some turnips from a Polish prisoner, and one night, he slipped through a hole in the fence with some others, to escape into a neighboring camp that had been abandoned. He returned, finding no food there.

People walked to avoid death. They wandered around by the hundreds all day, some men in striped prison shirts but no pants, women huddled in blankets. They milled about aimlessly, stepping around half-clothed corpses.

Temkin was sinking. His strength slipped each day, but he tried to keep walking, to keep upright, to move, because lying down meant the end. The war would be over any day now, he kept telling himself. But after several more days, he was too weak to stand. He finally had to lay down, and he waited to die, with comrades beside him. Within hours, they all heard artillery fire nearby, or were they hallucinating? He thought Allied tanks had to be coming soon. Word spread that the SS guards were high-tailing it out of the camp. In the towers, guards hung white flags.

"*Tanki, tovarishchi, tanki!*" someone yelled in Russian. "Tanks, comrades, tanks!"

It was April 15, 1945, and British troops had arrived to liberate the camp. Britain's 11th Armoured Division had landed at Normandy after D-Day, and its tanks rolled through France, north to Belgium and into the Netherlands, before pushing into Germany. The war-hardened soldiers were sickened by what they saw at Bergen-Belsen. They couldn't even estimate the tens of thousands of skeletal prisoners near death. They desperately needed food and medical care. More than 13,000 corpses were decomposing in plain sight.

Bergen-Belsen would become notorious. A diarist named Anne Frank had died there weeks before Temkin arrived, just shy of her sixteenth birthday. Her memoir of persecution, *The Diary of a Young Girl*, would later become an international best seller. Film of a bulldozer blade pushing piles of skin-and-bone bodies at Bergen-Belsen remains some of the most shocking imagery from the Nazi era. That footage was shown at the main Nuremburg trial, which would begin shortly after liberation.

With potato soup and other rations, Temkin was quickly on the mend. His youthful age must have helped him. He could finally stand again. One of the first things he wanted to do was get out of prison clothes, for the first time since 1941. He hurried to the storage rooms where the SS kept civilian clothing. There were heaps of clothes and shoes. He tried on shirts and pants until he found something that fit.

Over the next few days, the British supplied doctors and nurses, food rations, and guards to try to restore order for a safe evacuation. At first, SS guards were forced to bury the dead. Eventually, the bulldozer. The sights all around were macabre.

Not waiting for official permission to leave the camp, Temkin and a friend, Rybaltchenko Grigorjewitsch, slipped through a hole in the fence. They wanted to rejoin their own troops and their families back home. For several weeks, the pair walked or rode by horse cart or by train through Germany. Along the way, farmers gave them food and put them up overnight. They encountered masses of former prisoners and Russian forced laborers marching eastward as well.

It was sometime later that he reconnected with his family, only to learn his father had been shot to death by German soldiers in the winter of 1942. His mother and three sisters survived.

Temkin managed to walk a nearly four-year tightrope, including the time served in two Zeppelin slave camps, largely because he had posed as someone else. Shortly after his capture in July 1941, he was interrogated at a prisoner-of-war camp in Hammelburg. An SS guard looked intently at Temkin, and then he asked Temkin's Russian interpreter a direct question: *Is das eine Jude?* Temkin understood the words: "Is that a Jew?"

Temkin froze. "I did not let anything show on my face," he would recall. "When the interpreter then translated the question, I answered that I was a Belorussian."

The SS man peered again at Temkin. He paused, then moved on. "Name?"

In that moment, Moisej Temkin knew the sound of his name itself was a death sentence. His surname and given name would signal his heritage: He was Jewish. Into his head flashed a friend from technical school. Temkin replied, "Michail Petrowitsch Mirontschik."

The interrogator wrote it down. Once the bogus name was entered into Temkin's records with his photo, it just stuck. And it was under the name Michail Petrowitsch Mirontschik that Temkin moved camp to camp, undetected as Jewish. The International Tracing Service, a clearinghouse of records on those imprisoned and persecuted during the Nazi regime, confirmed that he was held in five concentration camps, including Friedrichshafen, under the name Michail Mirontschik. Camp records list his faith as Catholic.

At some point after the war, Temkin decided to write out an account of his years as a prisoner in Nazi Germany. Written in Russian, it amounts to about ninety pages. In Russia, prisoners who survived the concentration camps of Germany were typically suspected of collaborating with the enemy and had to prove otherwise. After the war, there were proceedings that either cleared one's name of collaborating or generated a sentence in a Russian prison camp. Temkin passed the Russian screening after his release and was reinstated to his officer's rank in the Red Army.

In 1947, Temkin married a woman named Tsilja, whom he met in the Ukraine, and they had two sons. He worked the rest of his career in Russian factories that made cameras and, later, typewriters. In 1993, he and his wife emigrated to Israel, where he died in October of 2006, just past his eighty-ninth birthday.

Temkin's memoir was published in Germany in 2017. His accounts, prisoner numbers, and narrative details were carefully checked and confirmed by German experts on each of the concentration camps. The details Temkin provided proved credible to them, jibing over and over with historical documents and eyewitness accounts.

Temkin would never forget his liberation. The morning after the British arrived, a car drove through Bergen-Belsen with loudspeakers on it. *All former prisoners. Come out to get milk, bread, sausage, butter, and chocolate.* Prisoners staggered out from barracks and tents to accept their rations. They were warned not to eat too much. Friends brought food to those too weak to get up.

"Our joy was boundless," Temkin recalled. "We embraced and kissed one another endlessly, laughed and cried with happiness."

Into his eighties, Hugo Eckener became still more brazen in deceit, revising history and burying his sinister war record. Not only had he misled investigators at Lakehurst on the *Hindenburg* disaster, but his autobiography renewed his false charge that America was partly responsible for the deadly accident because it had denied him fireproof helium. And he continued to portray himself as anti-Nazi and safety-conscious, while painting his rival, the deceased Lehmann, as the opposite on both counts.

Unfortunately, three generations of researchers didn't question Eckener's self-exculpatory memoir, didn't read it with an adequately critical eye, which rendered key parts of the *Hindenburg* history simply wrong. In his autobiography, Eckener added a late footnote: While the French-zone tribunal charged him with being a Nazi, an American-zone panel later absolved him. Case closed, he argued. And subsequent Zeppelin histories simply fell into line. Some authors apparently figured the Zeppelin trail ended with the Lakehurst tragedy and ignored the World War II years. Outfoxed by Eckener, authors chronicling Zeppelin history unknowingly passed on fiction as fact. Writing a history of the *Graf Zeppelin*, published in 1958 shortly after Eckener's death, one author dedicated the work to Dr. Eckener, saying, "May his airmanship and depth of character serve as inspirations for the future."

One important history of the airship age, published in the early 1970s, noted that the "outspokenly anti-Nazi" Eckener actually faced execution along with Hitler's other enemies in the Night of the Long Knives purge of 1934, but he happened to be away from Germany at the time. Source: Eckener, himself. So, how did Eckener survive the war years? "Presumably," the author speculated, "his great international reputation and the affection in which he was held in America in particular, saved him from being executed or imprisoned."

In the early 1990s, another book reflected: "Eckener, with his cosmopolitan, international outlook, his many contacts in America and other countries, and his deep loathing for the Nazi gangsters and their savage methods, resisted as best he could, but he dared not openly defy the new regime lest it imprison him and take over direct control of the entire Zeppelin organization." In 2002, a *Hindenburg* history declared: "Perhaps no other man in Germany could have said what he did and kept his job—or his life."

But within Germany, the Eckener pretense began to crack by the late 1990s, as researchers scrutinized Nazi military and denazification records. In one academic text on the rocket industry in 1997, author Georg Metzler wrote that he was astonished to discover that a person of Hugo Eckener's international stature employed concentration camp prisoners at Zeppelin company operations. Christa Tholander, a German researcher who has spent two decades studying the camp in Friedrichshafen, has in her writings and public talks discussed Eckener's role in Zeppelin's use of camp prisoners.

The Eckener autobiography, which threw other authors off track, was published in 1949, a pivotal year for Germany after the war. The British, French, and American occupation zones at that time fused into one, the Federal Republic of Germany, whose capital was located in Bonn. Political parties were licensed by Allied officials, and the country was toddling toward self-rule.

It was then that some Nazis stepped out of the shadows. One of the first was Otto Ernst Remer, Hitler's bodyguard. To keep the Nazi government in Berlin from falling apart, Remer was the man who had interfered with the 1944 bomb plot against Hitler.

In the summer of 1949, German militarists and nationalists formed a political group called the Association of Independent Germans in the town of Bad Godesberg. They vowed to fight for German unity and to "protect the honor of those who did their duty for the Fatherland." Remer was one of the signers of the new group's manifesto, which argued that denazification laws had "driven millions of decent men and women into despair." Another signatory, news reports noted, was Hugo Eckener, the grand old man of Zeppelin fame.

Remer quickly became a hated man in official Germany. In October of 1949, he emerged as deputy director of a neo-Nazi group called the *Sozialistische Reichs-Partei*, or SRP. Remer himself lambasted the "shit democracy" American occupiers had forced on Germany. He dismissed stories about Nazi atrocities as propaganda. He alleged that the crematories at Dachau were an American fabrication, built after the war, to vilify Germany. Films of concentration camps were faked as well, he claimed. He was an early champion of Nazi denial. In 1952, when the SRP began to attract membership in the thousands, the party was outlawed by the West German constitutional court, which categorized it as the direct descendant of the Nazi Party.

Eckener's association with Remer raised red flags with U.S. Army intelligence. It had already been looking into his wartime activities as part of its Paperclip background check, but its investigation seemed to escalate in 1949. Army records didn't reveal anything about his connection with the V-2 rocket or slave labor, but they do reflect other activity that concerned investigators.

A classified army dossier compiled in the early 1950s revealed that Eckener began working with the Abwehr, the Third Reich's military intelligence operation, possibly as an officer, in Bucharest, Romania, in September 1940. Army investigators found that he acted as an Abwehr operative in Berlin in May 1941 and March 1942. They tracked his Abwehr work to Istanbul, Turkey, in May 1942, and Sofia, Bulgaria, the following July.

At one point, the dossier also shows, Eckener was on the Administrative Council of the German Institute for Foreign Relations, which, it said, "was used by the Nazis during the war for propaganda purposes." Included in his file, too, was a news article about how Eckener had been Hitler's personal guest at the launching of the battleship *Graf Zeppelin* in December 1938.

There were enough warning signs in his dossier that it became declassified decades later in an extraordinary operation to shed light on war crimes. In 1999, the U.S. government established a body called the Nazi War Crimes and Japanese Imperial Government Records Interagency Working Group. It was charged with finding and recommending for declassification any classified U.S. records relating to German and Japanese war crimes. Eckener's dossier was one that the group identified. Declassified, it now resides at the National Archives, in a folder with its old designation, CLASSIFIED, in red capital letters on the cover. The trove of once-secret records, according to the National Archives, was released to help historians and scholars better comprehend World War II, war crimes, the Holocaust, and the postwar work of Allied intelligence agencies.

When Eckener testified in the hangar near the *Hindenburg*'s crash site in 1937, he kept the eyes of investigators squarely on the ship's final moments in New Jersey, kept the inquiry on American soil. That diverted attention from Germany, where evidence was neatly concealed not only of the *Hindenburg*'s structural defect, but also of Eckener's own early work on behalf of the Nazis and their troubling rearmament. Because the design flaw that doomed the *Hindenburg* never came up, American investigators were left stumped, grasping at speculation. The investigation never crossed the Atlantic, where some answers rested in Zeppelin construction and maintenance documents, leaving a mystery for posterity.

Dr. Eckener's speculation about an overly sharp turn on the *Hindenburg* has been the leading explanation for the disaster since 1937. The Commerce Department investigators, who published his theory, were apparently unaware that Eckener had anything to hide. No evidence has ever surfaced that the ship was sabotaged.

In August of 1954, at the age of eighty-six, Eckener died of a heart ailment in Friedrichshafen. Johanna, his wife, died in 1956. Eckener's Paperclip file was also not declassified until 1999. One item in it is an obituary from the *Sunday Star* in Washington, DC, dated August 15, 1954. "During the war," it said, "Dr. Eckener remained quietly at his home. Politically, he made little news in Germany after the war."

Leonhard Adelt, who warned the *Hindenburg* investigative committee about the gasbag peril, died during an air raid near Dresden in late February 1945. He survived the *Hindenburg* disaster, only to perish at age sixty-three in the historic firestorm that engulfed the city. The author and veteran newspaper reporter probably never told his wife, Gertrud, about Lehmann's disclosure concerning the gasbag damage, perhaps to protect her.

While Gertrud and Leonhard were still in America recovering from the tragedy at Lakehurst, she would recall, "My mother in Dresden got a visit by two Gestapo men who told her that her daughter must have spread news or hints about the *Hindenburg* catastrophe" that weren't sanctioned by the Propaganda Ministry. "They read all the letters I had written . . . from America but of course these letters didn't contain anything that was interesting, and so they left," Gertrud recalled.

The other person who definitely knew about Adelt's damning letter to the *Hindenburg* investigators was Charles Rosendahl. He worked to cover it up in the spring of 1937, just as investigators were desperate for answers on what caused the mysterious fire on the *Hindenburg*. His character assassination of Adelt, in writing to the head of the investigative board, seemed to have stopped cold the promising line of inquiry around the *Hindenburg*'s structural flaw. He simply could not abide any threat to his beloved airships.

Rosendahl remained a fanatic of the antiquated technology that was the airship, and he would swear until his dying day that the *Hindenburg* had been sabotaged. He helped two authors develop books, one in 1962, the other a decade later, proposing that the *Hindenburg* was sabotaged, though neither summoned credible evidence of any kind. One of the books became a sensational movie in 1975, starring George C. Scott and Anne Bancroft.

In the summer of 1962, Rosendahl, a retired vice admiral, released a statement to the press lambasting what he saw as a navy decision to put airships in mothballs for good. Rosie was the advocate for what had once been called lighter-than-air craft, while his enemies were heavier-than-air proponents, favoring airplanes. "After long sniping at airships from behind Pentagon bulwarks, the indifferent, uninformed, prejudiced, blinder-wearing heavier-than-air overlords of the airship, seemingly fearful that airships might succeed, have now twanged their final, poisoned pencil shafts into the sides of the two remaining blimps," Rosendahl's statement said.

Fully twenty-five years after the *Hindenburg* crumpled to the ground at the base he commanded, Rosendahl was still spitting mad. He argued that the navy had failed taxpayers by not fully exploring how the airship could contribute to national defense. The conclusion of his press statement suggests something other than what he evidently intended: "When the whole story is written—as it is sure to be—the tale of the airship will not be one of the most flattering chapters in the history of our generally great Navy."

In the final years of his life, Rosendahl tried, unsuccessfully, to establish a national airship museum at Lakehurst. He died one day shy of eighty-five, of a heart ailment in May 1977. He had been living for several years in retirement with his wife, Jean, at their estate near Lakehurst.

Knut Eckener was sixty-two years old and bedridden in Constance, Germany, in the winter of 1967. It was at that time that Horsehead, the brutal SS guard, was indicted by West Germany prosecutors. The crimes connected to the V-2 rocket at its Dora concentration camp were so horrific that justice still cried out, into the Age of Aquarius, into the Space Age.

Erwin Busta, known to Temkin and other prisoners as Horsehead, was one of three former SS guards at Dora who were arrested for war crimes in a lengthy trial whose witnesses would include Albert Speer and Wernher von Braun. None of this could have been welcome news to Knut Eckener, who already had heart troubles. His father had been dead for years, but could incriminating information come out, after all that time, about him?

Von Braun and V-2 partner and close friend Arthur Rudolph had ridden their Paperclip assignments into pioneering America's space program. Both were leaders in developing the promising Saturn V rocket that was the best chance of achieving John F. Kennedy's dream to put people on the moon before the decade of the 1960s was out.

But there was a dark side to the moon program. Von Braun and Rudolph had hidden their advocacy of prison labor to produce the V-2 rocket during the war. Two decades after 1969's historic moon landing by American astronauts, scholars and prosecutors began digging deeper into the past of the two German men behind that historic triumph. In time, memos and other documents surfaced showing that, despite their denials, they had willfully backed the exploitation of concentration camp prisoners.

Von Braun died in 1977, under a cloud of suspicion about his war days. In 1984, Rudolph was allowed to leave the United States rather than stand trial for war crimes. Their records in Nazi Germany, along with those of some other scientists recruited to the U.S. after the war, tarnished the entire Paperclip program.

Albert Speer, Hitler's armaments minister, spent twenty years in prison and was released in 1966 at age seventy-one. After his time served in the notorious Spandau Prison in western Berlin, he completed a tell-all memoir, *Inside the Third Reich*, published in 1969. His pen dripped remorse, though he denied knowledge of the Nazis' vast extermination operations. As a leader in the Reich, Speer recalled telling the judges at the Nuremburg trial that he had to share in responsibility for all that had happened. He called himself "inescapably contaminated morally." He closed his eyes so he didn't have to take responsibility. The Third Reich aimed at world domination, he said, and his hard work only prolonged that war. Following a stroke, Speer died in London in 1981.

Horsehead and the other two SS men were indicted in the executions of more than a hundred Dora prisoners. In 1958, a special inquiry service on Nazi crimes was created in Germany to prosecute cases not taken up by the Allied courts. The trial would bring more than 300 witnesses to the stand between late 1967 and 1970. Shortly after it began, Knut Eckener died, in 1968. Horsehead, sixty-four at the time, and another guard were sentenced to more than seven years in prison.

In the aftermath of the trial, and the apparent willingness of West German prosecutors to dig deep into the past for suspected war criminals, a whole new myth around Hugo Eckener as anti-Nazi surfaced. Willy von Meister apparently started it. A close associate of Hugo Eckener, von Meister translated Eckener's testimony before the *Hindenburg* investigators. He made himself available for interviews in the early 1970s by authors researching Zeppelin history. Given his intimate knowledge of the Zeppelin business and his contacts with executives, most notably Eckener, von Meister could have known about the Zeppelin slave workers in the war.

The story von Meister passed on is that his former boss, Hugo Eckener, was so clever an anti-Nazi that he outwitted Hitler at the Chicago World's Fair in 1933. At that time, the *Graf Zeppelin* was required to display a swastika on the port, or left, side of its tail fin and the traditional German red, white, and black colors on the other side, the starboard. Von Meister said that Eckener ordered the *Graf Zeppelin* flown around the city clockwise to hide the offending swastika from the thousands of fairgoers on the ground.

This apparently never happened, though it became a staple of later histories. Eckener himself never mentioned this maneuver, though he spent pages and pages of his memoir on the Chicago World's Fair flight and anti-Nazi worries in that city. Chicago newspaper accounts and photos at the time make it clear the *Graf Zeppelin* circled the fair in both directions. Even the *Graf Zeppelin's* flight log fails to confirm any such scheme.

After Ernst Lehmann died from injuries in the *Hindenburg* fire, the Nazis buried him in Frankfurt at a grave site with other crew members who died. Lehmann's widow, Marie, apparently did not think her husband would have wanted to be memorialized by the Nazis, and, in any event, he had previously expressed a desire to be buried with his little son, Luv, who had died in 1936. Sometime after her husband's burial, she had his body moved from Frankfurt to a cemetery in Grassau, where she lived at the time. Marie died in 1975, and the cemetery plot is where the Lehmanns rest, with their son, today.

After the war, Marie kept up with Jean Rosendahl, Rosie's wife. Marie wrote to her in February 1948 from Grassau, near Austria, in the American zone. Her handwritten letter, to the Rosendahl estate in Toms River near Lakehurst, began:

*Jean dearest and dear Rosie:*

*I learned by letters from Von Meister . . . that Rosie retired from the Navy and that you moved to Toms River.*

*But then, frankly speaking, I did not dare to write once more, thinking you probably did not want to get into touch with your old German friends after all the most terrible things that had occurred in our country.*

*I felt ashamed to belong to this nation. But my friendship and gratitude towards you had never changed. How could I ever forget what you did for Luv and me during those sad days in May 37?*

Marie wrote that her son from her first marriage was killed in Russia in January 1942, and that her daughter, who had been away in Asia for nearly eight years, had gotten married and was returning at last to Germany.

*I am afraid my letter is getting too long for the censor. Please do write to me as soon as possible. . . . Thank you once more from all my heart for the delicious parcel; it is a real godsend and such a great help in the daily struggle for food.*

Eight years later, Marie and Jean were still pen pals. In a letter dated July 5, 1956, Marie wrote about the delight she had with her grandson.

The little boy was a particular admirer of both the Little Captain, a man he had never met, and his memoir, the account Ernst Lehmann had published just before his fatal trip on the *Hindenburg*.

> *Jean Darling,*
> *My little grandson is fine. . . . There is nothing more interesting in his life than the airship and Luv. He never gets tired to look at the innumerable airship pictures, and he never gets tired to listen when I read to him Luv's book.*

# Acknowledgments

Five years ago, I stepped onto a Zeppelin and landed in a German concentration camp.

It was an entirely unexpected destination, and I encountered several surprising people along the way. One of the notables: Mark Heald, an eyewitness to the *Hindenburg* disaster as an eight-year-old boy in New Jersey. In his nineties now, he is a retired physics professor, and he kindly let me record his recollections for my podcast, the *Hidden Hindenburg*, which details my quest to solve this mysterious tragedy. He may well be its last living witness.

The story behind the *Hindenburg* disaster was embedded in numerous German texts: telegrams, Nazi memos, personal letters, technical documents, even poems. Kathy DiCenzo and her colleagues at KD Translations thoughtfully rendered thousands of words for me into English, some from paragraphs originally in a dense, old German font called Fraktur, some scrawled in jagged handwriting.

Thomas Kuhn, a university student in southern Germany, assisted me through a trove of German documents at the Zeppelin Museum archive in Friedrichshafen. Elsewhere, he helped retrieve the nearly forgotten text of Hugo Eckener's 1934 radio endorsement of Hitler. While we were on this raft together, we realized that we share a common affection for Mark Twain.

After I had initially been informed there were no *Hindenburg* maintenance records at the Zeppelin Museum archive, archivist Barbara Waibel found some and alerted me to their existence. Kathrin Wurzer at the archive also helped me attain some of the most important documentation for this book.

I might never have learned about the memoir of Moisej Temkin, the Russian prisoner of war forced into labor in Germany, but for Andre Scharf at the archives of the Dachau memorial camp. I am grateful to Mr. Temkin's sons, Aleksandr and Benjamin, for allowing me to publish passages of their father's dark and extraordinary memories, along with his photo.

Several German researchers have painstakingly unearthed the disgraceful details of slave labor in Friedrichshafen, the cradle of the Zeppelin world. Among them are Christa Tholander, Oswald Burger, Georg Metzler, and Martin Ebner. Kathryn Deschler at the German Historical Institute provided me with copies of several critical passages from the diaries of Joseph Goebbels.

In America, two researchers in particular provided invaluable background for this work. Michael Neufeld revealed the sinister history of the dreaded V-2 rocket, and Linda Hunt uncovered much of the sad chapter of the importation to the United States of Nazi scientists after World War II.

After months and months of exhaustive research, of being stuck in the abstract, I treasure one moment when I got to touch a concrete piece of this history. At Wichita State University, in Box 16 of a special airship collection, is a *Hindenburg* artifact: a metal girder fragment, a little over four inches long, more than an inch wide. To lighten its weight, it has holes punched in it, like Swiss cheese. I picked it up. Light as a pencil. Photos weren't allowed, so I drew my own sketch.

A surviving piece of Hindenburg girder. MICHAEL MCCARTHY

As with my previous book, my agent, Jim Hornfischer, was the first champion of this work, and editor Gene Brissie at Lyons Press was immediately enamored with the idea of the definitive history of the *Hindenburg*. My production editor, Meredith Dias, carefully choreographed all the text and images for this work.

A grateful nod to my early journalism professor Dr. Avis Meyer of St. Louis University. He introduced me to one of my favorite books, *All the King's Men*, by Robert Penn Warren. There's a line in it that has served as a mantra my whole career as a reporter and author: "Truth was what I sought, without fear or favor. And let the chips fly."

My son, Matthew, brought his historical insight to an early version of this book, and daughter Sadie, who spent time studying in Berlin years ago, translated some German speeches for me. Daughters Eastin and Gabrielle endured my endless talk of Zeppelins over the past few years. My wife, Marci, was with me tirelessly for every step—except one. I couldn't persuade her to ride on one of the new (helium-filled) Zeppelins hovering once again over Germany. Maybe someday.

MM
South Haven, Michigan

# Appendix

*LEONHARD ADELT, A FRIEND AND EDITOR OF CAPTAIN ERNST LEHMANN, WROTE a whistleblower letter to Hindenburg investigators three weeks after the disaster. Both men were on the final flight. Adelt survived. Captain Lehmann died shortly afterward. Investigators solicited eyewitness accounts from passengers. Adelt's three-page reply, handwritten, in German, resides in the National Archives. Adelt recounts revelatory conversations with Lehmann and mentions the official captain on the Hindenburg's last flight, Max Pruss. The author's translation, below, represents the first time this letter has been published.*

River Road, Mays Landing, N.J.
May 30, 1937.

Department of Commerce,
Investigation Board, Lakehurst

1) The last lightning bolt that I saw came down starboard from the *Hindenburg* without audible thunder, as the airship was advancing through the edge of the storm to the landing site; given the time and the distance, it cannot have any connection with the catastrophe.

2) My wife and I were at the reading-room observation window closest to the gangway (starboard), watching the rear landing cable being thrown out, when a soft, muffled thud came from the direction of the front of the airship, and a bright red glow appeared outside. Almost simultaneously with the second thud, which was audible near us, the airship struck the ground hard. The tilt threw us from the window against the gangway wall. I shouted to the passengers, "Through the window!," and jumped through the observation window closest to the gangway (stairs + hallway) with my wife as the burning frame broke apart above us.

The fact that we first noticed the fire only when it had already raced above our heads from the stern to the front of the airship indicates how quickly it spread; even an automatic fire alarm or an alarm given to the passengers by airship staff could not have given any more warning.

3) Captain Lehmann—contrary to newspaper reports—was not with us at the moment of the catastrophe. We first saw each other again in the Lakehurst naval hospital, when we were receiving provisional treatment for our injuries. I asked him briefly, "What was that?" He answered just as briefly, "Lightning strike."

Lehmann had full confidence in Pruss, whom he described to me as "our best captain," and had asked me to see to it that only Pruss was identified as the commander in the press, and not incorrectly him. He was worried, however, since a gas cell had been found to have worn through on the upper hanging side when the *Hindenburg* was overhauled over the winter. "It occurs to me as if I actually was the 'Rider of Lake Constance,'"* he told me. "What if the damage had happened during a trip or were to happen again to another gas cell!" His concern was increased by the fact that the young next generation lacked the decades of practical experience that the older people had in fixing things, and it was primarily for this reason that he came along on the trip, in order to keep an eye on them.

In the light of these things that he said, I understood and understand Lehmann's answer, "Lightning strike," as meaning that he conjectured that ignition of an oxyhydrogen mixture by an electric spark was the cause of the catastrophe.

Leonhard Adelt

*Translator's note: This passage refers to "Der Reiter am Bodensee" [The Rider on Lake Constance], the title of a poem. The little ballad describes a horseback rider who mistook the snow-covered frozen lake for a field, and, on realizing his danger only after he had ridden across it, dies from shock.

# NOTES

All quotations in the text are cited. Other than that, the author offers citations for every fact that is particularly revelatory in this history, or potentially challengeable, or otherwise worthy of further research into the Zeppelin era or early twentieth-century aviation.

*Air*
   2. *For our struggle is . . . .:* Ephesians 6:12.

*Chapter 1: Dealing with Demons*
   3. *The silvery Zeppelin glided . . . .:* Eckener, *Im Zeppelin*, 260.
   3. *Back in Germany . . . .:* Goebbels, Teil 1, Bd. 2/III, 219.
   3. *Eckener looked down . . . .:* Eckener, *Im Zeppelin*, 260.
   4. *"Everything in Germany . . ."*: Eckener, *Im Zeppelin*, 260 (author translation). There is an adequate English translation of Eckener's autobiography by a well-regarded historian of the Zeppelin age, the late Douglas Robinson. However, in reading Robinson's version of Eckener's book, one encounters not only translation errors, but omissions of large portions of the original text, notably Eckener's lengthy discussion of his historical experiences with, and sentiments about, the Nazi Party. Therefore, the author primarily used his own translation of the text as a fuller, more contextual, and more reliable version of Eckener's account of his life.
   4. *Hours earlier, a black . . . .:* The account of the Night of the Long Knives uses contemporaneous news accounts, along with descriptions from Gallo, Maracin, and Ullrich.
   6. *"Find Klausener and kill him."*: Gallo, 229.
   7. *"Take six men . . ."*: ibid., 242.
   7. *"Yes, I am General . . ."*: ibid., 236.
   8. *"Shoot them! . . ."*: ibid., 229.
   9. *"By order of the Führer . . ."*: ibid., 271.
   9. *"Hitler . . . has begun to kill. . . ."*: Maracin, 144.
   10. *"Mutinies are judged . . ."*: Gallo, 306.
   10. *"Since the Marshall's . . ."*: ibid., 300.
   11. *"savagery . . . disregard for all . . ."*: Maracin, 145.
   11. *"dirty swindler . . ."*: Ullrich, 472.
   11. *"Everywhere we're falling . . ."*: ibid., 471
   11. *Goebbels himself had ridden . . . .:* de Syon, 176.
   12. *Invited to the White House . . . .:* Several books on the *Hindenburg* and Hugo Eckener recount how President Coolidge once christened Eckener as a "Modern Columbus," but

that appears not to have happened. The author could find no newspaper account from the time that verified this. It doesn't seem like something reporters would have missed, the U.S. president's hailing a world aviation celebrity as the new Columbus. One German author even titled his 1979 biography *Hugo Eckener. Ein moderner Columbus.* In Eckener's own autobiography, he does not mention being called a "Modern Columbus," though he did refer to a "reception by President Hoover at the White House, where he spoke of the great adventurers, Vasco da Gama and Magellan, as having been put in the shade by our exploits ..." (Eckener, *My Zeppelins,* 169).

12. *Meeting with Goebbels ...:* Goebbels, Teil 1, Bd. 2/III, 219.

### Chapter 2: "The Pope"

15. *"Were it possible to solve ..." :* Meyer, *Airshipmen,* 31.
17. *"I am not a circus rider ..." :* ibid., 33.
17. *"I detest any notion ..." :* ibid., 41.
18. *"frightfulness":* Fegan, 19.
18. *"Zeppelin, fly ...":* ibid., 16.
18. *"All England must burn!":* Meyer, *Airshipmen,* 45.
19. *"Rush help, making for ...":* "Transatlantic Flight," 911.
23. *Crewmen began searching the aircraft ...:* Lehmann, *Zeppelin,* 212.
23. *"The last words we heard ...":* ibid., 214.
23. *"Now we know how Christopher ...":* ibid., 219.
23. *"a diamond merchant's ...":* ibid.
24. *"trailblazing exploit ...":* ibid., 220.
24. *... written receipt:* Meyer, *Airshipmen,* 140.
25. *"Practically every storm ...":* *Rigid Airship Manual,* ix–2.
25. *"because it came to us ...":* Topping and Brothers, 99.
27. *"This is a question which ...":* "National Advisory Committee," 5.
27. *"When more ships and crews ...":* ibid., 6.
27. *"For as soon as ...":* ibid.
27. *"But soon after the enterprise ...":* ibid., 5.

### Chapter 3: "Noble Wine"

30. *They began communicating only ...:* Meyer, *Airshipmen,* 137.
30. *He worked tirelessly ...:* Haddow and Grosz, vii.
30. *At one point, he hired an inventor ...:* ibid., 202.
31. *most of the money ... aristocratic friends.:* Meyer, *Airshipmen,* 37.
32. *"just a façade":* ibid., 132.
32. *No genuine German ...:* ibid., 133.
33. *"The German people were more ...":* ibid., 135.
34. *"pots and pans":* de Syon, 128.
34. *"a fabulous silvery fish ...":* Eckener, *My Zeppelins,* 142.
35. *Zep Fights for Life ... ignores Navy calls:* Vaeth, 17, 18.
35. *Amid the uncertainty ... and crew.:* ibid., 18.

36. *"If the airship . . ."*: Botting, 129.

36. *"Eckener should never have sent . . ."*: ibid., 119.

37. *the behavior of its rudders in the air could be erratic:* Lehmann, *Zeppelin*, 239.

37. *After dinner . . . horn-shaped speaker.:* Botting, 163.

38. *"As a last resort."*: ibid., 7.

38. *"Russia thrilled us . . ."*: Drummond-Hay, 25.

38. *"I can't tell you now . . ."*: *Racine (WI) Journal-Times*, May 8, 1936. Though the article was published in 1936, reporter Louis Lochner recounted historically his encounter with Captains Eckener and Lehmann on the world flight in 1929.

38. *"Maybe you think . . ."*: ibid.

38. *"It's simply uncanny . . ."*: ibid.

39. *"I want a manicure . . ."*: Botting, 187.

39. *He couldn't fathom . . . :* ibid., 219.

39. *"The spirit of high adventure . . ."*: *New York Times*, August 30, 1929.

40. *the president made Eckener . . . :* *New York Times,* May 12, 1937. Though the article was published in 1937, the reporter recounted historically the remarkable encounter between President Hoover and Eckener in 1929.

41. *"No cigarettes. No exceptions."*: Van Orman and Hull, 190.

41. *"My nearly uncontrollable . . ."*: ibid.

42. *"Our group would never . . ."*: Duggan, *LZ129*, 4.

44. *the* Graf Zeppelin *had a huge . . . :* *New York Times*, August 6, 1933.

44. *"presidential timber"*: *New York Times*, August 13, 1933.

45. *"We met during . . ."*: ibid.

45. *Eckener was working in his garden . . . :* Eckener, *Im Zeppelin*, 16–17.

46. *Colsman himself actually hired Eckener . . . :* Colsman, 77.

46. *"Does your Excellency . . ."*: ibid. (author translation).

46. *"It was rather a strange . . ."*: Goebbels, Teil 1, Bd. 2/III, 219 (author translation).

47. *. . . assaulted a man in Berlin . . . from New York.:* *Decatur (IL) Daily Review*, August 22, 1933.

47. *"press attachés"*: Goebbels, Teil 1, Bd. 2/III, 219 (author translation).

47. *Grudgingly, he had to ask Goebbels . . . :* ibid.

48. *"seems rather strained"*: ibid. (author translation).

48. *"What is happening in Germany . . ."*: *Chicago Daily Tribune*, September 3, 1933.

48. *"We found the key . . ."*: ibid.

48. *"We plan that we will . . ."*: ibid.

49. *"The much-criticized Hitler . . ."*: *New York Times*, October 27, 1933.

49. *"We have a new Zeppelin . . . suggestions?"*: *Chicago Daily News*, October 26, 1933.

51. *workers complained . . . :* Duggan, *LZ129*, 16.

51. *"Who votes against Hitler . . ."*: *Rochester (NY) Democrat and Chronicle*, August 12, 1934.

51. *"Nazi 'three-minute men' . . ."*: *Oshkosh (WI) Northwestern*, August 14, 1934. The *Oshkosh Northwestern* is one of several newspapers that carried the syndicated report. The *Guardian*, London, also reported that Eckener's speech had begun being aired, August 14, 1934. Häffner, 197, noted that denazification officials said that the

Eckener-endorsement speech occurred on August 19, 1934, which would have been the last day of a six-day broadcast campaign.

51. *"demonstrate to the world . . ."*: ibid.

52. *"One firm will has to command . . ."*: *Schwäbische Zeitung*, September 30, 1950 (author's translation, published here it is believed for the first time in English). As debate raged after World War II about the future of the remnants of the Zeppelin organization, some politicians resurrected the text of Eckener's pro-Hitler speech.

53. *working in Akron, Ohio:* Karl Hürttle's résumé was provided to the author in 2017 during his visit to the Zeppelin Museum in Friedrichshafen by Barbara Waibel, archive director.

53. *"Some concern is felt . . ."*: Lewis and Dick, 124.

54. *"safety measures demanded"*: *Protokoll*, 1 (author translation).

54. *"Other than the protection . . ."*: ibid., 2.

54. *Dr. Dürr explained . . . gas cells.*: ibid., 2–3.

## Chapter 4: A Quivering Cover

55. *"God would surely never . . . ."*: de Terzi, 20–26.

56. *"document in stone . . ."*: Ladd, 146.

57. *In the first . . . top of the ship.*: Duggan, *LZ129*, 60.

57. *In flight, the outer cover . . . only one-fifth of it.*: *Airship Aerodynamics*, 28–29.

57. *"The outer cover is not . . ."*: Lewis and Dick, notes on Flight 1, March 4, 1936.

57. *"It appears that flutter . . ."*: ibid.

58. *"The outer cover still . . ."*: Lewis and Dick, notes on Flight 4, March 17, 1936.

58. *Eckener invited aboard:* New York Times, September 26, 1935.

58. *"The Olympics without America . . ."*: ibid.

58. *"Believe me, we wish . . ."*: ibid.

59. *"If the French had invaded . . ."*: Ullrich, 510.

59. *"I think that a substantial . . ."*: Shirer, 59.

60. *"Dr. Eckener canceled . . ."*: Goebbels, Teil 1, Bd. 3/II, 47.

60. *at a considerable profit of nearly 90,000 Reichsmarks:* Duggan, *LZ129*, 66.

60. *"The ship then began . . ."*: Scott Peck to Ernst King, March 24, 1936.

60. *the wind speed . . . eight knots . . . .*: ibid.

61. *"rather than take a chance"*: New York Times, March 27, 1936.

61. *"Without direct news . . ."*: Ogden (UT) Standard-Examiner, April 5, 1936.

62. *"I never protested . . ."*: ibid.

62. *"I always say, 'Heil, Hitler!'. . ."*: Cincinnati Enquirer, April 16, 1936.

62. *"They wandered about . . ."*: Scott Peck to Ernst King, April 11, 1936.

62. *"The mud was over . . ."*: ibid.

62. *Admiral King had written . . . single bed.*: Willie von Meister to Ernst King, April 18, 1936.

63. *"The officers are quite free . . ."*: Scott Peck to Ernst King, April 11, 1936.

63. *"I would not want the Zeppelin . . ."*: ibid.

63. *Lehmann had fully tested . . . .*: Lehmann, *Zeppelin*, 218.

63. *Lehmann had backup plans....:* Scott Peck to Ernst King, March 24, 1936. In the letter, Peck informed the admiral, "If Rio is not ready, the *Graf Zeppelin* will make the flight. In this case, it is expected that the LZ 129 will make the next scheduled trip, which is two weeks or later."

64. *"The situation looked quite serious...":* Scott Peck to Ernst King, April 11, 1936.

64. *He quickly considered trying... "I admit... perplexity.":* Eckener, *Im Zeppelin,* 284 (author translation).

64. *Eckener was on board solely....:* Dick and Robinson, 111, 118; *San Francisco Chronicle,* April 11, 1936; *Salt Lake Tribune,* April 10, 1936; *Cincinnati Enquirer,* April 10, 1936; *Fresno Bee,* April 9, 1936; *Napa Valley Register,* April 9, 1936.

64. *A confidential government memo....:* Duggan, *LZ129,* 5.

64. *"expert financial management...":* ibid.

65. *"Count Zeppelin could not...":* Colsman, 80 (author translation).

65. *"The commander on board...":* Lehmann and Adelt, *Luftpatrouille,* 66 (author translation).

## Chapter 5: Begging for Helium

66. *"I wanted to pinch myself...":* San Francisco Chronicle, May 10, 1936.

67. *"You needn't be so...":* Miller, 311.

67. *"Here, I'll show you.":* ibid.

67. *... 1,750 locomotives... one of them.:* Lehmann, *Zeppelin,* 292.

69. *"It was all quiet...":* New York Times, May 9, 1936.

70. *"I had the impression...":* Lochner, 105.

71. *"Ah!"... "That's what I want now.":* Santa Ana Register, May 9, 1936.

72. *... would "double up" on beds.:* Ernst King to Willie Von Meister, May 14, 1936.

72. *The next day... silver cup.:* New York Times, May 11, 1936.

72. *he wrote a letter resigning....:* Italiaander, 338.

72. *Captain Lehmann replied... "Your devoted E. A. Lehmann.":* ibid.

73. *He began showing up...* Heereswaffenamt...: Metlzer, 23.

74. *he ordered the engines slowed... town of Keighley.:* New York Times, May 12, 1937. The article recalls a trip a year earlier.

74. *"It is the miracle...":* Ullrich, 513.

74. *During one flight.... Lakehurst.:* Mark Heald to Michael McCarthy, email September 8, 2015, and in-person interview December 19, 2019. It was remarkable to speak with a living witness of the *Hindenburg* disaster. Heald and the author were careful to use only details of the account that were sharply recalled, noting that the eyewitness was only eight at the time. The author recorded him for a podcast, also titled *The Hidden Hindenburg.*

74. *Dr. Eckener explained... triple the price.:* Sitzung vom 20. November 1936. This account is based on the six pages of minutes of a conference between Zeppelin company executives and the Nazi Air Ministry in Berlin. It is an extraordinary document, revealing how Nazi aviation officials desperately warned Zeppelin officers about the need for helium in their airships—six months before the *Hindenburg* was destroyed. Credit to John Duggan, author of *LZ129 Hindenburg: The Complete Story,* for unearthing it.

76. *"Over the blue . . .":* Lehmann and Adelt, *Luftpatrouille,* 6 (author translation).
76. *"If I were not . . .":* ibid. (author translation).
77. *"a cathedral":* ibid. (author translation).
78. *"But the moral effect . . .":* ibid., 200 (author translation).
78. *"Asked for my technical opinion . . .":* ibid., 58 (author translation).
79. *"The appearance of our airship . . .":* Lehmann, *Zeppelin,* 304. This quotation does not seem to be in the author's edition of the German text.
79. *struck on the nose by lightning:* ibid., 149.
79. *"Lightning . . . obeys the laws . . .":* Lehmann and Adelt, *Luftpatrouille,* 162 (author translation).
80. *Lehmann confessed something . . . :* Leonhard Adelt to Hindenburg Investigation Board, May 30, 1937, 3. This remarkable letter was penned in German by Adelt just weeks after the tragedy and mailed to Lakehurst investigators. The translation into English by investigators contains several puzzling errors, including the very first line incorrectly rendered as "The first lightning which I saw," which, when properly translated from the German, in fact, reads "The *last* lightning which I saw." A big difference. The text of this work uses the author translation of the Adelt letter. Both the German original and the investigators' translation into English reside in the National Archives and Records Administration, RG 197, Records of the Bureau of Air Commerce, records relating the investigation of the *Hindenburg* disaster, General Records, Box 2, Folder 622.20, C-1 New Jersey, Lakehurst, Advisory Board.

## Chapter 6: Twine and Tape

81. *The lengthy worklist . . . :* Sauter, 1–6 (author translation). In addition to the report cited, there is also an English translation of the *Hindenburg* overhaul report, prepared by Goodyear engineers Dick and Lewis, that resides in the Douglas Robinson Collection, Box 9, Folder 2, at the University of Texas, Dallas.
82. *The overhaul . . . maiden season.:* Duggan, *LZ129,* 279.
82. *The overhaul men checked . . . fire extinguishers.:* Sauter, 1–6.
82. *In thick, looping . . . :* Albert Sammt to DZR, December 29, 1936.
83. *try a simulation . . . "The conclusion drawn . . . chafing of the cell.":* Lewis and Dick, 30a. This one-page document, titled "Gas Cell Chafing, LZ 129," is notable for its raw language around the damage to the *Hindenburg*'s gas cell, its hand-drawn diagrams of where the abrasions occurred and where they were "worst," and the efforts to analyze and repair them. It resides in the Douglas Robinson Collection, University of Texas, Dallas, Box 9, Folder 1. The document may have been overlooked or merely dismissed as inconsequential a half century later, when Harold Dick and Douglas Robinson cowrote their book, *The Golden Age of the Great Passenger Airships,* and mentioned on page 148, "the winter inspection had shown some chafing so there could have been some type of leakage in the past and no resulting problems."
84. *"We recommend reporting damage . . .":* Karl Rösch to Ernst Lehmann, January 20, 1937 (author translation).
84. *they devised . . . gas-cell damage.:* Lewis and Dick, 30a.

85. *the workers painstakingly tied . . . wiring crossed. :* ibid.

85. *painting the entire top . . . a lacquer.:* Karl Hürttle to Karl Rösch, May 4, 1937.

85. *Lehmann even lined up a plane . . . :* Dick and Robinson, 144–45.

85. *Udet kept crashing . . . :* Dick and Robinson, 142; Duggan, *LZ129,* 87; *New York Times,* March 12, 1937.

86. *Dick told him the probable cause . . . :* Dick and Robinson, 87.

87. *Immediately, Captains Pruss and Sammt . . . steady the cover.:* Duggan, *LZ129,* 55. The author was unable to find this correspondence based on the citation provided by Duggan, LZA 16/39, but did find a subsequent letter that summarized them, Karl Hürttle to Karl Rösch, May 4, 1937.

87. *Should anything happen to him . . . :* Herbert Baum to Barbara Waibel, August 9, 2007 (author translation).

90. *"the desire to correct the stability . . .":* Karl Hürttle to Karl Rösch, May 4, 1937 (author translation).

90. *"to stretch the test panels . . .":* ibid. (author translation).

90. *"We believe that it would be . . .":* ibid. (author translation).


*Fire*

92. *The day will come when . . . :* Chardin, 86–87.


*Chapter 7: Headwinds*

93. *"It was like riding . . .":* *Pittsburgh Press,* May 7, 1937.

93. *"wretched sailor on the sea.":* Mather, 591.

94. *"One felt no motion . . .":* ibid.

95. *U.S. Naval Air Station, Lakehurst, N.J., Weather Bulletin:* Weather Bulletin, 1.

95. *"a board full of nails":* Adelt, 69.

95. *"Now, aren't you glad . . .":* *Sunday Star* (Washington, DC), August 8, 1937.

96. *"Condition still unsettled . . .":* Transcript, 17. There are fourteen archival boxes of materials and documents housed at the National Archives and Records Administration, principally related to the Commerce Department's ultimately inconclusive investigation of the *Hindenburg* accident. Undoubtedly, the 1,278-page transcript of the hearing held at Lakehurst, New Jersey, shortly after the tragedy is the richest source of eyewitness accounts of weather and conditions both inside and outside the ship, as well as expert and technical testimony on the observations made known to investigators.

97. *"Recommend landing now.":* Transcript, 18.

97. *"The ship is riding . . . :* Morrison, recording, May 6, 1937.

99. *"It's practically standing . . . ".:* ibid.

99. *Outside the fence . . . saw it, too.:* Mark Heald to Michael McCarthy, email, September 8, 2015.

99. *Near the mooring mast . . . ship is doomed.:* Lehmann, *Zeppelin,* 327, 334.

99. *"It burst into flames!" . . . ". . . the humanity!":* Morrison, recording, May 6, 1937.

## Chapter 8: "This Is the End"

100. *Joseph Spah dangles from a window frame . . . :* In interviews, Spah's own account changed over the decades. The author chose the most likely, least sensational one, the one given the day after the accident. To the outside of the *Hindenburg*, Spah said, "I held on by one hand and when the ship started falling, I turned loose. I landed on my feet, bounced into the air and fell on my face . . ." (*Pittsburgh Press*, May 8, 1937). Other accounts include ". . . hanging from the ship, two men were holding onto Spah's coat but lost their grip. Spah let go about 50 feet from the ground and broke an ankle . . ." (*Long Island Star-Journal*, March 25, 1957), and ". . . Spah grabbed a rope which dangled from the hydrogen-filled aircraft and held on as two other passengers fell to their death in front of him. 'I climbed down the rope but it was 40 feet too short.'" (*Lexington [KY] Leader*, December 29, 1975).

100. *"Through the window!":* Leonhard Adelt to Hindenburg Investigation Board, May 30, 1937, 1.

101. *"Come on . . ." . . . ". . . get my wife.":* Toland, 325.

101. *"This is the end.":* New York Herald Tribune, May 27, 1937.

101. *"Navy men, stand fast! . . .":* Toland, 328.

102. *"I can't believe it . . .":* ibid., 333. Many published accounts, including newspaper reports, of what Captain Lehmann uttered as he staggered from the burning ship have him blurting out, "I don't understand it." There was no reporter near the burning wreckage to hear precisely what he said, and it is very doubtful Lehmann would have said he did not understand what happened. Some accounts use the "don't understand" phrase to suggest he was blindsided by the fire—and then to suggest further that that indicated sabotage. In fact, Lehmann must have been struck, even in the seconds after the ship hit the ground, that the very thing he had dreaded, the very reason he decided to ride the *Hindenburg* on that very trip—the remote possibility of catastrophe from leaking gasbags—had indeed happened. The author offers the reader in the text, "I can't believe it," because it comes from an eyewitness, Harry Bruno, a friend of Lehmann's who was on the field after the disaster, who would have heard exactly what Lehmann said, and who Toland interviewed for his book.

## Chapter 9: Sincere Regrets

103. *"I can't talk . . .":* Morrison, recording, May 6, 1937.

103. *"A moment of spectacular madness.":* Lincoln (NE) Star, May 7, 1937.

103. *One man ran . . . and fell dead.:* Time, May 17, 1937.

104. *"What caused it?" . . . "Lightning.":* Adelt, 72.

104. *"The best she can hope . . . .":* Sunday Star (Washington, DC), August 8, 1937.

104. *Hoover made an extraordinary offer . . . Eckener refused.:* New York Times, May 11, 1937, and May 12, 1937.

105. *"A higher power . . .":* New York Times, May 8, 1937.

105. *"A horrific accident . . .":* Goebbels, Teil 1, Bd. 4/III, 128, May 8, 1937.

105. *"I always insisted airships are safe . . .":* Plain Speaker (Hazelton, PA), May 7, 1937.

106. *"The new German Zeppelin . . .":* ibid.

106. *"We could still smell . . .":* Chapman.

106. *"He was my oldest . . .":* New York Times, May 8, 1937.

106. *"He is deeply shaken . . .":* Goebbels, Teil 1, Bd. 4/III, 129, May 8, 1937.

107. *"Captain Lehmann has succumbed . . .":* ibid., 130, May 9, 1937.

107. *U.S. Naval Air Station, Lakehurst, N.J., Log Book:* Log Book.

108. *"glad news.":* Ernst Lehmann to Charles E. Rosendahl, February 8, 1935.

109. *he censored photos . . . :* Althoff, 98.

109. *For damage control . . . :* ibid.

110. *Trimble allowed Rosendahl . . . :* Transcript. Rosendahl's testimony runs on pages 12–44.

110. *"Obviously, I have no knowledge . . .":* New York Sun, May 10, 1937.

111. *"The ship appeared . . .":* Transcript, 51.

111. *The official report . . . and 5:30.:* "Exhibit 74 L."

111. *Hitler issued surprise orders . . . matter of months.:* New York Times, May 11, 1937.

112. *He offered a fond . . . :* New York Times, May 12, 1937.

112. *"From the ashes . . .":* ibid.

112. *On the Europa, Hugo Eckener wrote . . . :* Hugo Eckener to Johanna Eckener, May 12, 1937, cited in Italiaander, 357.

113. *"I sincerely regret . . ." :* ibid. (author translation).

113. *"In actuality, we have always been able . . .":* ibid. (author translation).

113. *He stayed at Rosendahl's . . . :* Eckener, *My Zeppelins,* 169.

114. *"You cared for my fellow . . .":* Hermann Göring to Jean Rosendahl. Göring wrote his letter in German, which was translated by the U.S. Navy into English. The letter was addressed to Mrs. J. W. Rosendahl and had no date beyond June of 1937.

114. *"Discussions concerning . . .":* New York Times, May 14, 1937.

114. *"As long as eight years . . .":* Duggan, *LZ129,* 39.

114. *he and the German team . . . stern of the ship . . . :* Trenton State Gazette, May 15, 1937.

115. *He suggested the FBI search . . . :* E. A. Tamm to J. Edgar Hoover, May 11, 1937.

115. *Rosendahl had ordered members . . . :* Airship Hindenburg Diary, May 9, 1937. An unnamed author, probably a Commerce Department investigator, kept a nearly daily journal of mostly behind-the-scenes meetings and letters and discussions, some between the FBI and the U.S. Navy, in the immediate aftermath of the disaster, from May 6 through May 29. The diary, which has no page numbers, was considered authentic enough by the Commerce Department staff to turn it over to the National Archives and Records Administration as part of its extensive and official investigative file on the *Hindenburg.*

115. *"Testimony to date . . .":* E. J. Connelly to J. Edgar Hoover, May 13, 1937. The FBI has made available on the internet hundreds of pages of documents related to its analysis of the *Hindenburg* tragedy, and they are a very good starting point. Ultimately, though, there are too many frustrating redactions, long portions of documents blacked out, sometimes for privacy reasons. The author won release of much more lightly redacted documents through a Freedom of Information Act request, initially denied but later upheld upon appeal. The agency seemed persuaded by the fact that several of the characters in the documents had clearly died and were no longer entitled to the agency's citing privacy concerns as a reason for redaction.

116. *They went to a movie theater . . . :* Airship Hindenburg Diary, May 15, 1937.

116. *Rosendahl called agent William Devereaux . . . "absolutely necessary.":* William Devereaux to J. Edgar Hoover, May 19, 1937. Devereaux gave FBI director Hoover a running, neutral synopsis of Rosendahl's attempts to steer investigators to a saboteur.

117. *"I have no knowledge . . .":* New York Sun, May 10, 1937.

### Chapter 10: "Noticeable Fluttering"

118. *"About four or five minutes . . .":* Transcript, 815.

119. *"Will you take the diagram . . ." . . . ". . . from the propeller.":* Transcript, 816–17.

119. *"Doctor, at this time . . .":* Transcript, 856. The succeeding quotations in the text, the question-and-answer testimony between investigators and Eckener, appear between pages 856 and 892 of the hearing transcript.

124. *"I would be very happy to know . . .":* New York Times, May 29, 1937.

124. *"That probably brought the ship . . .":* ibid.

124. *"There have been ignitions . . .":* Transcript, 1,151.

124. *"Where the hydrogen . . .":* ibid.

124. *Rosendahl assured them he had not.:* Transcript, 1,171.

125. *A soft, muffled thud . . . :* Leonhard Adelt to Hindenburg Investigation Board, May 30, 1937, 1 (author translation).

126. *"I asked him briefly . . .":* ibid.

126. *"He was worried . . .":* ibid.

126. *"It occurs to me . . .":* ibid.

126. *In the light of these things . . . :* ibid.

126. *"DER REITER . . .":* ibid.

127. *"You, no doubt . . .":* South Trimble to Charles Rosendahl, June 9, 1937.

127. *"With regard to the letter . . . see you in Washington.":* Charles Rosendahl to South Trimble, June 11, 1937. The extraordinary correspondence, in which the chief investigator suggests calling Adelt as a witness and Rosendahl dismisses that idea, assassinating Adelt's character in the process—all documenting a navy cover-up—appears in the National Archives and Records Administration records on the *Hindenburg* disaster, Box 1, Folder C-1, "Advisory Board."

128. *considerable losses . . . 1936 season.:* Duggan, *LZ129,* 239.

128. *the official report blamed . . . landing procedure.:* "Commerce Department Report," 35.

### Chapter 11: Broken Water

129. *Knut Eckener joined the Nazi Party . . . :* Staatsarchiv Sigmaringen 13 14/g/1044 (2025), cited in Ebner, section on Knut Eckener. (Ebner's text, *Die Entnazifizierung Von Zeppelin, Maybach, Dornier & Co.,* available only as an electronic book, does not have page numbers. In accord with accepted practice on such texts, these citations will offer a chapter title or section heading to help direct the interested reader to a given passage.) Also, Häffner, 197.

130. *"a stroke of genius.":* Eckener, *My Zeppelins,* 177.

130. *"Now it's the Czechs' turn . . .":* Ullrich, 722.

130. *The Japanese military . . . volcano fumes.: New York Times*, May 11, 1938.

131. *"I cannot understand what leads . . .":* Stein, 52.

131. *"deliberate unfriendliness" . . . ". . . possible point.":* ibid.

131. *"I cannot believe for a moment . . .": Pantagraph* (Bloomington, IL), April 26, 1938.

131. *"Perfectly absurd . . .":* ibid.

132. *"One such Zeppelin might . . .":* George Messersmith to Cordell Hull, et al., May 9, 1938.

132. *"We would not ship . . .":* Ickes, 391.

133. *"If those governments . . .": New York Times*, July 18, 1938.

133. *Eckener formally gave . . . bordering countries.:* Sammt, *Mein Leben*, 158.

133. *Hitler gave Eckener . . . :* Nielsen, 233.

134. *"I wish this ship to carry forth . . ." . . .* "Sieg Heil!".: Duggan, *Airships*, 220.

134. *Eckener stepped . . . hallowed grounds.:* Meyer, *Airshipmen*, 219.

134. *Eckener personally oversaw the modifications to the LZ 130.:* Dick and Robinson, 152.

134. *workers re-tensioned the fabric . . . :* Lewis and Dick, 46. All the revisions laid out in the succeeding paragraphs in the text come from the technical papers compiled by Goodyear's Harold Dick and George Lewis and are covered by pages 46–48 of their materials held at the University of Texas, Dallas, and Wichita State University.

135. *"From the ground . . .":* Lewis and Dick. These notes appear in a section called "LZ 130," 4.

135. *Eckener reportedly . . . over Czechoslovakia.:* Meyer, *Airshipmen*, 219.

135. *The dining room . . . radio transmissions.:* ibid.

136. *Four Messerschmitt fighter planes . . . :* Sammt, *Mein Leben*, 158.

136. *He assumed that they were related . . . signal-monitoring equipment.:* Lewis and Dick. These are Harold Dick's notes on unnumbered pages regarding test flights of the LZ 130.

137. *"a good German . . .": News-Herald* (Franklin, PA), December 8, 1938.

137. *invited as Hitler's personal guest.: New York Times*, December 9, 1938.

138. *"How can any American . . ." . . . ". . . benighted and bestial.": New York Times*, December 23, 1938.

139. *Air Ministry amassed huge crowds . . . :* Duggan, *Airships*, 222.

139. *Sammt stopped his engines . . . :* Sammt, *Mein Leben*, 158.


*Chapter 12: "Enjoy the War"*

142. *The entourage from the Peenemünde . . . :* Tholander, "Dachau," 179.

142. *After speaking . . . showed interest.:* ibid.

142. *he began working with the Abwehr . . . Bulgaria.:* Dossier, unnumbered page with stapled index cards reporting various political and military affiliations.

142. *He also began scouting . . . Passau.:* Becker and Eggerer, 533.

142. *Eckener scouted remote spots:* ibid.

143. *"An airplane carrying Hitler . . .":* Shirer, 562.

144. *"Before us in a clearing . . .":* Speer, 367.

144. *"I was thunderstruck . . .":* ibid.

144. *"We all froze . . .":* ibid.

144. *"gravest doubts":* ibid.
145. *"I . . . managed at length . . .":* Dornberger, 72.
145. *"I breathed again.":* ibid., 77.
145. *Suddenly, Hitler showed . . . :* Speer, 367.
145. *Puffing on . . . leaving Friedrichshafen.:* Italiaander, 381.
146. *it installed artificial fog machinery . . . wafting vapor.:* Neufeld, *Von Braun,* 154.
146. *At two the next morning . . . Johanna, that evening.:* Italiaander, 382.
147. *Hitler was still not convinced . . . :* Dornberger, 78.
147. *Hitler ordered Speer to form . . .":* Metzler, 33.
148. *At this point . . . safe after reading.:* Aktennotiz, 1. Stamped "*Geheim,*" or "Secret,"
Peenemünde Army Institute Memo No. T 2/43 is a list of the A-4 Special Committee
working group leaders, dated February 9, 1943. The name Eckener appears on the first
page of the list in relation to Group 12, responsible for the middle section of the rocket.
148. *As a ten-year-old . . . ". . . friends would be killed.":* Speer, 6.
148. *Zeppelin and Daimler-Benz were responsible . . . :* Metlzer, 32.
149. *Eckener's own salary . . . in Friedrichshafen.:* Staatsarchiv Sigmaringen 15/621 (Bd.1),
cited in Ebner, section on Hugo Eckener.
149. *"Enjoy the war . . .":* Ordway, 69.
150. *In 1942, 782 workers . . . :* Annual Reports for the Zeppelin Company (*Angaben im
Geschäftsjahr*) 1942 and 1943, LZA 06/0660, cited in Tholander, "Dachau," 184.
150. *Zeppelin, under Eckener's leadership . . . 1,000 of them men.:* Annual Report for the
Zeppelin Company (*Angaben im Geschäftsjahr*) 1943, LZA 06/0660.
150. In early 1943 . . . *never returned.:* Petersen, 263.
150. *paid a fraction . . . deducted by Zeppelin:* Tholander, "Dachau," 203.
150. *For violating race-separation . . . concentration camp.:* Herbert, 128.
150. *von Braun visited Friedrichshafen . . . build the rockets:* Petersen, 248.
151. *"construction of fuel tanks . . .":* ibid.
151. *After checking . . . mining industry.:* Petersen, 249.
151. *After that denial . . . the A-4 Special Committee.:* Neufeld, *Rocket,* 188; Allen, 213.
151. *It also put Eckener . . . camp network.:* Petersen, 249.
151. *Starting in February 1943 . . . :* Petersen, 249–50; Neufeld, *Rocket,* 188–89; Tholander, *Fremdarbeiter,* 531, with a map of the prison camp "Don," 237.
151. *The committee sent a delegation . . . :* Neufeld, *Von Braun,* 143.
152. *Dr. Dürr, Eckener's longtime . . . :* Tholander, *Fremdarbeiter,* 183.0
152. *"This system has worked . . .":* Neufeld, *Rocket,* 187.
152. *on the cover of* Berlin Illustrated . . . *:* Berliner Illustrierte, May 13, 1943.
152. *hailed as "armaments experts":* ibid., cover caption.
153. *Hitler for the first time . . . :* Speer, 368.
153. *He turned to Dornberger . . . could do with them.:* Dornberger, 100.
153. *"No defense against the rocket . . .":* ibid., 105.
153. *After years of hesitation, Hitler suddenly . . . :* ibid., 106.
153. *Speer immediately recommended to Hitler . . . :* Dornberger, 151.
153. *"God help us . . .":* Speer, 368.
153. *Two Polish janitors . . . :* Garliński, 52–53.

154. *"a weapon which is not yet known . . ."*: Jones, 58.

154. *"this rocket business"*: ibid., 333.

154. *"I saw it once . . ."*: ibid.

155. *Eisenhower worried it would be difficult . . .*: Eisenhower, 260.

### Earth
158. *In a century of Zeppelins . . .*: Stainton, 2.

### Chapter 13: Illicit Fruit
159. *Moisej Temkin was captured . . .*: Temkin, 39.

159. *an SS shooting range . . . and 1942:* Berben, 120.

159. *He came to a wide courtyard . . .*: Temkin, 63.

159. *Gestapo men ordered . . . onto a truck.*: ibid., 63–64.

160. *"Do you all know . . ."*: ibid., 67 (author translation).

160. *Sometime after Dachau . . . regime enemies.*: Berben, 6.

161. *"Tolerance is a sign . . ."*: ibid., 231.

161. *"Communists, bastards . . ."*: Temkin, 79 (author translation).

162. *Doctors hastily . . . he died.*: Berben, 59.

163. *He had to respectfully beg . . .*: Tholander, "Dachau," 191.

163. *Anyone who cheated . . . severely beaten.*: ibid., 198.

163. *The bombers did not touch . . .*: Angeben, 2.

164. *Construction of the Friedrichshafen camp . . .*: Metzler, 37; Königseder, Benz, and Distel, 328.

164. *Zeppelin agreed . . . Hall 3 . . .*: Tholander, "Dachau," 180.

164. *It was massive, 750 feet long . . .*: ibid.

164. *"This facility . . ."*: Angeben, 1.

164. *"continue to be the main business . . ."*: ibid.

164. *Under an ambitious production schedule . . .*: Tholander, *Fremdarbeiter*, 229.

164. *Using slave labor . . . war effort.*: Tholander, "Dachau," 184.

165. *Of the nearly 800 German Zeppelin . . .*: ibid., 185.

165. *Dachau pulled skilled laborers . . .*: ibid.

165. *The tall SS lieutenant . . . a whip . . .*: ibid., 188

165. *Grünberg came to Friedrichshafen . . .*: ibid., 187.

166. *Some prisoners so feared . . .*: Berben, 61.

166. *He carried boards . . .*: Temkin, 129.

167. *"Doubtful cases . . ."*: Berben, 233.

167. *The SS hounds were generally well-fed . . .*: ibid., 71.

167. *The guards courted . . .*: ibid., 233.

167. *Under Rule 11 . . .*: ibid.

168. *"Then we slept . . ."*: Temkin, 133 (author translation).

168. *One day a Polish prisoner . . . aluminum containers.*: Tholander, "Dachau," 200–201.

169. *Alles in Ordnung . . .*: Berben, 21.

169. *Two men, Otto Jung . . . prisoner number 932.:* Burger, *Zeppelin,* Teil 2, 61–62, with personal details retrieved via Stevemorse.org, which contains numerous biographical records compiled by the Nazis on Dachau prisoners.

169. *The punishment order cited . . . :* Burger, *Zeppelin,* Teil 2, 61.

170. *My dear child . . . Your H:* ibid., 61–62 (author translation).

### Chapter 14: The German Missile Crisis

171. *There was the one air attack . . . :* Allen, 214.

171. *Hugo Eckener returned at least twice . . . :* Rees interview.

171. *"He was very much interested . . .":* ibid.

171. *One dismissed . . . a hoax.:* Jones, 358.

172. *It also missed its objective . . . :* Sellier et al., 29.

172. *requisitioned some 30,000 . . . that August . . . :* Allen, 214.

173. *"It was decided by those . . .":* Angaben für, 4 (author translation).

173. *Knut Eckener, as operations director . . . production machines.:* Metzler, 54.

174. *Zeppelin transferred 335 . . . Saulgau:* Tholander, "Dachau," 210.

174. *surrounded by barbed wire . . . prisoners and guards.:* Königseder, Benz, and Distel, 477.

174. *"It appears that the final stage . . .":* Jones, 351.

174. *The surprising intelligence came from . . . :* ibid., 354.

175. *Over drinks each night . . . :* *Washington Post,* December 28, 1998, interview with the former spy, who was then seventy-nine years old.

175. *"I kept saying . . .":* ibid.

175. *To impress her . . . :* ibid.

175. *"During the last six months . . .":* Ordway, 168.

175. *A British home security . . . :* Jones, 445. Incidentally, the official's name is Herbert Morrison, the same as the famed announcer of the dramatic *Hindenburg* recording.

176. *bombing German secret-weapons sites . . . :* Ordway, 127.

176. *"We bombed the suspected . . . .":* Eisenhower, 259.

176. *a third of the workforce . . . :* Crew and Ulrich, 233.

176. *final reckoning . . . 1,202 of them from Dachau:* Geschäftsbericht, 3.

176. *"We recall with gratitude . . .":* ibid. (author translation).

176. *"The civilian laborers' camp . . . small circle.":* Angaben aus, 5.

177. *12.8 million Reichsmarks . . . another 5.4 million RM:* ibid., 1; Angaben für, 1.

177. *the* Graf Zeppelin *. . . only 1.7 million RM . . . :* Duggan, *LZ129,* 239.

177. *"We were fully occupied . . .":* Geschäftsbericht, 1.

### Chapter 15: "An Inside Job"

178. *"Prisoners ran around . . .":* Temkin, 132 (author translation).

178. *"Many prisoners died . . .":* ibid. (author translation).

178. *Gearing up for an Allied invasion . . . :* *Evening Sun* (Hanover, PA), April 28, 1944.

178. *Months earlier . . . 5,000 people.:* Angaben aus, 2.

179. *Two dozen of the 1,200 . . . :* Königseder, Benz, and Distel, 328.

179. *Some also had to defuse . . . :* ibid.

179. *Germany had more. . . . war industries.:* Berben, 88.

179. *He was appointed an* Abwehrbeauftragter . . . : Staatsarchiv Sigmaringen 13 14/g/1044, cited in Ebner, section on Knut Eckener.

180. *"What an inspiring murder . . .":* Longmate, 97.

180. *Some 2,000 army officers . . . :* Lee, 4.

180. *"A bomb attempt was made . . .":* Evening Review (East Liverpool, OH), July 20, 1944.

181. *In Friedrichshafen, seventy-two people died:* Catalogue of Camps, 629.

181. *"The depressing effect . . .":* Eisenhower, 259.

182. *About 700 prisoners were forced . . . :* Königseder, Benz, and Distel, Bd. 2, 514.

182. *Within the first six . . . poor hygiene.:* Burger, *Zeppelin,* Teil 2, 86.

182. *ninety-seven corpses were stuffed . . . had dog bites.:* ibid.

182. *Wassilij Sklarenko . . . ". . . deeply affected.":* Burger, *Stollen,* 55.

182. *He was among 762 prisoners vacated . . . :* Catalogue of Camps, 629; "New Arrivals from Dachau labor camp Friedrichshafen for September 30, 1944, with prisoner files," SS Operations Administration Support, Mittelbau, RG-04.006m_Reel 17_0008.jpg, United States Holocaust Memorial Museum Collections Division, Archives Branch.

182. *People in nearby . . . "zebras.":* Zeidler and Schafft, 56.

182. *Armaments Minister Speer . . . was under way.:* Ordway, 70.

183. *It also brought tears . . . sun again.:* Sellier et al., 127.

183. *prisoners had to sleep on straw . . . "like two cats.":* Zeidler and Schafft, 28.

183. *Desperate, forced to live like beasts . . . laid across.:* U.S. v. Kurt Andrae et al., 7.

184. *prisoner camp wouldn't be built . . . :* Wagner, 80.

184. *"The noise bores . . .":* Neufeld, *Rocket,* 210.

184. *Within six months, a staggering 3,000 prisoners died . . . :* ibid., 211.

184. *At first, the corpses . . . its own incinerator.:* Béon and Neufeld, 11–12.

184. *A prisoner named Jacky . . . gray bodies near a door:* ibid.

185. *At Dora, he became prisoner number 91408.:* Temkin, 34.

185. *encountered the first . . . with black skin.:* ibid., 136.

185. *One prisoner could see . . . word: liberation.:* ibid.

186. *The tunnels were humid . . . :* Buggeln, 106.

186. *When they left the tunnel . . . :* Temkin, 140.

186. *When he saw someone sleeping . . . :* ibid.

186. *"beaten or even stabbed . . ." exclusive domain:* Hunt, 66.

186. *"I have never before . . . :* Wegener, 95.

187. *Twelve accused saboteurs . . . :* Neufeld, *Rocket,* 262.

187. *"Most of their bodies . . .":* Béon and Neufeld, 147.

188. *Apparently, the original . . . mass extermination.:* U.S. v. Kurt Andrae et al., 17.

188. *Temkin vividly remembered . . . water through the window.:* Temkin, 144.

189. *"We awaken to find . . .":* Béon and Neufeld, 209.

189. *"a softer cushion . . .":* ibid., 210.

189. *The route of the train . . . :* U.S. v. Kurt Andrae et al., 19.

189. *The SS called on a local Nazi . . . :* Buggeln, 273.

189. *Pointing rifles, the guards . . . :* U.S. v. Kurt Andrae et al., 20.
190. *After dousing . . . set the building afire.:* ibid.
190. *1,016 of the evacuated prisoners had been burned to death.:* ibid.

## Chapter 16: Swastikas in the Closet
191. *"We must establish incredible facts . . . :* Thacker, 162.
191. *"Colonel, you'd better . . .":* Collins interview.
191. *"terribly angry . . .":* ibid.
192. *The American military. . . the victims.:* Minneapolis Star, April 23, 1945.
192. *Over a few days . . . and Czechs.:* Arizona Republic, April 15, 1945.
192. *"Things came to a head . . .":* Des Moines Register, April 17, 1945.
192. *"the bowels of hell" . . . ". . . burning kilns with them.":* Baltimore Sun, May 4, 1945.
193. *Winston Churchill . . . summary execution.:* Thacker, 161.
193. *"Fair hearings for the accused . . .":* ibid.
194. *Eckener gave an interview . . . :* The Bee (Danville, VA), July 26, 1945, a widely circulated dispatch from the Associated Press.
194. *"the Zeppelin builder" . . . ". . . Adolf Hitler.":* ibid.
195. *"at his villa . . ." . . . ". . . did not like us.":* ibid.
195. *"If anybody believes . . .":* Salem (OR) Journal, October 13, 1945.
196. *It was charged . . . production.:* Ebner, section on denazification.
196. *some half-million Fragebogen . . . overwhelmed.:* Biddiscombe, 171.
196. *The local tribunals . . . .and clerks.:* Ebner, section on denazification.
197. *a clerk wrote to the district office . . . in a gym.:* ibid.
197. *Eckener tap-danced . . . entire war record.:* Fragebogen, Eckener. Eckener's mandatory questionnaire resides in the Eckener, Hugo "Paperclip" file, which was declassified April 12, 1999, at the National Archives and Records Administration, Records Group 330, Stack 230.
197. *By the end of that year . . . manual labor.:* Hoover, 271.
197. *Asked if he ever belonged . . . honorary title of "Professor.":* Fragebogen, Eckener.
197. *Knut confessed to joining . . . in 1944.:* Staatsarchiv Sigmaringen 13 14/g/1044 (2025), cited in Ebner, section on Knut Eckener.
197. *French proceedings more often ended . . . :* Taylor, 322.
197. *At one point, Eisenhower . . . Nazi supporters.:* Biddiscombe, 166.
198. *"spiritually and practically devoted . . . :* ibid., 164.
198. *roughly one in ten Germans . . . :* Doyle, 22.
198. *"I was unwilling . . .":* Fragebogen, Müller (author translation).
198. *For the next three years, Müller . . . and magazines.:* ibid.
199. *But one week later . . . denazification panel.:* Eau Claire (WI) Leader, October 8, 1946.
199. *"a fanatical Nazi.":* Lee, 147.
199. *"We may expect that the number . . . :* Hunt, 10.
200. *Within a few months . . . Springfield, Massachusetts.:* Burlington (VT) Free Press, April 30, 1947.
200. *His application cited as character references . . . :* Basic Personnel Record. Hugo Eckener's Basic Personnel Record, which is undated, resides in the Eckener, Hugo "Paperclip"

file, which was declassified April 12, 1999, at the National Archives and Records Administration, Records Group 330, Stack 230.

200. *one defendant in that case would hang . . . .: Nevada State Journal* (Reno), May 23, 1947.

201. *"I am very sorry to say . . ." . . . unannounced destination.: Burlington (VT) Free Press*, April 30, 1947.

201. *conducted virtually no background checks.:* Hunt, 61, 115, 116, 121, 265.

201. *Each German expert . . . scraps of intelligence.:* ibid., 25.

201. *Hoover, who repeatedly . . . weapons installations.:* ibid., 112.

202. *"beating a dead Nazi horse.":* ibid., 110.

202. *rocket operation that killed some 20,000 slave workers.:* U.S. v. Kurt Andrae et al., 20.

202. *"The transplantation of . . ." . . . ". . . political leadership.": Newsweek*, December 9, 1946; subsequent quotations appear on pages 64–69.

203. *"Though the other nations . . .": Life*, December 9, 1946; subsequent quotations appear on pages 49–52.

203. *He was to be paid 30,000 German marks . . . :* Special Contract. The Special Contract for the Employment of German Nationals with the War Department of the United States awarded to Hugo Eckener on March 10, 1947, resides in the Eckener, Hugo "Paperclip" file, which was declassified April 12, 1999, at the National Archives and Records Administration, Records Group 330, Stack 230. This document is the citation for subsequent details in the text regarding Eckener's work, physical characteristics, contacts, responses to questions, and declaration of truthfulness.

204. *"several hundred having to do . . .": Fragebogen*, Eckener (author translation).

205. *"I have also often spoken . . .":* ibid. (author translation).

205. *"My son, Knut Eckener . . .":* ibid. (author translation).

205. *"I have not directly . . .":* ibid. (author translation).

205. *"The statements on this form . . .":* ibid.

206. *"Subject has no governmental . . .":* Security Report. The Security Report for Hugo Eckener issued March 26, 1947, by the Office of the Military Government of the United States is on a form titled "Security Report on German (or Austrian) Scientists or Important Technicians" and resides in the Eckener, Hugo "Paperclip" file, which was declassified April 12, 1999, at the National Archives and Records Administration, Records Group 330, Stack 230.

206. *"Based on available records . . .":* ibid.

206. *Rosendahl. . . . subsidize airships.: Nebraska State Journal* (Lincoln), July 13, 1947.

207. *When Eckener arrived in Akron . . . : Akron (OH) Beacon Journal*, May 4, 1947.

207. *"Ostensibly acting only as . . .":* Nurnberg, 25.

208. *"the use of prisoners of war . . . :* ibid., 44.

208. *"part of the slave labor program . . .":* ibid.

208. *Another Farben officer was cited . . :* ibid., 45.

208. *"enclosed with barbed wire . . .":* ibid., 46.

209. *Erich Bachem . . . rejected an offer by Himmler . . . :* Metzler, 63.

209. *Then on May 19, 1947 . . . underground installation.:* Hunt, 19.

209. *another defendant . . . in the prison hospital.:* Nevada State Journal (Reno), May 23, 1947.

209. *a camp founded solely to supply the war machine.:* Hunt, 72.

210. *Zeppelin's Knut Eckener . . . at least one meeting there . . . :* Metzler, 188.

210. *Rickhey knew about forty-two boxes . . . :* Hunt, 60.

210. *closer to 18,000 to . . . evacuations.:* U.S. v. Kurt Andrae et al., 20.

210. *the Nordhausen concentration camp . . . :* Allen, 223; Béon and Neufeld, xii.

210. *Conditions tunneling out the factory. . . . :* ibid., 1–17. The Andrae indictment is the citation for subsequent details in the text including number of prisoners, shortage of blankets, decomposing bodies, beatings with iron bars and other weapons, twelve-hour work shifts, drinking urine in desperation, and the other mentioned miseries.

211. *as the surname Eckener appeared . . . A-4 Special Committee.:* Aktennotiz, 1. Stamped "*Geheim,*" or "Secret," Peenemünde Army Institute Memo No. T 2/43 is a list of the A-4 Special Committee working group leaders, dated February 9, 1943. The name Eckener appears on the first page of the list in relation to Group 12, responsible for the middle section of the rocket.

211. *"The leader of the Special Committee . . . :* Allen, 223.

212. *The Army Acceptance Office . . . from Luftschiffbau Zeppelin.:* Petersen, 342.

212. *Whenever a prisoner was accused . . . with a footstool.:* U.S. v. Kurt Andrae et al., 14–17. The gory details of the hangings described in the text are covered in three pages of the indictment cited.

### Chapter 17: "I Don't Believe in War"

213. *Litchfield explained that Eckener . . . :* Baltimore Sun, October 31, 1947.

213. *Eckener was never a Nazi . . . :* ibid.

214. *His information, he said, was that Russia . . . :* Nebraska State Journal, July 13, 1947.

214. *In the two years since . . . in nearly 500 cases.:* United States Army Investigation, 1.

214. *Their statute of limitations . . . :* Hunt, 105.

214. *Eckener told his American . . . :* Outgoing Classified Message. This classified memo resides in the Eckener, Hugo "Paperclip" file at the National Archives and Records Administration.

215. *To HQ EUCOM, Frankfurt Germany . . . :* Bosquet Wev to J. Edgar Hoover, November 25, 1947.

215. *"Dr. Eckener was repatriated . . ."*: ibid.

215. *"I don't believe in war.":* Palm Beach (FL) Post, December 7, 1947.

216. *Rickhey's defense attorney requested . . . :* Hunt, 70.

216. *Rickhey asked the court to credit . . . :* ibid.

216. *The regional committee, reviewing the case . . . :* Ebner, section on Hugo Eckener.

216. *That panel charged that . . . August of 1934.:* ibid.

216. *So, he argued that he did write . . . :* Eckener, Im Zeppelin, 263.

217. *the Gestapo was looking to eliminate . . . :* ibid., 260.

217. *he was branded an opponent . . . :* ibid., 244.

217. *Eckener contended that Hitler . . . :* ibid., 249.

217. . . . *spared a known enemy of the Nazis.*: Even Robinson, an admirer of Eckener's who seems to have been completely in the dark about his conduct in the war years, was given pause by this bold assertion. In his book *Giants in the Sky*, Robinson added a footnote, on page 282: "I cannot put much stock on the story that Eckener was spared because President Hindenburg, on his deathbed in July 1934, made Hitler promise not to harm him. I do not doubt the testimony of his physician, Professor Sauerbruch, in relating Hindenburg's words, but cannot imagine that such a promise would deter a man who murdered millions from liquidating a single inconvenient opponent." *Giants in the Sky* also has a phenomenal historical reference, Appendix A, that lists the dimensions, materials, and ultimate end (burned, crashed, dismantled) of every single one of the world's 161 "rigid" airships flown between 1897 and 1940.

217. *"contrary to the existing . . .":* Ebner, section on Hugo Eckener (author translation).

217. *In late 1946 . . . administrative jobs.:* ibid.

217. *The committee was eager to fine . . . the city.:* ibid.

217. *Early on, Eckener not only failed . . public opinion.:* ibid.

218. *Knut played a decisive role . . . :* Ebner, section on Knut Eckener.

218. *"great anger":* ibid. (author translation).

218. *Knut Eckener noted that he only joined . . . :* ibid.

218. *"personally against the Party":* ibid.

218. *He claimed not to have known that the parts . . . :* ibid.

218. *He also said . . . of the Gestapo.:* ibid.

218. *One firm will has to command . . . :* *Schwäbische Zeitung*, September 30, 1950.

219. *He said Dr. Eckener's resistance claims . . . :* Ebner, section on Hugo Eckener.

219. *"There must be thousands . . . :* ibid. (author translation).

219. *the French tribunal declared Eckener . . . :* *Corpus Christi Caller-Times*, January 23, 1948.

219. *Hugo Eckener . . . voting privileges.:* ibid.

219. *Ludwig Dürr, for one, was found innocent . . . :* Ebner, section on Hugo Eckener.


## Chapter 18: "Hunger Cages"

220. *He privately tossed off . . . :* Shirer, 59.

221. *He was living . . . :* *Akron (OH) Beacon Journal*, August 7, 1949.

222. *"So, I had Hindenburg . . .":* Eckener, *Im Zeppelin*, 249 (author translation).

223. *Face to face with the agitated . . . :* ibid.

223. *Eckener relayed how the* Graf Zeppelin. . . : ibid.

223. *When the* Graf Zeppelin *finally arrived . . . :* ibid., 257.

224. *"Everything in Germany has turned . . .":* ibid., 260.

224. *"consummate criminal":* ibid., 262.

225. *"I considered it a tasteless . . .":* ibid., 265.

225. *To make the election aerial tour . . . :* ibid.

225. *Eckener asserted that he berated . . . :* ibid. Eckener made this assertion, which has been retold in history after history, though there was no corroboration of his berating Lehmann by eyewitnesses on the field that day who should have seen this public blowup and who subsequently wrote accounts of the accident, including U.S. Navy observer

Scott Peck, Goodyear consultant Harold Dick, and, of course, Captain Lehmann himself.

225. *"I . . . said something like this . . ."*: ibid.

226. *a surprise gust of wind . . . field that day.*: Scott Peck to Ernst King, March 27, 1936; Lehmann, *Zeppelin*, 299.

226. *A newspaper account . . . to the air.*: *New York Times*, March 27, 1936.

227. *"A true patriot!"*: Goebbels, Teil 1, Bd. 3/II, 47.

227. *In December 1948, Eckener . . . full years.*: *Der Spiegel*, December 18, 1948.

227. *"I never protested . . ."*: *Ogden (UT) Standard-Examiner*, April 5, 1936.

227. *"I always say 'Heil, Hitler!' . . ."*: *Cincinnati Enquirer*, April 16, 1936.

227. *He quickly considered . . . "I admit . . . perplexity."*: Eckener, *Im Zeppelin*, 284 (author translation).

228. *Eckener, who was solely . . .*: Dick and Robinson, 111, 118. *San Francisco Chronicle*, April 11, 1936; *Salt Lake Tribune*, April 10, 1936; *Cincinnati Enquirer*, April 10, 1936; *Fresno Bee*, April 9, 1936; *Napa Valley Register*, April 9, 1936.

228. *Nazi Air Ministry even urged Eckener . . .*: *Sitzung vom 20. November 1936*.

228. *He admitted as much, in a letter . . .*: Hugo Eckener to Johanna Eckener, May 12, 1937, cited in Italiaander, 357.

229. *His memoir would recount . . .*: Eckener, *My Zeppelins*, 173.

230. *"Since we could not fly without . . ."*: ibid., 181

230. *"Every director of any industrial . . ."*: Eckener, *Im Zeppelin*, 274 (author translation).

230. *The Zeppelin was conceived by the Count . . .*: ibid., 307.

230. *Of the 119 Zeppelins . . .*: Robinson, *Famous*, 307.

230. *Eckener trained more than a thousand . . .*: Dick and Robinson, 15.

230. *"All England must burn!"*: Meyer, *Airshipmen*, 45.

231. *Before Winston Churchill addressed . . . suburban New Cross.*: *Baltimore Sun*, April 27, 1945.

231. *In the final reckoning . . . or exhaustion.*: Neufeld, *Rocket*, 264.

231. *he denied being a party member . . .*: Eckener, *Im Zeppelin*, 274.

231. *"I laughed about my punishment"*: ibid. (author translation).

231. *The tribunal's ruling came . . .*: *Evening News* (Harrisburg, PA), August 4, 1948.

232. *"The defendant did not want . . ."*: Italiaander, 478 (author translation).

## Epilogue

233. *It had become a dumping ground . . . 60,000 prisoners.*: "Bergen-Belsen," 1.

233. *He had seen calamities . . . Bergen-Belsen.*: Temkin, 148.

233. *They would tie string or straps . . .*: ibid., 146.

233. *For days, Temkin licked at drops . . .*: ibid., 150.

234. *His strength slipped each day . . .*: Temkin, 152.

234. *"Tanki, tovarishchi, tanki!"*: ibid.

234. *More than 13,000 corpses . . .*: "Eleventh Armored Division," 1.

234. *A diarist named Anne Frank . . .*: Sellier et al., 329.

234. *He hurried to the storage rooms . . .*: Temkin, 153.

235. *Not waiting for official permission . . .*: ibid., 154.

235. *only to learn . . . sisters survived.:* ibid., 163.

235. Is das eine Jude?: Temkin, 43.

235. *"I did not let . . .":* ibid. (author translation)

235. *"Name?":* ibid.

235. *"Michail Petrowitsch Mirontschik.":* ibid.

236. *At some point after the war . . . Nazi Germany.:* Temkin's diary is available in its original Russian on the internet at http://militera.lib.ru/memo/russian/tyomkin_mv01/text.html (accessed August 23, 2019).

236. *In 1947, Temkin married . . . two sons.:* Temkin, 27.

236. All former prisoners . . . *"Our joy . . . cried with happiness.":* Temkin, 152.

237. *Eckener added a late footnote . . . :* Eckener, *Im Zeppelin,* 274.

237. *"May his airmanship . . .":* Vaeth, vi.

237. *"Presumably, his great international . . .":* Robinson, *Giants,* 282.

237. *"Eckener, with his cosmopolitan . . .":* Dick and Robinson, 16.

237. *"Perhaps no other man in Germany . . .":* Archbold, 123.

237. *In one academic . . . camp prisoners:* Metzler, 62.

237. *Christa Tholander, a German researcher . . . :* *Südkurier,* December 12, 2014, and August 12, 2016.

238. *"protect the honor of those . . ." . . . Zeppelin fame.:* *New York Times,* June 23, 1949.

238. *He dismissed stories . . . he claimed.:* Lee, 49, 50.

238. *In 1952 . . . the Nazi Party.:* ibid., 84.

239. *A classified army dossier . . . "was used by . . . propaganda purposes.":* Dossier, unnumbered page with stapled index cards reporting various political and military affiliations.

240. *"During the war . . .":* *Sunday Star* (Washington, DC), August 15, 1954.

240. *Leonhard Adelt . . . died during an air raid . . . :* Hoehling, 178. While Hoehling's conclusion that the *Hindenburg* was sabotaged is completely without basis, it is clear that he did much credible research, as corroborated by the author's own research.

240. *"My mother in Dresden . . .":* ibid., 211.

241. *He helped two authors . . . :* Rosendahl is gratefully cited in the acknowledgments of the two major books promoting the sabotage theory, Michael Mooney's *The Hindenburg,* page 240, and *Who Destroyed the Hindenburg?* by A. A. Hoehling, page 227.

241. *"After long sniping . . .":* Statement.

241. *"When the whole story is written . . .":* ibid.

241. *Knut Eckener was sixty-two years old . . . :* Dick and Robinson, 186.

242. *Von Braun and Rudolph had hidden . . . :* Neufeld, *Von Braun,* 163, 165; Hunt, 77.

242. *"inescapably contaminated morally.":* Speer, 376.

243. *Horesehead . . . seven years in prison.:* *Independent Press-Telegram,* May 9, 1970.

243. *The story von Meister passed on . . . :* It is one of the best known, and repeated, stories purporting to show Hugo Eckener's resistance to the Nazis. It also apparently never happened. The tale is that he piloted the *Graf Zeppelin* in such a way as to hide swastikas painted on its fins from crowds at the World's Fair in Chicago in 1933. At the time, the *Graf* flew with the red, white, and black striped flag of German merchant ships on its starboard fins and the Nazi swastika on its port ones. So, by circling with only the starboard side showing, a pilot, if he so desired, could effectively hide the swastikas

from people on the ground. The lore has a curious provenance. Eckener himself never mentioned this stunt, though he spent several pages of his autobiography specifically on antics surrounding the Chicago World's Fair. Rather, the story seems to have been started by F. W. (Willy) von Meister, a special assistant to Eckener for many years. Historian Henry Cord Meyer interviewed von Meister apparently in mid-1973. Based on that discussion, on page 203 of *Airshipmen, Businessmen and Politics 1890–1940*, Meyer wrote that the *Graf Zeppelin* arrived and landed at an airfield north of the city. "On departure, he (Dr. Eckener) took the *Graf* on a long, low circular clockwise flight around the edge of the city [of Chicago] showing inwardly the traditional red-white-black colors on the starboard side of the fins." Eckener later said to von Meister, as he reported to Meyer, "Do you think I wanted to show my friends the swastika?" News reports in 1933 make it clear, however, that Eckener stayed in Chicago for a dinner and other meetings, while Lehmann sailed the *Graf Zeppelin* back to Akron. Meyer evidently had his doubts about this and other matters he and von Meister had discussed. On page 261, in an endnote, Meyer offered: "Possibly von Meister rearranged, and may have embellished, the details of his comments in order to make the stories more dramatic."

Author Cheryl Ganz wrote that she interviewed von Meister in July 1976. Her version of the World's Fair stunt, reported in *The 1933 Chicago World's Fair*, published in 2008, had the event taking place on the approach to Chicago, not the departure. On page 137, she wrote: "Approaching Chicago at daybreak on September 26, 1933 [it was actually October] Commander Hugo Eckener ordered the *Graf Zeppelin* . . . to fly west beyond the city and then circle clockwise, although a northerly route from Indiana with an approach to Chicago from the east over Lake Michigan would have been more expeditious. . . . Willy von Meister, the United States special representative of Luftschiffbau Zeppelin G.m.b.H., the Zeppelin company, was in the control car with Eckener during the approach to Chicago. He asked why Eckener had not taken the shorter circle. 'And let my friends in Chicago see the swastikas?'"

News reports clearly state that the Zeppelin did, indeed, fly over Lake Michigan on approach and it also circled the city in both directions, meaning Chicagoans would have certainly seen the swastika side. "From St. Joseph, Mr. Eckener charted a course to the south, striking the west coast of Lake Michigan several miles south of Chicago. Until 7 a.m. the zeppelin nosed its way up the coast, its motors almost idling" (*Chicago Freeport Journal-Standard*, October 26, 1933). "The big ship settled at the Curtiss-Reynolds airport . . . its blunt, silver nose pointed to the east, it was Germany's official visit to the center of progress. . . . flaunting the swastika of the Nazi" (*Chicago Daily News*, October 26, 1933). "The dark shadow of the *Graf* first appeared out of the fog and smoke of South Chicago at 6 AM. It followed the shoreline to the Loop" (*Chicago Harold and Examiner*, October 27, 1933). "[The *Graf Zeppelin*] was first reported over Chicago when it was seen flying slowly northward over the lake, just east of 31st St., at about 5:30 AM. It circled slowly over the city for more than an hour and then headed directly for the airport" (*Chicago Daily Times*, October 26, 1933). A photograph of the *Graf Zeppelin* pointed northward along the Lake Michigan coastline appears in the *Chicago Daily Times* of October 26, 1933, page 19. There was also a firsthand report by Merrill Meigs, an aviation buff and the general manager of the *Chicago American*, who joined the *Graf* in Akron and flew on its approach to Chicago: "While the ship moves slowly over the lake, inside of Chicago, we had a magnificent breakfast" (*Chicago American*, October 26, 1933).

Finally, the *Graf Zeppelin* logbook itself (LZA 16/385) says nothing about flying the ship clockwise, counterclockwise, or otherwise. The times in the log are on a twenty-four-hour clock, always synchronized to the time in Germany. The entire notation, along with some wind measurements, around the flight in question is: *Graf proceeded from Akron, 2342, hit "St. Josef" at 0345, proceeded over "Lake Michigan," was over Chicago at 545, Landed at 0700, over Chicago 725, over Chicago 0913, Berrien Springs, 1000.* Why would von Meister offer this account? Consider that Nazi war-crimes trials perked up and continued in the 1960s and 1970s. It is very possible that von Meister and others connected with the Zeppelin enterprise did not want investigators and prosecutors to start nosing around in the rocket work in Friedrichshafen, trying to determine who knew what. The colorful tale of the *Graf Zeppelin*'s hiding its swastika in Chicago lent strong credence to the idea that Eckener was a Nazi opponent, which certainly would have thrown investigators off the scent.

244. *Lehmann's widow . . . with their son, today.:* Herbert Baum to Barbara Waibel, August 9, 2007 (author translation).

244. *Jean dearest . . . struggle for food.:* Marie Lehmann to Jean Rosendahl, February 22, 1948.

245. *Jean Darling . . . :* Marie Lehmann to Mrs. C. E. Rosendahl, July 5, 1956.

### *Appendix*

249. *River Road . . . Leonhard Adelt:* National Archives and Records Administration, RG 197, Records of the Bureau of Air Commerce, records relating to the investigation of the *Hindenburg* disaster, General Records, Box 2, Folder 622.20, C-1 New Jersey, Lakehurst, Advisory Board (author translation).

# References

Adelt, Leonhard. "The Last Trip of the Hindenburg." *Reader's Digest*, November 1937.
———. Letter to Hindenburg Investigation Board, May 30, 1937, in its original German. Hindenburg Investigation Files, National Archives and Records Administration, Washington, DC. (Author translation into English.)
———. Letter to Hindenburg Investigation Board, May 30, 1937, translated into English by investigative staff. Hindenburg Investigation Files, National Archives and Records Administration, Washington, DC.
*Airship Aerodynamics: Technical Manual.* Honolulu, HI: University Press of the Pacific, 2003. Reprint of the 1941 U.S. War Department booklet.
Airship Hindenburg Diary, n.d. Hindenburg Investigation Files, National Archives and Records Administration, Washington, DC.
Aktennotiz Nr. T 2/43. Bundesarchiv, Militärarchiv, RH 8/1210.
Allen, Michael Thad. *The Business of Genocide: The SS, Slave Labor, and the Concentration Camps.* Chapel Hill: University of North Carolina Press, 2004.
Althoff, William F. *USS Los Angeles: The Navy's Venerable Airship and Aviation Technology.* Washington, DC: Potomac Books, 2004.
*Angaben aus dem Geschäftsbericht 1943* [Information from the annual financial report for the Zeppelin company 1943], Archiv Luftschiffbau Zeppelin GmbH, Friedrichshafen (LZ Archiv). Documents are located in folders classified with two numbers, separated by a backslash; in this case, LZA 6/660.
*Angaben für den Geschäftsbericht 1943*, Geheim, Information for annual financial report for the Zeppelin company 1943], [Secret] LZA 6/660.
Archbold, Rick. *Hindenburg: An Illustrated History.* Edison, NJ: Wellfleet Press, 2005.
Basic Personnel Record, Hugo Eckener, Headquarters, European Command, undated.
Basil, Saint. *St. Basil the Great: On the Holy Spirit.* Crestwood, NY: St. Vladimir's Seminary Press, 1980.
Baum, Herbert. Letter to Barbara Waibel, August 9, 2007. Personal correspondence Ms. Waibel, a Zeppelin archivist, shared with the author.
Becker, Winfried, and Elmar W. Eggerer. "'Walderke' Und 'Oberilzmühle' Die Passauer KZ- Außenlager Und Ihr Umfeld 1942–1945." In *Passau in Der Zeit Des Nationalsozialismus: Ausgewählte Fallstudien.* Passau: Universitätsverlag, 1999.
Béon, Yves, and Michael J. Neufeld. *Planet Dora: A Memoir of the Holocaust and the Birth of the Space Age.* Boulder, CO: Westview, 1998.
Berben, Paul. *Dachau 1933–1945: The Official History.* London: Norfolk Press, 1975.
"Bergen-Belsen." Holocaust Encyclopedia, United States Holocaust Memorial Museum, Washington, DC. Accessed June 4, 2017. https://encyclopedia.ushmm.org/content /en/article/bergen-belsen.
*Berliner Illustrierte Zeitung*, May 13, 1943.

Biddiscombe, Alexander Perry. *The Denazification of Germany: A History 1945–1948.* Stroud, UK: Tempus, 2007.

Bornemann, Manfred. *Geheimprojekt Mittelbau: Vom Zentralen Öllager Des Deutschen Reiches Zur grössten Raketenfabrik Im Zweiten Weltkrieg.* Bonn: Bernard und Graefe, 1994.

Botting, Douglas. *Dr. Eckener's Dream Machine: The Historic Saga of the Round-the-World Zeppelin.* New York: Henry Holt, 2001.

Buggeln, Marc. *Slave Labor in Nazi Concentration Camps.* Oxford: Oxford University Press, 2015.

Bureau of Air Commerce. Airship "Hindenburg" accident investigation § (1937).

Burger, Oswald. *Der Stollen.* Eggingen: Isele, 2015.

———. "Zeppelin und die Rüstungsindustrie am Bodensee." 1999: *Zeitschrift für Sozialgeschichte des 20. und 21. Jahrhunderts,* 1987, no. 1, 8–49, and no. 2, 52–87.

Catalogue of Camps and Prisons in Germany and German-Occupied Territories, September 1–May 8, 1945. International Tracing Service: Arolsen, Germany, July 1949/April 1950/March 1951.

Chapman, William (former government inspector). Oral testimony recorded by WCVA radio station in Culpeper, Virginia, in March 1977.

Chardin, Pierre Teilhard de. *Toward the Future.* New York: Harvest Harcourt, 1973.

Collins, James L. (former colonel, U.S. Army, liberator of Nordhausen in 1945). Interview recorded by Linda Hunt, undated. Accession Number 2003.44.2.16, RG-50.702.0016, United States Holocaust Museum, Washington, DC.

Colsman, Alfred. *Luftschiff Voraus!* Berlin: Deutsche Berlags-Anstalt, 1933.

"Commerce Department Report on the Hindenburg Disaster." Air Commerce Bulletin, U.S. Department of Commerce, vol. 9, no. 2, August 15, 1937.

Connelly, E. J. Letter to J. Edgar Hoover, May 13, 1937. FBI Hindenburg Investigative Files, Washington, DC.

Crew, David, and Herbert Ulrich. "Labor as Spoils of Conquest, 1933–1945." In *Nazism and German Society, 1933–1945.* London: Taylor and Francis, 2013.

Crouch, Tom D. *The Eagle Aloft: 2 Centuries of the Balloon in America.* Washington, DC: Smithsonian Institution Press, 1983.

de Syon, Guillaume. *Zeppelin!: Germany and the Airship, 1900–1939.* Baltimore, MD: Johns Hopkins University Press, 2007.

de Terzi, Francesco Lana. *Prodomo, ovvero saggio di alcune invenzioni nuove,* cited in Rolf Strehl, *Der Himmel hat keine Grenzen: Das große Abenteuer der Luftfahrt,* 20–26. Düsseldorf: Econ, 1962.

Devereaux, William. Letter to J. Edgar Hoover, May 19, 1937. FBI Hindenburg Investigative Files, Washington, DC.

Dick, Harold G., and Douglas H. Robinson. *The Golden Age of the Great Passenger Airships: Graf Zeppelin & Hindenburg.* Washington, DC: Smithsonian Institution Press, 1985.

Dornberger, Walter. *V-2.* New York: Bantam Books, 1979.

Dossier. Eckener, Hugo. File AE532193. Declassified. Department of Defense, Department of the Army, U.S. Army Intelligence and Security Command, U.S. Army

Central Security Facility, U.S. Army Investigative Records Repository, Nazi War Crimes Interagency Working Group. National Archives and Records Administration, Record Group 319, Box 177.

Doyle, Peter. *World War II in Numbers*. London: Bloomsbury Publishing, 2014.

Drummond-Hay, Grace. "Round the World in Twenty Days." *World Traveler Magazine*, December 1929.

Duggan, John. *Airships in International Affairs 1890–1940*. London: Palgrave Macmillan, 2014.

———. *LZ129 Hindenburg: The Complete Story*. Ickenham: Zeppelin Study Group, 2002.

Ebner, Martin. *Die Entnazifizierung Von Zeppelin, Maybach, Dornier & Co.* Amazon Media EU, 2013.

Eckener, Hugo. *Im Zeppelin über Länder Und Meere: Erlebnisse Und Erinnerungen*. München: Morisel, 2013.

———. Letter to Johanna Eckener, May 12, 1937, cited in Italiaander, 357. (Author translation.)

Eckener, Hugo, and Knut Eckener. *My Zeppelins: With a Technical Chapter by Knut Eckener*. Translated by Douglas Robinson. London: Putnam, 1958.

Eisenhower, Dwight D. *Crusade in Europe*. Norwalk, CT: Easton Press, 2001.

"Eleventh Armored Division." Holocaust Encyclopedia, United States Holocaust Memorial Museum, Washington, DC. Accessed June 4, 2017. https://encyclopedia.ushmm.org/content/en/article/the-11th-armoured-division-great-britain.

"Exhibit 74 L: Weather Conditions Afternoon of May 6, 1937," n.d. Hindenburg Investigation Files, National Archives and Records Administration, Washington, DC.

Fegan, Thomas. *The "Baby Killers": German Air Raids on Britain in the First World War*. Barnsley, UK: Pen & Sword Military, 2012.

*Fragebogen*, Gerhard Müller, Military Government of Germany, March 5, 1946.

*Fragebogen*, Hugo Eckener, Military Government of Germany, April 14, 1946.

Gallo, Max. *The Night of the Long Knives*. New York: Harper & Row, 1972.

Garliński Józef. *Hitler's Last Weapons: The Underground War against the V-1 and V-2*. London: Julian Freedman, 1978.

*Geschäftsbericht für das Jahr 1943* [Annual financial report for the Zeppelin company 1943], LZA 6/660.

Goebbels, Joseph. *Die Tagebücher Von Joseph Goebbels*. Edited by Elke Fröhlich. München: Saur, 2004.

Göring, Hermann. Letter to Jean Rosendahl, June 1937. University of Texas, Dallas, Vice Admiral Charles E. Rosendahl Collection.

Haddow, G. W., and Peter M. Grosz. *The German Giants: The Story of the R-Planes 1914–1919*. London: Putnam, 1969.

Häffner, Michaela. *Nachkriegszeit in Südwürttemberg: Die Stadt Friedrichshafen Und Der Kreis Tettnang in Den Vierziger Und fünfziger Jahren*. München: Oldenbourg, 1999.

Heald, Mark. Letter to Michael McCarthy, September 8, 2015.

Herbert, Ulrich, and William Templer. *Hitler's Foreign Workers: Enforced Foreign Labor in Germany under the Third Reich*. Cambridge: Cambridge University Press, 2006.

Hoehling, A. A. *Who Destroyed the Hindenburg?* Boston: Little Brown, 1962.

Hoover, Herbert J. *Addresses upon the American Road.* New York: D. Van Nostrand Co., 1946.

Hunt, Linda. *Secret Agenda: The United States Government, Nazi Scientists, and Project Paperclip, 1945 to 1990.* New York: St. Martin's Press, 1991.

Hürttle, Karl. Letter to Karl Rösch, May 4, 1937. LZA 16-0326.

Ickes, Harold L. *The Secret Diary of Harold L. Ickes* (3 vols.). Vol. 2, *The Inside Struggle: 1936–1939.* New York: Da Capo Press, 1974.

Investigative records concerning the May 6, 1937, accident resulting in the destruction by fire of the German airship, *Hindenburg.* Transcripts, 197.2.1. Records of the Bureau of Air Commerce, National Archives and Records Administration, Washington, DC.

Italiaander, Rolf. *Ein Deutscher Namens Eckener: Luftfahrtpionier Und Friedenspolitiker: Vom Kaiserreich Bis in Die Bundesrepublik.* Konstanz: Stadler, 1981.

Jones, R. V. *The Wizard War: British Scientific Intelligence 1939–45.* New York: Coward, McCann & Geoghegan, 1978.

Kershaw, Ian. *Hitler: A Biography.* New York: W. W. Norton, 2010.

King, Ernst. Letter to Willie von Meister, May 14, 1936. University of Texas, Dallas, Douglas Robinson Collection.

Königseder, Angelika, Wolfgang Benz, and Barbara Distel. *Der Ort Des Terrors/Der Ort Des Terrors. Geschichte Der Nationalsozialistischen Konzentrationslager Bd. 3: Sachsenhausen, Buchenwald.* München: C. H. Beck, 2016.

Ladd, Brian. *The Ghosts of Berlin: Confronting German History in the Urban Landscape.* Chicago: University of Chicago Press, 2018.

Lee, Martin A. *The Beast Reawakens: Fascism's Resurgence from Hitler's Spymasters to Today's Neo-Nazi Groups and Right-Wing Extremists.* London: Routledge, 2016.

Lehmann, Ernst A. Letter to Charles E. Rosendahl, February 8, 1935. University of Texas, Dallas, Vice Admiral Charles E. Rosendahl Collection.

———. *Zeppelin: The Story of Lighter-than-Air Craft.* Croydon, UK: Fonthill Media, 2015.

Lehmann, Ernst A., and Leonhard Adelt. *Auf Luftpatrouille Und Weltfahrt.* Berlin: Wegweiser-Verlag, 1936.

Lehmann, Marie. Letter to Jean Rosendahl, February 22, 1948. University of Texas, Dallas, Vice Admiral Charles E. Rosendahl Collection.

———. Letter to Mrs. C. E. Rosendahl, July 5, 1956. University of Texas, Dallas, Vice Admiral Charles E. Rosendahl Collection.

Le Maner, Yves, Sellier André, and Waltraud Gros. *Bilder Aus Dora: Zwangsarbeit Im Raketentunnel, 1943–1945.* Bad Münstereifel: Westkreuz-Verlag, 2001.

Lewis, George, and Harold Dick. "Technical Notes Translated from Zeppelin Company Documents on LZ 129 and LZ 130," n.d. Working papers housed at the University of Texas, Dallas, Robinson Collection, Box 9, Folders 1 and 3, as well as the Harold G. Dick Airships Collection at Wichita State University, Box 15, Folder 3, and Box 3, Folder 10.

Lochner, Louis P. "Aboard the Airship Hindenburg: Louis P. Lochner's Diary of Its Maiden Flight to the United States." *The Wisconsin Magazine of History* 49, no. 2 (1965): 101–21.

Log Book, U.S. Naval Air Station, Lakehurst, N.J., May 6, 1937. University of Texas, Dallas, Vice Admiral Charles E. Rosendahl Collection.

Longmate, Norman. *Hitler's Rockets: The Story of the V-2s.* New York: Skyhorse, 2009.

Maracin, Paul R. *The Night of the Long Knives: 48 Hours That Changed the History of the World.* Guilford, CT: Lyons, 2007.

Mather, Margaret. "'I Was on the Hindenburg.'" *Harper's Monthly Magazine*, November 1937.

McNab, Chris. *Hitler's Masterplan: Facts, Figures and Data for the Nazi's Plan to Rule the World.* London: Amber Books, 2018.

Messersmith, G. S. [Washington]. Memorandum to The Secretary [Cordell Hull], The Undersecretary [Sumner Welles], the Counselor [R. Walton Moore], [James Clement] Dunn, and [J. Pierrepont] Moffat, May 9, 1938. Special Collections, University of Delaware Library.

Metzler, Georg. *"Geheime Kommandosache": Raketenrüstung in Oberschwaben: Das Aussenlager Saulgau Und Die V2 (1943–1945).* Bergatreute: Eppe, 1997.

Meyer, Henry Cord. *Airshipmen, Businessmen and Politics 1890–1940.* Washington, DC: Smithsonian Institution Press, 1991.

Michel, Jean, and Nucéra Louis. *Dora.* London: Sphere, 1981.

Miller, Webb. *I Found No Peace: The Journal of a Foreign Correspondent.* Harmondsworth, UK: Penguin Books, 1940.

"Minutes of the Discussion on Safety Measures for LZ 129 and Future Airships," January 21, 1936. Zeppelin Museum, Friedrichshafen, Germany.

Mooney, Michael Macdonald. *The Hindenburg.* New York: Dodd, Mead & Co., 1972.

Morrison, Herb. "Hindenburg Disaster." On *Historic Voices: The 30s & 40s.* Saland Publishing, 2007, compact disc.

"National Advisory Committee for Aeronautics: Report of Meeting of October 16, 1924," Washington, October 16, 1924. University of Texas, Dallas, Vice Admiral Charles E. Rosendahl Lighter-Than-Air Collection, Box 40, Folder 2.

Neufeld, Michael J. *The Rocket and the Reich.* Washington, DC: Smithsonian Books, 1995.

———. *Von Braun: Dreamer of Space, Engineer of War.* New York: Vintage, 2008.

"New Arrivals from Dachau labor camp Friedrichshafen for September 30, 1944, with prisoner files," SS Operations Administration Support, Mittelbau. RG-04.006m _Reel 17_0008.jpg. United States Holocaust Memorial Museum, Collections Division, Archives Branch.

Nielsen, Thor. *The Zeppelin Story.* London: Allan Wingate, 1955.

*Nurnberg Military Tribunals: Indictments.* Office of Military Government for Germany (U.S.), Nuremberg, 1948. U.S. v. Carl Krauch et al., also known as the IG Farben Trial.

Ordway, Frederick I., and Mitchell R. Sharpe. *The Rocket Team.* Burlington, ON: Apogee Books, 2003.

Outgoing Classified Message, Restricted, War Department, HQ EUCOM, Frankfurt, Germany, Nr. War 90163, November 12, 1947.

Peck, Scott. Letters to Ernst King, April 11, 1936, and March 24, 1936. University of Texas, Dallas, Douglas Robinson Collection.

Petersen, Michael. "Engineering Consent: Peenemünde, National Socialism, and the V-2 Missile, 1924–1945." PhD diss., University of Maryland, College Park, 2005.

*Protokoll zur Besprechung über Sicherheitseinrichtung für LZ 129 und die zukünftigen Lufts-chiffe,* January 21, 1936. Archiv Luftschiffbau Zeppelin GmbH, Friedrichshafen (LZ Archiv), LZA 17/246.

Rees, Eberhard (former technical plant manager, Peenemünde). Interview recorded by Michael Neufeld, Huntsville, Alabama, November 8, 1989. National Air and Space Museum, Archives Division, MRC 322, Washington, DC.

*Rigid Airship Manual.* Washington, DC: U.S. Government Printing Office, 1928.

Robinson, Douglas H. *Famous Aircraft: The LZ 129 "Hindenburg."* New York: Arco, 1964.

———. *Giants in the Sky: A History of the Rigid Airship.* Seattle: University of Washington Press, 1979.

Rösch, Karl. Letter to Ernst Lehmann, January 20, 1937. LZA 16-0323.

Rosendahl, Charles H. Letter to South Trimble, June 11, 1937. Hindenburg Investigation Files, National Archives and Records Administration, Washington, DC.

Sammt, Albert. Letter to Deutsche Zeppelin Reederei f.a.b.H. (DZR), December 29, 1936. Kurhaus und Winder-Sportplatz, Freudenstadt, Germany.

———. *Mein Leben Für Den Zeppelin.* Wahlwies: Verl. Pestalozzi Kinderdorf, 1994.

Sauter, Rudolf. *Zusammenstellung der Überholunsarbeiten während der Winterliegezeit des Luftschiffe "Hindenburg,"* Frankfurt, December 17, 1936. LZA 16-0323.

Schwartz, A. Brad. *Broadcast Hysteria: Orson Welles's War of the Worlds and the Art of Fake News.* New York: Hill and Wang, 2015.

Security Report, Hugo Eckener, Office of the Military Government of the United States Security Report on German (or Austrian) Scientists or Important Technicians, March 26, 1947.

Sellier, André, Stephen Wright, Susan Taponier, Michael J. Neufeld, and Jens-Christian Wagner. *A History of the Dora Camp.* Chicago: Ivan R. Dee, 2003.

Shirer, William L. *Berlin Diary.* London: Sphere, 1970.

*Sitzung vom 20. November 1936 betreffend Luftschiffragen, Reichsminister der Luftfahrt, LB 1, Nr. 6046/36,* Confidential. To the Foreign Office, December 14, 1936. Political Archives, Foreign Office, Bonn.

Special Contract for the Employment of German Nationals with the War Department of the United States, Hugo Eckener, March 10, 1947.

Speer, Albert. *Inside the Third Reich: Memoirs.* New York: Simon & Schuster Paperbacks, 1970.

Stainton, Leslie. *Lorca: A Dream of Life.* New York: Farrar, Straus, Giroux, 2000.

Statement by Vice Admiral C. E. Rosendahl, U.S. Navy retired, August 31, 1962. University of Texas, Dallas, Vice Admiral Charles E. Rosendahl Collection.

Stein, Harold. "The Helium Controversy." In *American Civil-Military Decisions.* Tuscaloosa: University of Alabama Press, 1963.

Tamm, E. A. Letter to J. Edgar Hoover, May 11, 1937. FBI Hindenburg Investigative Files, Washington, DC.

Taylor, Fred. *Exorcising Hitler*. London: Bloomsbury Publishing, 2014.

Temkin, Moisej Beniaminowitsch. *Am Rande Des Lebens: Erinnerungen Eines Häftlings Der Nationalsozialistischen Konzentrationslager*. Edited by Reinhard Otto. Translated by Tatjana Szekely. Berlin: Metropol, 2017.

Thacker, Toby. *The End of the Third Reich: Defeat, Denazification & Nuremberg, January 1944–November 1946*. Stroud, UK: Tempus, 2008.

Tholander, Christa. "Als Dachau Im Juni 1943 Nach Friedrichshafen Kam— KZ-Häftlinge, Die V2 Und Das Unternehmen Luftschiffbau Zeppelin GmbH." *Friedrichshafener Jahrbuch für Geschichte Und Kultur*, Band. 6, 2014.

———. *Fremdarbeiter 1939 Bis 1945: Ausländische Arbeitskräfte in Der Zeppelin-Stadt Friedrichshafen*. Essen: Klartext Verl., 2001.

Toland, John. *The Great Dirigibles: Their Triumphs and Disasters*. New York: Dover, 1972.

Topping, Dale, and Eric Brothers. *When Giants Roamed the Sky: Karl Arnstein and the Rise of Airships from Zeppelin to Goodyear*. Akron, OH: University of Akron Press, 2001.

"The Transatlantic Flight of R 34." *Flight: The Aircraft Engineer & Airships* XI, no. 550 (July 10, 1919): 897–912.

Trimble, South. Letter to Charles E. Rosendahl, June 9, 1937. Hindenburg Investigation Files, National Archives and Records Administration, Washington, DC.

Ullrich, Volker. *Adolf Hitler: Ascent, 1889–1939*. London: Bodley Head, 2016.

United States Army Investigation and Trial Records of War Criminals, U.S. v. Kurt Andrae et al. (and related cases), April 27, 1945–June 11, 1958 (pamphlet). National Archives and Records Administration, 1981.

U.S. v. Kurt Andrae et al., Case No. 000-50-37, April 15, 1948, 7708 War Crimes Group, European Command, APO 407.

Vaeth, J. Gordon. *Graf Zeppelin*. New York: Harper, 1958.

Van Orman, Ward Tunte, and Robert Hull. *The Wizard of the Winds*. Saint Cloud, MN: North Star Pr., 1978.

von Meister, Willie. Letter to Ernst King, April 11, 1936. University of Texas, Dallas, Douglas Robinson Collection.

Wagner, Jens-Christian. *Produktion Des Todes: Das KZ Mittelbau-Dora*. Göttingen: Wallstein Verlag, 2015.

Weather Bulletin, U.S. Naval Air Station, Lakehurst, N.J., May 6, 1937. University of Texas, Dallas, Vice Admiral Charles E. Rosendahl Collection.

Wegener, Peter P. *The Peenemünde Wind Tunnels: A Memoir*. New Haven, CT: Yale University Press, 1996.

Wev, Bosquet. Letter to J. Edgar Hoover, November 25, 1947. National Archives and Records Administration, Washington, DC. In the Eckener, Hugo "Paperclip" file.

Zeidler, Gerhard, and Gretchen Engle Schafft. *Commemorating Hell: The Public Memory of Mittelbau-Dora*. Champaign: University of Illinois Press, 2011.

# Index

relationship with Eckener,
72–73
relationship with
Rosendahl, 108
says lightning caused fire, 104
senses problem with
*Hindenburg* before
landing, 98
trains Zeppelin pilots during
WWI, 18–19
Lehmann, Marie, 112–113,
116–117, 244–245
Lenz, Philip, 101
Lewald, Theodore, 58
Lewis, George, 53–54
liberation, 187, 234
*Life* magazine, 203
lightning, 54, 79–80, 97, 104, 125
Lindbergh, Charles, 138
Litchfield, Paul, 50, 136
acts as character reference for
Eckener, 200, 206–207
at Goodyear, 207
testimony before Air Policy
Commission, 213–214
Litomisky, Otakar, 183
Lochner, Louis, 38, 62, 70
London, 175, 181, 231
*Los Angeles,* 28, 98, 108
construction of, 20–22
first transoceanic flight,
22–26
Rosendahl censors mishap
on, 109
Luce, Clare Booth, 192–193

Luftschiffbau Zeppelin. *See*
Zeppelin factory
Luther, Hans, 32, 49
LZ 126. *See Los Angeles*
LZ 127. *See Graf Zeppelin*
LZ 128, 40, 42–43
LZ 129, 43, 46–47, 49–50, 53–54.
*See also Hindenburg*
LZ 130, 75, 90, 105–106
Göring accelerates
construction of, 108
Göring decides to use it as
spy weapon, 130
grounded by Hitler, 111
helps Nazis gather
intelligence to prepare
attacks, 140
Hitler allow hydrogen use
in, 133
named *Graf Zeppelin,* second
generation, 133–134
observation car allows spying,
139–140
outer covering revisions, 119,
134–135
outfitted with espionage
equipment, 133
rebuilt to use helium,
131–132
test flights, 135
LZ 131, 75
LZ 132, 75

Mann, Thomas, 11
Martini, Wolfgang, 139